Reagan's first four years

Dedication

This book is dedicated to the memory of John D. Lees, who died as it was being completed.

All of the contributors wish to record their appreciation of a fine scholar and friend, whose contributions to the study of American politics will be sadly missed.

Reagan's first four years
A new beginning?

edited by
JOHN D. LEES and MICHAEL TURNER

Manchester University Press

Distributed exclusively in the USA and Canada by St. Martin's Press, New York

Copyright © Manchester University Press 1988

Whilst copyright in the volume as a whole is vested in
Manchester University press, copyright in the individual
chapters belongs to their respective authors, and no chapter
may be reproduced whole or in part without the express
permission in writing of both author and publisher.

Published by
Manchester University Press
Oxford Road, Manchester M13 9PL, UK
Distributed exclusively in the USA and Canada
by St. Martin's Press, Inc.,
Room 400, 175 Fifth Avenue, New York, NY 10010, USA

British Library cataloguing in publication data
Reagan's first four years. A new beginning?
    1. United States—Politics and government—1981
    I. Lees, John D.   II. Turner, Michael,
    1942 Sept. 9–
    353'.072'09   E876

Library of Congress cataloging in publication data applied for

ISBN 0 7190 2539 7 (hardback)
        0 7190 2540 0 (paperback)

Printed and bound in Great Britain by
Biddles Ltd, Guildford and King's Lynn

Contents

Contributors

John D. Lees was, at the time of his death, Reader in American Politics, Department of American Studies, University of Keele, England.

Michael Turner is Lecturer in Politics, Department of Applied Social Studies, Paisley College of Technology, Paisley, Scotland, and was formerly Associate Director of the State University of New York's Washington Semester Programme in Washington, DC.

Nigel Ashford is Senior Lecturer in Politics, Department of Politics and International Relations, North Staffordshire Polytechnic, Stoke-on-Trent, England.

Joseph J. Hogan is Senior Lecturer in Public Administration, School of Social Studies, Robert Gordon's Institute, Aberdeen, Scotland.

Introduction

This study does not purport to be a comprehensive overview of the first term of President Reagan. Rather it is a survey and an analysis of the major political events and the changes that occurred in American national government following the 1980 election which put Ronald Reagan into the White House. The emphasis is on the impact of the Reagan administration and a new public philosophy on the central political insitutions and organisations – the Executive Office of the President, Congress, the federal bureaucracy, the courts and interest groups – who in their different ways help to determine the policy agenda and policy outcomes in Washington. Economic and budgetary developments, while of considerable importance, are also complex, and are the proper subject for more specialist study elsewhere. Hence they are considered only in so far as they help to explain the nature of the political changes which occurred.

The main objective of what follows is to provide a considered evaluation of the first four years, in terms of the goals of those inside and outside of the Republican party who helped to make Reagan president, and the real objectives (as opposed to the rhetoric) of his administration. In marked contrast to the Carter presidency, there has been an abundance of 'instant' interpretation and assessment of the so-called 'Reagan Revolution' by academics in the United States. However, Ronald Reagan and his presidency also attracted considerable and continued attention outside the United States. He is a puzzle, even a source of wonderment, to many unfamiliar with the day-to-day workings of government in Washington but conscious of the potential impact of decisions made in that process on their lives, and on the governments they help to elect.

What we seek to provide here therefore is an explanation by non-American specialists in the study of American government, primarily for a non-American audience, of a very particular American phenomenon. Essentially we seek to monitor the performance of the Reagan administration in the first term and provide a balanced assessment of a presidency which produced the kind of specific and extreme responses, emotions and reactions engendered in their different ways in the recent past by presidents such as Franklin D. Roosevelt, John F. Kennedy and Richard M. Nixon. Along the way we also attempt to understand and appreciate the elusive qualities which help to make some presidents, and their administrations, more 'successful' as well as more popular than others. Is this success a factor of how an administration handles economic issues, or of how a president communicates his ideas and his style of governing to people inside and outside government, or what? It would appear that the combination of a strong president and a distinct and new programme of policies can still achieve more than merely incremental change, contrary to the assumptions of many students of the presidency and the policy process in the 1970s. But did Reagan's first term lay the foundations of a permanent break from the past and a new conservative era? Did the new beginning produce anything more than a reordering of the balance of interest group influence, and a readjustment in the purposes and priorities of the use of the power of the federal government rather than a reduction in its role and function? These are some of the questions raised by the evidence in the chapters which follow, which are considered in particular in the final part of the study.

In the course of producing this study, all the contributors have profited from the collective activities of organisations such as the American Politics Group and the individual thoughts and sagacity of many contacts in Washington, DC, some of whom would like to remain anonymous. John Lees wished to acknowledge the financial support of the Nuffield Foundation, which permitted him to visit Washington and to understand better the activities discussed in particular in Chapters 8 and 10. Michael Turner would like to acknowledge financial support from the Foreign Policy Research Institute of Philadelphia, the American Politics Group and the United States Information Agency, London, which enabled him to make visits to Washington to research defence and foreign policy issues raised in Chapters 6 and 7, as well as the operations of the administration discussed in Chapter 3. Nigel Ashford would like to acknowledge financial assistance from the American Politics Group, the Heritage Foundation and the Marguerite Eyer Foundation which allowed him to visit the United States to study at first hand the movements and issues discussed in Chapters 1 and 2. Finally, Joseph Hogan would like to acknowledge financial support from the United States Information Agency, London, and the Political Studies Association of the UK which enabled him to visit Washington to research the budgetary and legislative activities dealt with in Chapters 4 and 5.

John D. Lees
Michael Turner

Part 1

The political environment of the Reagan administration

1 Nigel Ashford

A new public philosophy

Every society is governed by a public philosophy, a set of widely accepted ideas which define the political agenda and the options considered within political debate. From the 1930s to the 1960s, the public philosophy of the USA was New Deal liberalism, of federal responsibility for the economy and the provision of basic welfare, anti-communist internationalism in foreign policy and a domestic culture of Americanism.

This was challenged in the 1960s and it appeared that a new public philosophy was emerging of a greatly expanded role for the federal government (as represented by the Great Society programmes), *détente* and neo-isolationism in foreign policy and cultural permissiveness (King, 1978, ch.1). The Reagan administration, however, sought to create a new conservative public philosophy based on a more limited role for the federal government, strong anti-communism and cultural conservatism. There has been a substantial shift in the political agenda in the late 1970s and 1980s, so that political debate is over issues such as the effect of taxation on incentives, the growing power of the Soviet Union and the social problems created by the decline of traditional institutions and lifestyles. Intellectual conservatism came to dominate the agenda of public policy debate but it remains uncertain to what extent this is a permanent change or simply a transitory phenomenon. Whether the conservative ideas discussed here have established themselves as the new public philosophy will be reflected in the following chapters, and in the degree to which the Reagan administration has established a new beginning.

Neo-conservatives

At the forefront of the emergence of conservatism as a respected intellectual force in America were a group of former New Deal liberals led by Irving Kristol, editor of *Public Interest*, and Norman Podhoretz, editor of *Commentary*. Their journals provided a regular forum for disillusioned liberals, supported by a massive output of books, magazine articles, pamphlets, seminars and newspaper columns. Neo-conservatism was a reaction to the radical liberalism of the 1960s and called for more scepticism towards government programmes, a vigorous anti-communism and more respect for traditional cultural values (Ashford, 1981).

They became convinced both by their own studies and those of Chicago economists that the Great Society had been a disaster. Not only were the programmes very expensive, they were counterproductive, making the conditions they were designed to treat even worse. One example was the growth of welfare dependency, where many of the poor had become so dependent on welfare that they had been rendered incapable of moving out of their poverty (Murray, 1984). They developed a Law of Unintended Consequences, that the unanticipated consequences of social action are always more important and usually less agreeable than the intended ones. They were sceptical about the ability of government to improve society, although they did not believe that nothing could be done, only that policies should be introduced with caution and humility, with a detailed assessment of costs and benefits, both before and after the policy is introduced. The neo-conservatives were very significant in creating the atmosphere of scepticism towards big government.

The US was felt by them to be suffering from a failure of nerve in foreign policy, lacking self-confidence in the virtues of America's role in the world and the will to act – all part of the post-Vietnam syndrome. Podhoretz attacked the New Isolationism, and urged the resumption of oppositon to the Soviet Union as the central thrust of foreign policy (Podhoretz, 1980). The first priority was to restore faith in the virtues of America and its role in the world. They saw America's national interest as intimately linked to the promotion of the values of democracy, liberty and human rights, and this established the essential morality of the aims of American foreign policy (although not always the means). Daniel Moynihan urged 'that it is for the US deliberately and consistently to bring its influence to bear on behalf of those regimes which promise the largest degree of personal and national liberty' (Moynihan, 1980, 21). Their second theme is the importance of ideas in international relations and the need for the US to go on the ideological offensive against the

Soviet Union, leading the international 'party of Liberty' (Moynihan, 1980, ch.5). Thirdly, neo-conservatives believe that the US must actively use international forums to put forward its case. Moynihan pursued this approach as US Ambassador to the UN in 1975-76, and Reagan's appointee, Jeane Kirkpatrick, acted in the same tradition, drawing criticism for a style described as aggressive and uncompromising (Kirkpatrick, 1983). A similar strategy was pursued by Max Kampelman as US Representative to the Conference on Security and Cooperation in Europe.

Neo-conservatives provided much of the intellectual attack on the counterculture and moral laxity, claiming that hedonism, the pursuit of instant gratification, leads to selfishness, the abdication of responsibility and social instability. The decline of the family is perceived as having negative consequences in such areas as education, crime, drugs and poverty. Government intervention has undermined the role of traditional institutions, such as the family, the church and the neighbourhood, described as mediating structures (Berger and Neuhaus, 1977). The role of the family could be strengthened against that of the 'expert' (Berger and Berger, 1983); the integrity of the neighbourhood should be respected and local values upheld (e.g. by allowing communities to define their own standards of pornography); and the separation of church and state could be interpreted to allow various churches to receive government aid in their social work. The neo-conservatives were therefore the intellectual wing of the pro-family movement.

The neo-conservatives were of considerable significance in presenting a new public philosophy covering the political, foreign and social realms. Whilst other intellectuals made important contributions to particular issue areas, the neo-conservatives were the only group to present an intellectually coherent conservative approach to public policy across the range of areas.

Free market libertarians

Federal programmes came under increasingly critical attention from free market economists. They claimed that these programmes usually failed to achieve their objectives at considerable costs (not only financial) and that problems could be better dealt with by greater use of the free market.

Milton Friedman is the best known exponent of this point of view. A well-respected economist, awarded a Nobel Prize in 1976 and President of the American Economic Association in 1977, he sought a wider audience for his ideas, with a regular column in *Newsweek* magazine and a successful TV series and book *Free To Choose* in 1980 (Friedman and Friedman, 1980). Friedman is most closely associated with monetarism, the idea that inflation is determined by the money supply. With inflation as the main economic problem of the 1970s, his ideas became widely accepted and strongly influenced the policies of the Federal Reserve Bank, the US body responsible for monetary policy, even before Reagan was elected. His ideas were further developed by 'rational expectations' monetarists, such as Thomas Sargent, who argued that traditional macro-economic management in the Keynesian tradition, which was the basis of economic policy since the New Deal, was no longer working.

Friedman has discussed a wide range of economic issues, and is only the best known of the Chicago school of economists who have critically examined government policies and their consequences and found them seriously wanting. The minimum wage has destroyed low-paid jobs and increased unemployment. Rent control has destroyed the private rental market and made it more difficult for the poorer single tenant to find a home. Occupational licensing has excluded more people entering these occupations to the disadvantage of the consumer. Protectionism has destroyed more jobs in other industries than those saved in the protected industries. The attempt to prevent unemployment through Keynesian demand management has been to create more long-term unemployment. The list of government failures is long in the empirical studies of the Chicago school.

The Chicago economists have proposed a series of policies to seek the same objectives but through greater use of the market. These include a negative income tax, whereby the poor would receive direct cash payments to ensure a minimum standard rather than the provision of services (e.g. food stamps); the privatisation of the social security system; the introduction of education vouchers which parents could spend at any recognised school; and the replacement of public housing by cash grants. At a time of growing disillusion with government, the Chicago school provided market-oriented alternatives to place on the political agenda.

One of their major areas was the effect of government regulations on the economy. The founding father of the deregulation movement was the Chicago economist George Stigler, awarded a Nobel prize in

1982. Stigler argued that many of the regulatory bodies, such as the Federal Trade Commission, protected existing companies against competition and thus hurt the consumer. Murray Weidenbaum of the Centre for the Study of American Business of Washington University, St. Louis, estimated that regulations cost $103 billion in 1979 or $500 per capita. Well-intentioned regulations were felt to be a significant cause of slow growth, inflation and unemployment.

Some free market libertarians felt that the market-oriented solutions of the Chicago school still involved too great a role for government. The Austrian school of economists led by Friedrich Hayek urged a more *laissez-faire* approach: an end to the legal privileges of trade unions such as the Sherman and Norris-LaGuardia Acts, a return to the gold standard and even the 'denationalisation' of money, whereby government would lose its monopoly of legal tender, US banks could create their own money and foreign currencies would be allowed to circulate freely. Reagan created a Gold Commission to examine the case for gold, but the idea was rejected by the monetarist majority on the Commission.

Free market libertarians recognised the existence of 'market failure', the imperfections of the market, but contrasted it with the far more extensive imperfections of 'government failure'. They argued that the free market maximised liberty, increased wealth and was the most effective problem-solver because it relied on man's natural desire to improve himself. The free market was restored to intellectual respectability and to the political agenda.

Supply-siders

If Reaganite economic policy is associated with any one policy it is tax cuts. The intellectual basis for tax cuts came from supply-side economics, which said that a reduction of taxation was the single most effective method of restoring growth. Supply-siders argued that taxation affects the relative prices of two major decisions: the trade-off between work and leisure and between saving and consumption. Higher taxation increases the cost of work and reduces the price of leisure, and increases the cost of saving and reduces the cost of consumption. The consequences are a reduction in work and saving and a rise in leisure and consumption, with the result that there is a decline in the production of goods and services and in the availability of capital (dependent on saving) necessary for investment. For supply-siders, taxation is the major cause of slow economic growth. Their concern with the effects of government on supply therefore contrasts with the Keynesian concern with demand (Buchanan, 1978).

Arthur Laffer of the University of Southern California developed the Laffer Curve which showed that above a certain point the rate of taxation is so high as to discourage so much production that the tax revenue is actually lower than if the rate of taxation were reduced. Laffer argued that America was above that point, so that tax reduction would eventually lead to higher revenue. Most supply-siders did not believe that tax cuts would pay for themselves, only that tax revenues would not fall to anything like the extent predicted by conventional economists. Supply-siders felt that inflation ('too much money chasing too few goods') could be cured by increasing the supply of goods rather than reducing the money supply. They therefore rejected the balanced budget views of traditional conservative economists, because they argued that deficits were not inflationary unless they were paid for by an increase in the money supply.

While supply-siders claimed that there is a long history of supply-side economics going back to Adam Smith, these ideas were virtually unknown in 1975. They were popularised by Jude Wanniski in the *Wall Street Journal* and his book, *The Way the World Works* (Wanniski, 1978); the neo-conservative Irving Kristol in his journal, *Public Interest*; George Gilder in his best-selling *Wealth and Poverty* (Gilder, 1981); and journalist Tom Bethell in the traditionally liberal magazine, *Harpers*. Particularly significant was the adoption of their ideas by the rising young Republican Congressman from New York, Jack Kemp. Several supply-siders entered the administration, including Paul Craig Roberts at the Treasury, who became disillusioned with the strength of anti-supply-siders within the administration and resigned (Roberts, 1984).

Public choice

Some economists and political scientists have sought to apply basic economic concepts to political behaviour. The individual is seen as rational, seeking to maximise his own interests within institutional limits. This approach is used to explain both the behaviour of political actors, such as politicians, bureaucrats and interest groups, and the policy outputs that emerge from the political process. This type of analysis is called Public Choice, and is led by James Buchanan and Gordon Tullock of the Centre for the Study of Public Choice at George Mason University in Virginia. The consequence, most public choice writers suggest, is that government is much bigger than the people want.

Politicians are seen as vote-maximisers, seeking re-election, and so one might assume that they would provide the policies that people want. However two factors prevent that: log-rolling and the political business cycle. Log-rolling is when legislator A agrees to vote for something legislator B wants in return for B's vote on something that A wants. This leads to 'pork barrel' legislation where specific benefits are provided for particular groups and constituencies rather than for the public interest. Morris Fiorina has used this approach to explain how Congress works (Fiorina, 1977). Political business cycles are when governments increase expenditure leading up to elections, to boost employment and create the impression of prosperity, and then have to reverse those policies after the election to avoid inflation, thus destabilising the economy. Politicians make promises to the voters while hiding their costs, so that elections become competitive vote-buying (Tullock, 1976).

Bureaucrats are assumed to favour empire-building or 'size-maximisation', as public choice describe it, because their salary, status and power are increased with the size of the agency and bureau. Bureaucrats are in a strong position to obtain their objectives because of their strategic location, their control of information, their low organisational costs and their ability to cooperate with interest groups. These factors lead to an oversupply of government services and the lack of incentives to be efficient. William Niskanen argued that '. . . All bureaus are too large. Bureaucrats produce outputs in excess of those that voters would demand if they were aware of the costs' (Niskanen, 1973, 33).

Most interest groups are portrayed as seeking the power of government to satisfy their particular wants rather than achieve them privately. Small and homogeneous groups like manufacturers and workers in the same industry will be easier to organise than large and diverse groups such as taxpayers. These organised groups, such as industries demanding protection or farmers seeking subsidies, will have a direct interest in being politically active on the issue, while the losers, consumers or taxpayers, have a weak interest in getting involved in any particular issue. It is a problem of concentrated benefits and dispersed costs.

The consequence of these factors, public choice theory suggests, is that the political system is biased in favour of big government. These ideas have become well-known among conservatives, either from reading public-choice writers or more popular versions of the same message. This helps to explain conservative suspicion of traditional bargaining politics. Congress is seen as representing special vested interests ranged against the administration's objective of less government, and therefore the President must appeal above the heads of Congress to mobilise the larger constituency of taxpayers and consumers. The career bureaucrats are seen as hostile to reducing government and some attempts have been made in the Reagan administration to provide the incentives to bureaucrats to be more efficient, based on the ideas of Niskanen who was a member of the President's Council of Economic Advisers from 1981 to 1985.

Interest groups are treated with suspicion and there is less attempt to find a compromise with them because of the bias towards bigger government that would result. Stuart Butler argues that the solution lies in building vested interests against bigger government (Butler, 1985). Buchanan and Tullock have argued that constitutional reform is the only effective means of correcting the bias. They are associated with the campaign for a constitutional amendment to achieve a balanced budget and a limit on taxation and spending powers, which has gained considerable support in Congress and state legislatures (Moore and Penner, 1980). They have also argued for a line-item veto, which would give the President the power to veto individual sections of an Appropriations bill (such as pork barrel amendments seeking local public works) and not the whole bill. Reagan has spoken out in favour of these changes, but not given it a high priority.

The new globalism

The position of the foreign policy right, reasserting an active global role for the US, is based on two principles. First, the relationship between the US and the Soviet Union is viewed as not simply between two superpowers, but rather between two nations who represent two wholly different and incompatible ideologies and sets of values. Second, the survival of the US as a free nation and of the rest of the free world depend on the strength of the US and that strength had suffered a major decline in recent years relative to the Soviet Union. These two principles led them to recommend an active policy of global ideological conflict and a massive build-up of US military force.

Fred Iklé, later Under-Secretary of Defence for Policy in the Reagan administration, stated that

To assure the survival of the US as a free nation is, of course, the first priority for America's defence and foreign policy. Other goals – to work towards a democratic and peaceful world order, to enhance America's trade and access to resources, to foster humanitarian action and moral values consistent with American traditions throughout the world – are largely supportive of this task (Duignan and Rabushka,1980,419).

The US is a nation based on certain values – limited government, the market economy and human rights – so the promotion of those values globally is of direct national interest, and is in direct conflict with the values and interests of the Soviet regime. To these writers the essential characteristics of the Soviet Union are that it is totalitarian (with the state seeking to control every aspect of political, economic and social life) and imperialistic, willing to use any means, including force, to extend its power. These characteristics led them to reject the concept of symmetry which postulates that the US and the Soviet Union are essentially similar. The consequences of this approach are threefold. Firstly, the US must declare its moral superiority over the Soviet Union through the speeches of its leaders and directly to the people of the world. This led to Reagan's reference in 1983 to the Soviet Union as an 'evil empire', to increased funding for Radio Liberty and Radio Free Europe which broadcasts behind the Iron Curtain, and to the creation of Radio Marti to broadcast to Cuba. Secondly, the US must actively promote its values to the Third World, in particular Latin America, which has led to support for democratisation in countries such as El Salvador, the creation of the National Endowment for Democracy and an emphasis on private sector investment rather than government-to-government aid or aid through multilateral agencies such as the UN. Thirdly, a distinction must be made between totalitarian and authoritarian states, because in the latter there are possibilities for development into free nations, as occurred in Spain, Portugal and Greece. It was the expression of this argument by Jeane Kirkpatrick in a *Commentary* article on 'Dictatorships and Double Standards' that drew her to Reagan's attention (Kirkpatrick, 1982).

The ability to deter Soviet intervention is dependent upon the relative strength of the two countries, and many experts were convinced that the military capabilities of the US had declined significantly in recent years, particularly but not only under the Carter administration. *Détente* was identified as a major cause of this decline because it had reduced America's vigilance while at the same time allowing the Soviets to build up their forces. Figures were produced to indicate that the US was inferior to the Soviet Union, both in strategic nuclear weapons, such as the number of launchers and destructive power, and in conventional warfare, in terms of manpower, hardware and firepower. The perception of US weakness encouraged Soviet adventurism in Africa, Afghanistan and elsewhere. Even more worrying was the belief that without swift action the USSR would be so much stronger that its leaders might risk a serious trial of strength in the late 1980s in the so-called 'window of opportunity'. From this point of view it was a matter of urgency to achieve a massive increase in defence expenditure to restore parity with the Soviet Union; not as an alternative to arms control talks, but as a necessary requirement to get the Soviets to talk seriously. The new globalists provided the intellectual framework for the foreign and defence policies of the Reagan administration.

The think-tanks

There were many conservative ideas and policy proposals in circulation, but how did they come to influence policy debate both inside and outside the Reagan administration? A significant role was played by several conservative research institutes or 'think-tanks', which provided an outlet for ideas, communicated them to policy-makers and provided informed personnel to staff the administration. The main institutes were the Heritage Foundation, the American Enterprise Institute (AEI), the Hoover Institution and the Committee on the Present Danger.

The Heritage Foundation is a relatively young body in the Washington policy community, but it has rapidly established itself as a major influence on conservative policy-makers. Many of its staff and associates joined the Reagan administration and it provided the names of conservative experts from its Resource Bank run by Willa Ann Johnson, a member of Reagan's transitional personnel office.

Heritage publishes the highly regarded journal *Policy Review* and in 1981 published *Mandate for Leadership*, a massive 1093-page set of specific recommendations which was frequently used by conservatives as a measuring rod of the Reagan administration's first-term performance (Heatherley, 1981). Two policy areas in which Heritage has been particularly significant are supply-side economics and the Strategic Defence Initiative (SDI). Thus it has provided a home and financial support both for the supply-side Institute for Research on the Economics of Taxation, founded by Norman Ture (who later joined the Treasury), and for the High Frontier project of Lt. Gen. Daniel Graham, which did the early political groundwork for what became the Strategic Defense Initiative (SDI) or 'Star Wars'.

In terms of the provision of Reagan personnel from the institutes, the AEI provided the largest number, including David Gergen, White House communications chief, and Lawrence Korb in the State Department. High profile appointments included AEI associate scholars Jeane Kirkpatrick as UN Ambassador and Murray Weidenbaum as Chairman of the Council of Economic Advisers. Two policy areas of considerable AEI influence were regulation and the role of the private sector. The AEI published regulatory studies by Weidenbaum and many others, set up the Centre for the Study of Government Regulation in 1977, published the journal *Regulation*, and the Centre's co-director James Miller III became Chairman of the Federal Trade Commission (and in 1985 Director of the Office of Management and Budget). Influenced by the neo-conservative interest in mediating structures and private sector alternatives to government as problem-solvers, the AEI published numerous studies in this area, including the major work, *Meeting Human Needs* (Meyer, 1982), and in response to a request from Reagan established the Center for the Study of Private Initiatives and inspired the White House Office on Private Sector Initiatives.

Reagan has long been associated with the Hoover Institution in California. Hoover Fellow Martin Anderson, as long-time domestic policy adviser to Reagan, became the head of the White House Office of Policy Development and was influential against the military draft and the Law of the Sea Convention and over welfare reforms (Anderson, 1978). Other Hoover associates include director Glenn Campbell as Chairman of the Intelligence Oversight Board, John Bunzel to the Civil Rights Commission and Edward Teller as an SDI adviser. Hoover published *The US in the 1980s* which was widely cited as indicating the direction of the administration's domestic and foreign policy (Duignan and Rabushka, 1980).

A strong foreign policy and defence posture was advocated by a number of policy institutes including Heritage, AEI, Hoover, Georgetown University's Center for Strategic and International Studies, Pennsylvania University's Foreign Policy Research Institute, the Ethics and Public Policy Center in Washington, DC and New York's National Strategy Information Centre. All these groups were brought together in the Committee on the Present Danger, which criticised reductions in the defence budget and the pursuit of arms negotiations from a position of weakness under the Carter administration. The Committee brought together considerable intellectual firepower and political experience, and was a significant factor in the defeat of SALT II. Some 32 members of the Committee received appointments in the administration, including Paul Nitze, Richard Perle and Fred Iklé (Tyroler, 1985).

A new public philosophy?

Throughout his political career, Ronald Reagan has articulated the political philosophy reflected in the intellectual ideas of those discussed above. As a politician seeking votes, he has spoken in a populist rhetoric and employed specific examples to illustrate his basic theme echoed frequently throughout his campaigns, to 'get the government off the people's backs'. This was a major theme of his Inaugural Address in 1981, when he said that 'Government is not the solution to our problem, government is the problem.' The development of these ideas amongst intellectuals gave respectability and substance to Reagan's rhetoric and a set of policy alternatives.

Reagan gave a major speech on the eve of his election which stated the philosophical convictions that would guide his presidency and reflected the influence of the conservative intellectuals.

Many Americans today, just as they did 200 years ago, feel burdened, stifled and sometimes even oppressed by government that has grown too large, too bureaucratic, too wasteful, too unresponsive, too uncaring about people and their problems.

I believe we can embark on a new age of reform in this country and an era of national renewal, an era that will reorder the relationship between citizen and government, that will make government responsive again to people, that will revitalize the values of family, work and neighbourhood and that will restore our private and independent social institutions. These institutions always have served as buffer and bridge between the individual and the state – and these institutions, not government, are the real sources of our economic and social progress as a people.

That's why I've said throughout this campaign that we must control and limit the growth of Federal spending, that we must reduce tax rates to stimulate work and savings and investment. That's why I've said we can relieve labour and business of burdensome, unnecessary regulations and still maintain high standards of environmental and occupational safety.

That's why I've said we can reduce the cost of government by eliminating billions lost to waste and fraud in the Federal bureaucracy – a problem that is an unrelenting national scandal. And because we are a federation of sovereign states, we can restore the health and vitality of state and local governments by returning to them control over programmes best run at those levels of government closer to the people (Smith *et al.*, 1980, 154).

Ronald Reagan, his 1980 election and his administration, all reflected the new conservatism of the intellectuals. Much of the remainder of this book examines to what extent and how these ideas were tranlated into policies, away from calm and serious intellectual debate in the rough and tumble of daily politics. Did Ronald Reagan in his first term create a new public philosophy, permanently altering the political agenda and the terms on which issues are debated?

References

Anderson, M. (1978). *Welfare: the Political Economy of Welfare Reform in the US*, Stanford, CA: Hoover Institution Press.

Ashford, N. (1981). 'The Neo-Conservatives', *Government and Opposition*, pp.353–69.

Berger, P. and Berger, B. (1983). *The War Over the Family*, London: Hutchinson.

Berger, P. and Neuhaus, R. (1977). *To Empower People*, Washington, DC: American Enterprise Institute.

Buchanan, J. *et al.* (1978). *The Economics of Politics*, London: Institute of Economic Affairs.

Butler, E. (1983). *Hayek*, London: Temple Smith.

Butler, S.(1985). *Privatizing Federal Spending*, New York: Universe Books.

Duignan P. and Rabushka A., eds (1980). *The US in the 1980s*, Stanford, CA: Hoover Institution Press.

Fiorina, M. (1977). *Congress: Keystone of the Washington Establishment*, New Haven, Conn.: Yale University Press.

Friedman, M. and Friedman, R. (1980). *Free To Choose*, London: Penguin.

Gilder, G. (1981). *Wealth and Poverty*, New York: Basic Books.

Heatherley, C., ed. (1981). *Mandate for Leadership*, Washington DC: Heritage Foundation.

King, A., ed. (1978). *The New American Political System*, Washington, DC: American Enterprise Institute.

Kirkpatrick, J. (1982). *Dictatorships and Double Standards*, Washington, DC: American Enterprise Institute.

Kirkpatrick, J. (1983). *The Reagan Phenomenon*, Washington DC: American Enterprise Institute.

Meyer, J., ed. (1982). *Meeting Human Needs*, Washington, DC: American Enterprise Institute.

Moore, W. G. and Penner R., eds (1980). *The Constitution and the Budget*, Washington, DC: American Enterprise Institute.

Moynihan, D. (1980). *Counting Our Blessings*, London: Secker & Warburg.

Murray, C. (1984). *Losing Ground: American Social Policy 1950–1980*, New York: Basic Books.

Niskanen, W. (1973). *Bureaucracy: Servant or Master?*, London: Institute of Economic Affairs.

Podhoretz, N. (1980). *The Present Danger*, New York: Simon & Schuster.

Roberts, P. C. (1984). *The Supply Side Revolution: an Insider's Account of Policymaking in Washington*, Cambridge, Mass. and London: Harvard University Press.

Smith, H., Clymer, A., Silk, L., Lindsay, R. and Burt, R. (1981). *Reagan: the Man, The President*, New York: Macmillan.

Tullock, G. (1976). *The Vote Motive*, London: Institute of Economic Affairs.

Tyroler, C., ed. (1984). *Alerting America: the Papers of the Committee of the Present Danger*, New York: Pergamon-Brassey.

Wanniski, J. (1978). *The Way the World Works*, New York: Basic Books.

A new Conservative majority?

Since the 1932 presidential election, a New Deal liberal Democrat coalition has dominated US government. The Democrats have had a majority in elective offices, party identification and voting behaviour at presidential, congressional and state levels. Through the 1960s and 1970s there was evidence that the coalition was unravelling, and there has been considerable discussion about whether there is a realignment, with the Republicans emerging as the new majority party, or a dealignment, with both parties in decline and no party dominant. Conservatives hailed the 1980 election as a major step towards realignment and a mandate for conservatism, while liberals saw it as a personal defeat for Carter that did not represent a permanent diminution in the strength of the Democratic party or liberalism. This chapter considers the decline of the New Deal coalition, the emergence of the New Right and the New Christian Right, some of the problems of the Carter administration and the results of the 1980 election.

The decline of the New Deal coalition

From 1896 to 1928, the Republicans were the dominant party, but with the Great Depression the Democrats under Franklin Roosevelt presented the New Deal as a solution to the depression. Whether economic recovery was due to the New Deal economic policies or to the Second World War is disputed but, whatever the cause, the Democrats were the beneficiaries and dominated electoral politics. This majority coalition consisted of blue-collar workers, urban voters, Roman Catholics and ethnics, Southern whites, blacks, intellectuals and the young. The Republicans had strength only among the old, the North East, businessmen and white Protestants, and were very much the minority party.

Gradually the Democrat coalition became unravelled. It began first with the South, as the growing liberalism of the national Democrat party alienated conservative Southern whites, who continued to support local Democrats but rejected Democrat presidential candidates. A major cause was the issue of race, but their differences with liberal Democrats extended over a wide range of issues. This alienation expressed itself in support for the Republican Barry Goldwater in 1964 (although these gains were swamped by losses elsewhere); for the independent George Wallace in 1968, who captured 13.5% of the national vote and defeated the official Democrat candidate in the Deep South; and an overwhelming vote for Nixon in 1972.

Other major constituencies of the Democratic coalition began to leave, according to Ladd, because of powerful economic, social and cultural changes, which had created 'the Inversion of the New Deal Class Order' and 'Liberalism Upside Down' (Ladd, 1978). He showed that, in contrast to the 1930s, it was the upper class and the well-educated who were the most liberal, especially on egalitarian and cultural issues, and the new middle class and urban working class the most conservative. 'The high social strata now consistently provide a greater measure of support for liberal programmes and candidacies than do the lower strata' (Ladd, 1978, 227). Scammon and Wattenberg identified, as a determinant of voting behaviour, the rise of the 'Social Issue', which covered a wide range of cultural and moral issues such as crime, race and sexual promiscuity, and they expressed concern that unless the Democrats demonstrated sensitivity to the position of the 'unyoung, unpoor and the unblack' on these issues, the party coalition would collapse (Scammon and Wattenberg, 1970).

Kevin Phillips, a conservative elections expert, predicted that because of demographic and ideological trends undermining the Democrats, there was an opportunity for an Emerging Republican Majority (Phillips, 1970). On the economy, the Democrats were now taxing the many for the benefit of the few, and, on the social issues, the Democrats represented a Liberal Establishment against a conservative people. Republican expectations of representing 'the Silent Majority' received encouragement from Nixon's 60.7% vote in the 1972 election. Such hopes were dashed by the Watergate affair, the economic depression begun in 1974 and the nomination of a cultural conservative as Democrat presidential candidate in Jimmy Carter, a Southern born-again Christian. Even Phillips concluded that the Republicans had failed to open their arms to social conservatives and thereby surrendered any possibility of majority status (Phillips, 1975).

Despite Carter's win in 1976 against President Ford, there continued to be signs that the Democrat coalition was in trouble. Firstly, party identification was in decline among voters. In 1952, 47 per cent identified with the Democrats; but by 1980 this had dropped to 41 per cent. The number of people describing themselves as Independents grew from 22 per cent to 34 per cent. More importantly, party identification was becoming less important as a predictor of voting behaviour, so that many were willing to split their ticket, voting for different parties at the presidential level (often Republican) and at the congressional and state levels (usually Democrat) (De Vries and Tarrance, 1972). Secondly, there was evidence that voters were becoming more influenced by issues (Nie *et al*, 1976). Many traditional Democrat voters were becoming disenchanted with the Democrats over the issues, associating the party with poor economic growth, a soft line on communism and cultural permissiveness.

The New Deal coalition was in trouble, but the Republicans had not demonstrated that they could create a new majority. Republican-voter identification was also falling, from 27 per cent in 1952 to 22 per cent in 1980. The party had won four out of the seven presidential elections from 1952 to 1976 and narrowly lost in 1960 and 1976, but at every other level it was weak. Since 1932 Republicans had controlled Congress only for a brief period from 1952 to 1954. The Democrats held the large majority of the Governorships, except for 1966–8, and dominated the state legislatures. The break-up of the Democrat coalition was no guarantee of Republican success and many experts predicted that dealignment, the decline of both parties, was more likely than realignment, the replacement of one major party by another (Ladd, 1978). The election of 1980 raised the question again as to whether the Republicans could begin to establish themselves as the new majority party, especially under the leadership of a strong conservative like Reagan.

The New Right

The view that conservatives could not win elections was challenged by a group of conservatives that became known as the New Right. The key figures were Richard Viguerie, a political fundraiser; Paul Weyrich of the Committee for the Survival of a Free Congress; Howard Phillips of the Conservative Caucus; and Terry Dolan of the National Conservative Political Action Committee (NICPAC). Their strategy was to win elections by the use of direct mail fund-raising, independent action by Political Action Committees, improved campaign organisations, the use of single issues, and the mobilisation of 'fundamentalist' voters (Viguerie, 1981).

Viguerie set up his own company to raise money for conservative candidates, organisations and causes by direct mail to potential contributors. Political money had traditionally been raised in large contributions from businesses, unions, interest groups or rich individuals, but this was made more difficult by the Federal Election Campaign Act of 1972. By the use of sophisticated techniques of targeting, Viguerie raised considerable sums from small contributions from a large number of people, many of whom were not involved politically in any other way. Dolan created NICPAC to raise money through direct mail and spent it in cash or contributions in kind in support of conservative candidates, amounting to $2.3 million in 1980. NICPAC has become particularly controversial for its hard-hitting, independent and negative campaigns (McIntyre, 1979). Instead of supporting specific conservative candidates, it often spends resources attacking liberal candidates. One example would be the distribution of leaflets outside churches on Sunday indicating that a particular liberal candidate was pro-abortion. Weyrich provided campaign expertise for conservative candidates in primary and general elections, such as research on issues, opinion polling and the use of volunteers. Election campaigns have become a highly professional business and the availability of advice and experienced campaigners has been a considerable benefit to suitably conservative candidates, particularly in the primaries. Weyrich has become active in organising coalitions in Washington, while Phillips has concentrated on organising at the grass-roots level in every congressional district.

All of them employ the 'single issue' strategy of finding the issue on which the person feels most strongly and using that to obtain a response. The issue might be taxes, abortion, gun control, unions or defence. They use that issue to get the person into a campaign or organisation and then 'educate' them into the conservative position on other issues. The New Right has found that 'social issues' such as abortion or crime are the most successful in obtaining a response. They believe that the party which gives sufficient attention to the social issues could become the new majority party, but they remain sceptical that the Republican party will (Rusher, 1975). By the use of single issues, the New Right has mobilised a substantial constituency of voters, contributors and activists. Critics complain that 'single issue' groups and individuals are intolerant of opponents and make political compromises impossible. Their most controversial tactic was their role in encouraging the participation of fundamentalist christians in politics, known as the New Christian Right.

In 1978 the New Right established itself as a major force. It led the opposition to the Panama Canal Treaty, mailing up to 9 million letters and spending over $3 million to make it a major issue. The New Right also helped to replace two liberal Senators with their own men, Gordon Humphreys in New Hampshire and Roger Jepsen in Iowa, and helped Jeffrey Bell to defeat liberal Republican Clifford Case in the New Jersey primary. In 1980 it claimed a major role in the election of Reagan and in the defeat of six liberal Senators, George McGovern of South Dakota, Birch Bayh of Indiana, Frank Church of Idaho, John Culver of Iowa, Warren Magnuson in Washington state and Gaylord Nelson in Wisconsin. How important the New Right was in these election victories is subject to dispute, but it was very successful in claiming and receiving the credit (or blame). It had successfully killed the idea that conservatives were losers.

During Reagan's first term, the New Right complained at the lack of progress in pursuing a conservative agenda, particularly on social issues, which took a low priority behind tax cuts and increased defence expenditure. Reagan himself has remained rather suspicious of the New Right, because of their failure to support him early in 1980, their excessive claims that he owed his election to them and the fear that they might lose him support among most Americans who do not share their strong views on the social issues.

The New Christian Right

Fundamentalist churches, which believe that the Bible is God-given truth and not simply illustrative tales, are the fastest-growing churches in America and currently claim over ten million members, with a considerable influence over the wider evangelical movement

such as the Southern Baptist Convention. Traditionally, fundamentalists have avoided political activity because of the fear that they will
be tainted by political secularism. However, a number of issues have
emerged to make them more politically conscious. The most important issue is abortion, which was declared a constitutional right in the
Supreme Court case, *Roe v. Wade*, in 1973. To a fundamentalist,
abortion is murder, so this issue has mobilised many of them into the
Right-to-Life movement and in support of candidates who promise
to act against abortion. Other issues of concern to them include the
1978 loss of automatic tax exemption for religious schools, the
promotion of homosexuality as an acceptable lifestyle, voluntary
school prayer, feminism as a threat to the traditional role of women,
and the widespread availability of pornography and its potential
effect on children.

Viguerie and Weyrich were influential in persuading some fundamentalist leaders that exercising influence on these issues required
participation in political activity. The Revd Jerry Falwell, head of
the highly successful Liberty Baptist Church in Lynchburg,
Virginia, organised the Moral Majority in 1979 to mobilise all those
concerned with moral decline, including not only fundamentalists
but also mainstream Protestants, Catholics and Jews. Other groups
included Christian Voice, which produced a report card on Congressional voting, and Religious Roundtable, led by Eddie McAteer,
which organised political seminars for fundamentalist preachers.

The New Christian Right (NCR) is able to reach a substantial
constituency through television and preachers. Christian TV and
Radio programmes attract a considerable audience. Falwell has his
Old Time Gospel Hour, attracting 1.4 million viewers, which mixes
readings from the Bible, the singing of hymns and traditional
preaching, with references to the moral decay of America due to
religious and political liberalism. Other TV preachers who present a
conservative political message include Pat Robertson, head of the
Christian Broadcasting Network, James Robison and Jim Bakker.
Meanwhile local preachers have considerable influence over their
congregations and provide a ready-made local organisation.

The Moral Majority claimed to have helped register 2.5 million
voters in 1980, and to have encouraged thousands of Christians to
participate in political activity. Critics complain that the NCR seeks
to break the separation of church and state established by the First
Amendment of the Constitution, and that it claims to present the

christian position on non-religious issues such as relations with Taiwan and tax cuts (Liebman and Wuthnow, 1983, ch.8). The NCR reply that the neutrality of the Constitution has been used to discriminate against religion and in favour of secular humanism, and that liberals did not complain of religious involvement in issues such as Vietnam and welfare. Its claims to have contributed decisively to the election of Reagan and other Republicans have been challenged, but the NCR has nonetheless succeeded in placing its concerns on the political agenda (Lipset and Raab, 1981).

The Carter administration

Conservatism gained considerable strength during the Carter administration as a reaction to the failures of the administration in two major areas: the economy and foreign policy.

The economy was felt to be in decline under Carter, in particular with the rate of inflation entering double digits for the first time, high interest rates and a sharp decline in the value of the dollar. In the face of this, Carter appeared to lack any economic strategy. The only economic policy with which Carter was associated was an energy policy, but his proposals were widely criticised and failed to pass Congress. Carter appeared to have no sense of direction, and this was seen to be confirmed by a speech to the nation in 1979 about a national crisis of confidence, which was felt to represent more a crisis of confidence within the administration than the nation.

By contrast the Republicans had an economic strategy and it was a popular one based on tax cuts. In June 1978, Proposition 13 was passed by the voters of California, by a margin of two to one, against the opposition of the political and economic establishment. Proposition 13 reduced local property taxes by over half. It was only the most visible sign of a popular tax revolt which led to tax reductions passed by many state legislatures or by referenda (Rabushka and Ryan, 1982). Supply-side economists argued that tax cuts were the most effective way of restoring the American economy. In 1977 Congressman Jack Kemp, a former professional football player and a Republican from the traditionally Democrat-union town of Buffalo, New York, introduced the Kemp-Roth Bill (co-sponsored by Senator William Roth of Delaware) as an alternative to the Carter budget. The bill proposed a three-year across-the-board tax reduction at 10 per cent a year. With evidence of popular support for tax

cuts, Kemp-Roth became the centrepiece of the Republican campaign in the 1978 elections. It was in 1978 that Reagan removed his
initial doubts and committed himself to supply-side economics,
partly because it fitted in with his upbeat image of America, that if
only the talents and energies of ordinary Americans could be released
then the economy would be revived, partly because he recognised
that tax cuts were a vote-winner, and partly because it was endorsed
by newspapers and journals in whom he had confidence, the *Wall
Street Journal*, *National Review* and *Human Events*. The importance
of tax cuts as a political strategy was that it identified the Republicans
as the party of economic growth, in contrast to its old image as
cold-hearted expenditure-cutters. On the economy the Republicans
therefore held the high ground.

In foreign policy, Carter came to power with the hope of shifting
attention from the struggle with the Soviet Union towards other
aspects of international relations. In a speech at the University of
Notre Dame in May 1977, he claimed that 'we are now free of that
inordinate fear of communism which once led us to embrace any
dictator who shared our fear'. The administration concentrated on
the standard of human rights of American allies, the peace process in
the Middle East, the signing of a Panama Canal treaty surrendering
control to Panama, the signing of an arms control treaty, SALT II,
with the Soviet Union and the improvement of relations with black
Africa.

Only in the Middle East was the Carter administration seen as
successful, with the achievement of the Camp David accord between
Israel and Egypt. The Panama Canal Treaty was eventually ratified
by the Senate, but only after a long struggle in which the New Right
mobilised itself in opposition, and with many Americans failing to
see any benefits in return for surrendering control of the Canal to the
Panamanian dictator General Torrijos. On the most important
foreign policy issue for the administration, the SALT II treaty with
the Soviet Union, the Senate refused to ratify the treaty, taking the
view that America's relative defence position had declined and that
the treaty would merely ratify that decline. Carter's weakness
towards the Soviet Union was underlined by the lack of an initial
response to the build-up of Soviet missiles in Western Europe, and
Carter's surprise decision not to deploy neutron weapons. The
emphasis on human rights was seen as weakening American allies,
and the person responsible for relations with Africa, UN Ambas-

sador Andrew Young, was forced to resign after several embarrassing episodes. Carter was forced to abandon his strategy of downplaying East–West conflicts after the Soviet invasion of Afghanistan in December 1979. The greatest blow came with the fall of the Shah of Iran and the holding of American hostages in Tehran. After an initial 'rallying around the President', Carter's inability to secure their release confirmed the now established image of an incompetent and indecisive President. Ronald Reagan provided a strong contrast in 1980.

The 1980 election

At the beginning of 1980, few commentators would have predicted with much certainty that Ronald Reagan would be the next President. The general view of most commentators was that he was too old and too conservative to win the Republican nomination, or the presidential election.

Reagan was an unusual conservative politician. He had been a moderately successsful Hollywood actor, a registered Democrat until 1962 and President of the Screen Actors Guild, the actors' union. He achieved national political attention through a late television broadcast for Goldwater in 1964, which was considered the best broadcast for the Republicans in the whole campaign and raised considerable sums from large numbers of small donations. Encouraged by Californian conservatives to enter politics, he surprised most commentators, as a Republican novice in a Democrat state at the age of fifty-five, by defeating experienced incumbent Democrat Governor Pat Brown. He was Governor of California for eight years from 1966 to 1974, easily winning re-election, and he made two unsuccessful attempts for the Republican presidential nomination in 1968 and in 1976.

By 1980 Ronald Reagan was considered by most commentators as unlikely to win the Republican nomination, faced as he was by a strong field of opponents. A few of the other eleven candidates were not very serious, but the field was an unusually strong one. They included: George Bush, who had an impressive political career as Director of the CIA, Ambassador in Peking and Chairman of the Republican National Committee; liberal Congressman John Anderson, who received considerable media attention; Howard Baker, Senate Republican leader and Watergate star; John Connally, Treasury Secretary under Nixon with a well-funded campaign; and conservative Congressman Phil Crane, with access to conservative organisations and the support of the New Right. There was also former President Ford, who was under great pressure to run as a candidate to stop Reagan. Despite this formidable field of candidates, two months before the Republican convention on 14 July all of the other candidates had dropped out of the race, except for Anderson who was building up for an independent campaign. At the Republican convention, Reagan won easily on the first ballot, confounding early predictions that there would be a deadlocked convention with many ballots and perhaps the entry of Ford as a compromise candidate. There was an attempt to persuade Ford to accept the vice-presidential nomination, but Ford's price was too high for Reagan. In contrast to Goldwater's campaign, Reagan worked hard to achieve party unity, both by the nomination of his main opponent Bush as his vice presidential running mate and by his conciliatory acceptance speech.

Press comment was that only centrist candidates could win, and that the history of presidential elections had shown that extreme candidates either of the left, such as McGovern in 1972, or of the right, Goldwater in 1964, were doomed to heavy defeat. Reagan was 'Carter's favourite opponent', because he represented the conservative minority within the minority party, he was sixty-nine years old, he lacked Washington experience, and he had not held elective office for six years. Hamilton Jordan, a close aide to Carter, summed up his campaign assessment: 'The American people are not going to elect a 70 year old, right-wing ex-movie actor to be president' (Ranney, 1981, 212). Even by the end of the campaign, election pundits stated that the election was too close to call, and there was considerable speculation that Anderson would prevent Carter from obtaining a majority in the electoral college and throw the election to the House of Representatives.

The result was stunning. Reagan won with a ten-point lead over Carter, with 50.8% of the vote to Carter's 41% and Anderson's 6.6%, and an electoral college landslide of 489 votes to 49. Carter was the first elected incumbent to be defeated since Hoover in 1932. The Republicans also gained 33 House seats, 4 Governorships, 189 state legislative seats and 5 state legislative chambers. Particularly satisfying for them was the twelve seat gain in the Senate, which brought them control for the first time since 1954 and involved the defeat of six senior liberals. The Democrat vote had declined in every state, and Reagan had won throughout the South with the sole exception of Carter's home state of Georgia. Even liberal Massachusetts, McGovern's single state in 1972, had gone for Reagan. No one could dispute the size of the Reagan victory, but the interpretation of the election results became a subject of controversy. Conservatives were quick to claim that the election was a conservative mandate, while liberals argued that it was a personal defeat for Carter and not a repudiation of the Democrat party.

A new Conservative majority?

The debate over the 1980 election result revolved around the questions as to what extent it demonstrated a shift in a conservative direction among the voters, whether it was simply a repudiation of the incompetent Carter administration, or to what extent it provided yet more evidence of a volatile electorate in an era of dealignment.

Evidence for the view that there had been a fundamental change was that the swing to the Republicans had occurred at all levels, presidential, congressional and state, suggesting more than a rejection of Carter, and that the defeated Democrats were largely from the liberal wing. Opinion polls showed that more people were describing themselves as conservative than liberal, thus a *New York Times* poll found 31 per cent describing themselves as conservative and only 18 per cent as liberal. The greatest gains had been among the Democrat core vote: union families, manual workers, Southerners, Jews, Catholics, the old and the non-college educated. James Q. Wilson believed that 'the Reagan candidacy is a candidacy based on issues, issues which the candidate has developed over the better part of two decades and which now, taken as a whole, command the assent of a very large proportion of the American people' (Wilson, 1980). Scammon and Wattenberg argued that it was an end of an era even before the results were announced (Scammon and Wattenberg, 1980). They pointed to poll results showing that between 1959 and 1978 the percentage of Americans who thought that 'big government' was the major cause of inflation went from 14 per cent to 51 per cent. By 1978, 76 per cent believed that 'Washington had become too powerful' and 84 per cent held that 'Washington was spending too much'. Support for increased defence spending rose from 11 per cent in 1971 to 60 per cent in 1979 (pre-Iran). However Scammon and

Wattenberg made it clear that these changes would not necessarily benefit the Republicans, only that they probably would unless the Democrats were responsive to this change in mood.

Supporters of the New Right claimed that it was the social issues that won Reagan the 1980 election, pointing to big conservative majorities on these issues (Pines, 1981). A 1979 Gallup poll found only 22 per cent backing abortion in all circumstances and only 19 per cent wanting to ban it in all circumstances, but 54 per cent favoured abortion only in very restricted circumstances, such as a threat to the woman's life, which was far more restrictive than the ruling of the Supreme Court. Gallup polls in 1980 also found a majority against the hiring of homosexuals as clergy and elementary school teachers; 76 per cent in favour of a constitutional amendment to allow school prayers; 79 per cent in favour of sex education in schools only with parental consent; and 70 per cent against the legalisation of marijuana. However, among those who claimed a conservative mood, there were considerable differences over the relative importance of the different issues. Libertarians and supply-siders believed that it was support for the free market and tax cuts which were central to the election victory. Neo-conservatives identified defence as a major cause of Democrat defection, while the New Right pointed to the social issues.

Liberals argued that the election result represented only a verdict on Carter (Sandoz and Crabb, 1981; Williams and Reilly, 1982). The Democrat vote had declined by 7 per cent, but the Republican vote had gone up only by 2.8 percent, and the liberal Anderson had achieved 6.6 per cent because Carter was the candidate. A CBS/*New York Times* poll found that 38 per cent of Reagan's voters said that 'it was time for a change' and 21 per cent wanted 'strong leadership', while only 18 per cent mentioned conservatism as a reason for voting for Reagan. When asked why Reagan had won, 63 per cent said it was a rejection of Carter and only 24 per cent that it was a mandate for conservatism. Carter's unpopularity was clear receiving a 63 per cent unfavourable rating in July, 1980, while in September, 1980, he was given low ratings for his handling of foreign policy (78 per cent) and the economy (85 per cent). Liberals pointed to polls which suggested that voters who wanted reductions in taxation did not support cuts in expenditure.

A third view was that there had been a fundamental shift in opinion but that this was a dealignment and not clearly a move to the right. Everett Ladd was a leading spokesman for this view. He showed that there had been considerable changes in the electorate and that the New Deal coalition was dead, but that the emergence of cultural conflicts created problems for both parties. There had been a class transformation, with the upper class more liberal especially on social issues and the working class more conservative, especially on social issues. While this created problems for the Democrats in retaining working-class votes, it also created problems for the Republicans in gaining them without losing middle-class votes (Ladd, 1981).

William Maddox and Stuart Lillie argued that the terms 'liberal' and 'conservative' were incomplete descriptions of the ideological spectrum because they suggest a one-dimensional view of politics (Maddox and Lillie, 1984). They proposed two issue-dimensions, on support for greater intervention in economics and social affairs. Liberals (interventionist in economics but not social issues) and conservatives (interventionist in social issues but not economics) should be joined as ideological labels by libertarians (non-interventionist in both) and populists (interventionist in both). They also suggested, though more tentatively, differences over foreign policy, with interventionist conservatives and populists and anti-interventionist libertarians and liberals. From this perspective, the problem for the parties is to put together a coalition of these groups. According to Maddox and Lillie, Reagan's support was distributed between 28 per cent libertarian, 32 per cent conservative, 11 per cent populist, 11 per cent liberal with 11 per cent other. They found that many Reagan voters were against interventionism abroad and social conservatism, and they argued that the economy was the primary issue for Reagan voters. They predicted that the parties will become increasingly divided, the Republicans between conservatives and libertarians, and the Democrats between liberals and populists, further supporting the dealignment thesis.

The debate on explaining the result of 1980 has been confused not only by partisan claims but also by the difficulty of correctly reading the data. Some points are clear. Attachment to the parties has declined, but is this a permanent decline or simply a sign of a period of transition? Hostility to big government and support for a strong defence grew significantly among the public, but is this a reflection of specific events or a more fundamental shift? The Democrat coalition has collapsed but is not yet replaced by a new Republican one.

Reagan successfully put together the coalition in 1980, but could he hold it together, or his successor? Whether the changes were short-term or fundamental would partly depend on the performance of the new Reagan administration. Therefore the actions of the administration were watched with considerable interest to see if they presaged a new era in American politics.

References

De Vries, W. and Tarrance, L. (1972). *The Ticket Splitter: a New Force in American Politics*, Grand Rapids, Michigan:Eerdsmeer.
Ladd Jr., E.C. with Hadley, C. (1978). *The Transformation of the American Party System*, 2nd edn, New York:Norton.
Ladd Jr., E.C. (1981). 'The Brittle Mandate: Electoral Dealignment and the 1980 Election' , *Political Science Quarterly*, pp.1–25.
Liebman, R. and Wuthnow, R., eds (1983). *The New Christian Right*, New York:Aldine.
Lipset, S. and Raab, E. (1981). 'The Election and the Evangelicals', *Commentary*, pp.25–31.
Maddox, W. and Lillie, S. (1984). *Beyond Liberal and Conservative: Reassessing the Political Spectrum*, Washington, DC:Cato Institute.
McIntyre, T. (1979). *The Fear Brokers*, New York:Pilgrim Press.
Nie, N., Verba, S. and Petrocik, J. (1976). *The Changing American Voter*, Cambridge, Mass. and London:Harvard University Press.
Phillips, K. (1970). *The Emerging Republican Majority*, New York:Doubleday.
Phillips, K. (1975). *Mediacracy:American Parties and Politics in the Communications Age*, New York:Doubleday.
Pines, B. Y. (1981). 'A Majority for Morality?' , *Public Opinion*, pp.42–47.
Rabushka, A. and Ryan, R. (1982). *The Tax Revolt*, Stanford, CA:Hoover Institution Press.
Ranney, A., ed. (1981). *The American Elections of 1980*, Washington, DC, American Enterprise Institute.
Rusher, W. (1975). *The Making of a New American Majority Party*, Ottawa, Ill.:Green Hill.
Rusher, W. (1984). *The Rise of the Right*, New York:Morrow.
Sandoz, E. and Crabb, C., eds (1981). *A Tide of Discontent:The 1980 Elections and Their Meaning*, Washington DC:Congressional Quarterly Press.
Scammon, R. and Wattenberg, B. (1970). *The Real Majority*, New York: Berkeley.
Scammon, R. and Wattenberg, B. (1980). 'Is this An End of An Era?' *Public Opinion*, pp.2–12.
Viguerie, R. (1981). *The New Right:We're ready To Lead*, Falls Church, VA:Carolina House.

Wilson, J. Q. (1980). 'Reagan and the Republican Revival' , *Commentary*,
   pp.25–32.
Williams, P. M. and Reilly, S. J.(1982) 'The 1980 U.S. Elections and After',
   Political Studies, pp.371–92.

Part 2

Managing the Reagan Policy Agenda

The Reagan White House, the Cabinet and the bureaucracy

The presidential office occupied by Ronald Reagan in January 1981, was an office which reflected considerably the massive expansion in the size and scope of the federal government's role in the wake of the New Deal measures of Franklin D. Roosevelt and the Great Society programmes of Lyndon B. Johnson. The proliferation of federal programmes prompted an aggrandisement of the modern presidency, which manifested itself by a swelling White House bureaucracy and by a vastly expanded presidential involvement to manage directly the machinery of government – which survived even the aftermath of Watergate (Cronin, 1980; Greenstein, 1979; Watson and Thomas, 1983).

Examining the advent of what was termed the 'administrative presidency' (Nathan, 1975) and its tendency towards a situation of presidential 'overload', a number of studies proposed the abandonment of managerialism and a restructuring of the office of President. Central to many of these proposals were the arguments put forward by one school of thought which advocated coupling a reduced presidential role with a collegial approach to decision-making requiring more substantive use of the president's Cabinet appointees (Hess, 1976; Porter, 1980). An alternative school argued, however, that the presidential role needed to be redeveloped by the adoption of a strategic approach which envisaged presidential focus on a few major priority policy goals to which the resources of the presidency should be directed (Heineman and Hessler, 1980; Heclo and Salamon, 1981; but see also Meltsner, 1981).

Essentially, Ronald Reagan's approach to the office of president was one which straddled both the 'collegial' and 'strategic' reform schools. As a political chief executive with considerable experience from his two terms as Governor of California (1967–1975), Reagan brought to the presidency a distinctly collegial style which required substantial use of his cabinet and which featured significant delegation of authority to individual Cabinet officers. His intentions on this as president were made clear on the eve of his 1980 election victory, when he pledged himself to 'a new structuring of the presidential Cabinet that will make Cabinet officers the managers of the national administration'. At the same time, it was also clear that within a Reagan administration Cabinet (and sub-Cabinet) appointees should be wholly committed to Reaganite goals. From the outset, therefore, the Reagan appointments process laid great stress on ideological commitment and loyalty to the Reagan agenda.

The overall policy agenda directly associated with Reagan was remarkably clear-cut and focused. In domestic terms, he had campaigned for the reduction of the role of government (by means of tax reductions, spending cuts, elimination of 'wasteful' federal programmes and economic deregulation). On foreign policy the agenda was no less clear-cut, with Reagan committed to rebuilding US military strength as a basis for restoring the United States to a position of leadership on the world stage. In office therefore Reagan as president employed a largely strategic approach which concentrated on the straightforward goals of the Reagan agenda.

Thus, the Reagan presidency can be viewed as an endeavour to combine the strategic approach of strong commitment to a focused policy agenda with a Cabinet-centred collegial style of government featuring committed political appointees pledged to ensure adherence to the goals of the Reagan agenda throughout the federal bureaucracy.

The Reagan White House

The structuring requirements of the Reagan presidency for its operation of the White House office and other units within the Executive Office of the President (EOP) were essentially fourfold: first, to ensure coherent management of the Reagan agenda; second, to provide a policy development process which would maintain a presidential focus; third, to obtain effective political implementation of the Reagan agenda on Capitol Hill; and, fourth, to accommodate the collegial executive style of Ronald Reagan.

As a former two-term governor of California, Reagan brought to the presidency the operational style of a presider rather than a manager, of a board chairman rather than a chief operations officer, and he had a distinct penchant for delegation (Hamilton and Biggart, 1984). Moreover, he had arrived in Washington for his inauguration in Januray 1981, having loudly proclaimed his determination to operate a system of Cabinet government. This determination appeared to have a firm edge to it, given his practice in the California governorship where he had employed a small Cabinet group as his main policy-making forum. In California, his approach had been straightforward:

As a political chairman of the board, Reagan liked to meet regularly with his five principal officers and his chief of staff. . . . These Cabinet meetings were his forum for debating policy options with his closest advisers. . . . Sometimes he would make decisions on the spot, sometimes later. And he delegated to the Cabinet officers the responsibility to carry out his decisions (Smith *et al.*, 1981, 167).

From the outset therefore the staffing and structuring of the Reagan presidency were of critical importance.

Mindful of the heavy criticism directed at Nixon and Carter for surrounding themselves with an inner circle of 'home-state' cronies, Reagan indicated at the outset of his 1980 campaign that a Reagan White House would not be comprised of 'nine Californians'. In the event, this pledge was implemented by the selection of his key EOP appointees on the basis of a judicious blend of talent, experience, ideological commitment and past personal association. Only two of his California gubernatorial staff were given major White House posts: Edwin Meese, as Counsellor to the President (with Cabinet rank), and Michael Deaver as Deputy Chief of Staff. For his White House Chief of Staff, Reagan appointed a Texan, James Baker, who had built up a considerable reputation for organisational and operational ability. Baker had been centrally involved in the campaigns of two former Reagan rivals (as Ford's chief delegate hunter in the Republican nomination race against Reagan in 1976, and as manager of Bush's unsuccessful challenge to Reagan in 1980), but as part of Reagan's 1980 presidential campaign-team he had quickly impressed the candidate by his preparation of him for the successful televised debate with Jimmy Carter. The two major White House policy adviser posts were given to specialists who had advised Reagan in both his 1976 and 1980 campaigns: as his national security adviser,

Reagan appointed Richard Allen (who had briefly served as a staff member of the National Security Council under Henry Kissinger in 1969); and, as his assistant for domestic policy, Reagan chose Martin Anderson (a conservative academic who had previously served as John Ehrlichman's assistant in the Nixon Domestic Council).

Elsewhere in the EOP, Reagan sought to recruit his key appointees on the same essential basis of talent, experience and commitment to the Reagan agenda. In some ways, the most surprising appointment was that of David Stockman to the vital post of Director of the Office of Management and Budget (OMB). Strongly committed to a radical-right perspective, Stockman was a young, two-term Congressman from Michigan who was widely credited with an almost encyclopaedic knowledge of the congressional budget process. An associate of Congressman Jack Kemp, one of Reagan's inner-circle of advisers, Stockman had drawn himself to Reagan's attention with a transition-team proposal in November, 1980, arguing for a swift and massive economic recovery programme which would seek to avoid a Republican 'Economic Dunkirk'. As his Chairman of the Council of Economic Advisers Reagan selected Murray Weidenbaum, an economist who not only possessed Washington experience (as a staff economist at the Bureau of the Budget [now OMB] between 1949 and 1957, and as Assistant Treasury Secretary between 1969 and 1971) but who was also committed strongly to free market economics and a vigorous policy of deregulation. For the post of US Trade Representative, Reagan appointed William Brock. A former member of Congress (with a total of fourteen years in both houses), Brock had exhibited considerable negotiating skills as Chairman of the Republican National Committee in working to rebuild the party over the four-year period capped by Reagan's 1980 presidential victory. Finally, as Director of the Central Intelligence Agency (CIA), Reagan chose his 1980 campaign manager, William Casey, who had previously served in the Nixon and Ford administrations (as Chairman of the Securities Exchange Commission, 1971–3; as Assistant Secretary of State for economic affairs, 1973–74; and as Chairman of the US Export–Import Bank, 1974–7). Casey possessed practical experience in the intelligence field, having worked for the Office of Strategic Services (the CIA's predecessor) during the Second World War and as Chief of Secret Intelligence under General Dwight D. Eisenhower.

Reflecting Ronald Reagan's collegial style as a chief executive, the White House was to be operated, not by a single dominant staff assistant (on the model of Haldeman in the Nixon White House), but rather by means of a 'troika' comprising Edwin Meese (as Counsellor to the President), James Baker (as Chief of Staff) and Michael Deaver (as Deputy Chief of Staff). Deaver was given charge of all of the President's scheduling, while Meese and Baker were assigned responsibilities which divided between them the substantive and the strategic elements of administration policy. Thus Meese would be concerned with oversight of the content and development of policy matters, while Baker would deal with the political aspects of obtaining policy support and approval on Capitol Hill and with interest groups and the American public.

As Figure 3.1 indicates, Meese was given charge over the president's two principal policy advisers: Richard Allen (on national security matters) and Martin Anderson (on domestic affairs) would both report to the president via Meese as presidential Counsellor. Thus Reagan implemented immediately his intention to downgrade the two major policy advisers' posts as part of his approach to operate a Cabinet-centred administration. Meese was also to act as the main White House liaison with Cabinet members through the Cabinet Secretariat directed under Meese's supervision by Craig Fuller (a former member of Deaver's California public relations firm). As Counsellor to the President with Cabinet rank, Meese would be able to deal with Cabinet members as an equal; but it was also made clear that all Cabinet officers retained the right of direct access to the president. Finally, Meese was charged with the responsibility of developing a process to enable the president to work directly with his Cabinet members on substantive policy issues.

As for the Baker side of the Meese-Baker White House division, as Figure 3.1 shows, this centred on responsibility for the various presidential units engaged with external political actors and included principally: the Office of Legislative Affairs (initially headed by Max Friedersdorf who had held the same post in the Ford administration); the Office of Public Liaison (initially directed by Elizabeth Dole who subsequently was appointed as Secretary of Transportation); the Office of Intergovernmental Affairs (which liaised with state and city governments); the Office of Political Affairs; and the Press and Speech Writing Offices. By agreement with Meese, Baker also assumed responsibility for the 'co-ordination and control of all in and out paperflow to the president' (see Barrett, 1983, 76–7). While at first sight this may appear to comprise a rather trivial

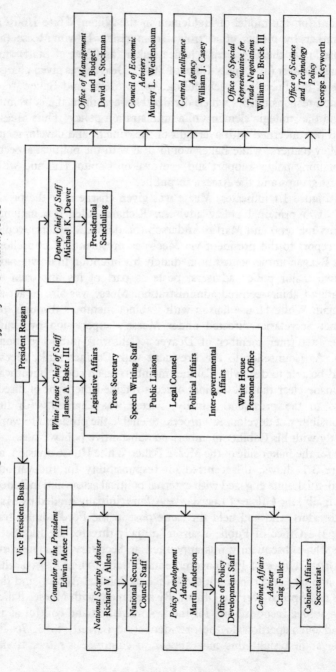

Figure 3.1: The Executive Office of the President, 1981

President Reagan

Vice President Bush

White House Chief of Staff
James A. Baker III

Deputy Chief of Staff
Michael K. Deaver
- Presidential Scheduling

Counselor to the President
Edwin Meese III

- Legislative Affairs
- Press Secretary
- Speech Writing Staff
- Public Liaison
- Legal Counsel
- Political Affairs
- Inter-governmental Affairs
- White House Personnel Office

National Security Adviser
Richard V. Allen
- National Security Council Staff

Policy Development Adviser
Martin Anderson
- Office of Policy Development Staff

Cabinet Affairs Adviser
Craig Fuller
- Cabinet Affairs Secretariat

Office of Management and Budget
David A. Stockman

Council of Economic Advisers
Murray L. Weidenbaum

Central Intelligence Agency
William J. Casey

Office of Special Representative for Trade Negotiations
William E. Brock III

Office of Science and Technology Policy
George Keyworth

consideration, the fact was that it guaranteed access for Baker to the various processes of presidential policy making. Control of the president's paperflow actually constitutes an enormous source of power: determining what the president sees and when he will see it are vital elements in presidential decision-making. The day-to-day task of dealing with the paperflow was assigned to Baker's deputy, Richard Darman. Darman was a former policy assistant to Elliot Richardson in four Cabinet departments during the Nixon and Ford administrations, and was regarded as a highly experienced Washington operative.

From the outset, it was evident that some means of co-ordinating the two sides of the Meese-Baker White House division would be needed. The matter was given considerable impetus by the pace of Stockman's endeavours in the first weeks of the adminstration in assembling the 'Reaganomics' package of spending, cutting and taxation proposals to generate economic recovery. Thus Meese and Baker issued a joint memorandum on 17 February 1981 to all Cabinet officers and senior White House personnel which stated:

To coordinate the efforts of all departments, agencies and offices involved, we need to pull together the various plans and activities related to the economic program. . . . The contact person for all material from the White House Staff will be Dick Darman. The contact for members of the Cabinet will be Craig Fuller (quoted in Barrett, 1983, 89).

Since Darman and Fuller occupied adjacent offices in the basement of the West Wing of the White House, both the Baker and Meese sides could keep themselves abreast of their respective counterpart's policy concerns.

The agreement on White House co-ordination was followed up four days later, on 21 February, by a paper from Darman to Baker arguing the clear and urgent need for the administration to develop a focused legislative strategy. This concern was prompted by the disparate activities of the Treasury, OMB and the Legislative Affairs Office, all of whom were moving off in different directions on the administration's legislative programme. Accepting the need for a coherent legislative strategy to ensure that all 'points of conflict, consistency, incompleteness, or opportunity' would be considered, Baker moved to create a Legislative Strategy Group (LSG). Initially, the LSG featured Baker and Meese as co-chairmen, thus under-scoring their equal status as the two major members of the White

House 'troika'. However, because all LSG meetings were held in Baker's office, Baker became in time the sole LSG chairman (illustrating again the potential for power or leadership within seemingly trivial factors). Besides Baker and Meese, the LSG's limited membership comprised: Michael Deaver (the third 'troika' partner); OMB Director David Stockman; the Assistant for Legislative Affairs (first Friedersdorf, then Kenneth Duberstein, and finally M. B. Oglesby); the Assistant for Communications, David Gergen; Richard Darman (as LSG secretary); and Craig Fuller (to assist in co-ordinating the work of the Cabinet with the LSG).

The principal role of the LSG was, from the outset, the consideration and coordination of the political dimensions of the policy strategies needed to build support for the administration's policy goals. However, because of its central position within the Reagan White House it was also able to function powerfully to shape the substance of policy. Nonetheless, while the LSG did achieve a position of considerable power throughout Reagan's first term, its character was essentially reactive – with its power ultimately resting on the capacity it possessed to react quickly as situations demanded (see chapter 4, below, for a fuller discussion of the LSG's role in legislative liaison).

On the policy development side of the White House, Meese was concerned with the task of ensuring that domestic policy in the Reagan presidency should be Cabinet-based rather than the product of strong EOP staff units as in previous administrations (see: Salamon, 1981; Turner, 1983). To that end, within the first weeks of the administration Meese developed a novel system of Cabinet Councils which was designed to sharpen the focus and degree of involvement of Cabinet members with policy matters – especially those concerned with cross-cutting issues affecting different departments and agencies. As explained in a White House press release on 26 February 1981, the new Cabinet Councils would operate as subgroups of the full Cabinet, with the president presiding as chairman of each Council. However, this new system was not intended to replace conventional Cabinet sessions: full Cabinet meetings would continue as in the past, focusing on broad issues of concern to the entire administration as well as on budgetary and fiscal matters.

Essentially, the purpose of the Cabinet Council system was to involve Cabinet officers, both individually and collectively in small groups, in 'an orderly process for reviewing issues requiring a decision by the president'. This was made explicit in the procedures laid down by Meese for the operation of the Council system:

* Each Cabinet Council will be chaired by the president.
* Each Cabinet Council has a designated chairman pro tempore who will guide the direction of the Council and will serve as the chairman of working sessions in which the president is not in attendance.
* An executive secretary will be appointed for each Cabinet Council from the Office of Policy Development. This individual, working with the Office of Cabinet Administration, will co-ordinate the activities of each Cabinet Council including the preparation and distribution of agendas and meeting summaries. This activity will be supplemented by a secretariat for every Cabinet Council, composed of the executive secretary, representatives of the member departments, and other personnel as needed, to prepare background materials, refine policy options and recommendations, and otherwise assist the Cabinet Council.
* Issues will be sent to Cabinet Councils by the Office of Cabinet Administration. Notification of such assignments will be communicated immediately to all Cabinet members to assure full opportunity to participate in consideration of each issue.
* Presidential decisions, made in or after Cabinet Council meetings, will follow full discussion by any Cabinet member who wishes to participate. Council meetings are open to any member of the Cabinet. Decisions will be reported to the full Cabinet as they occur. When full Cabinet review is required, the matter will be set for a full meeting of the full Cabinet (White House Fact Sheet, February 26, 1981).

   Initially, five Cabinet Councils were created:
1. – Cabinet Council on Economic Affairs (CCEA)
2. – Cabinet Council on Natural Resources & Environment (CCNRE)
3. – Cabinet Council on Commerce and Trade (CCCT)
4. – Cabinet Council on Human Resources (CCHR)
5. – Cabinet Council of Food and Agriculture (CCFA)

In 1982, two further Councils were created: on 29 Janurary the Cabinet Council for Legal Policy (CCLP) was established; and, on 22 September, after an internal White House evaluation had concluded that management policy and management oversight within the executive branch was too fragmented and uncoordinated, the Council for Management and Administration (CCMA) came into being (*Strategic Evaluation Memorandum* #18, 1982, 40).

   A major strength of the Cabinet Council system lay in the capacity of each Council to deal effectively with the increasing number of issues cutting across the jurisdictional boundaries of individual Cabinet departments and agencies. As Figure 3.2 indicates, by assigning to each individual Council as 'principal members' the various cabinet officers whose departments could be expected to claim some jurisdiction on a given area of policy, the Council system was intended to promote coherent policy deliberations on cross-cutting issues and thus to minimise debilitating jurisdictional 'turf' battles. At the same time, the formal assignment of 'principal memberships' to each Council was not meant to create exclusive policy groupings. On the contrary, all Cabinet officers remained free to participate in the work of any Councils to which they had not been formally assigned. Illustrating this point is the fact that Alexander Haig, as Secretary of State, served as a 'principal member' of three Cabinet Councils while Caspar Weinberger, as Secretary of Defense, had no such assignments, yet in the first fifteen months of the new system Weinberger attended more Council meetings (twelve) than Haig (nine).

The frequency of Cabinet Council sessions held at Cabinet officer level varied considerably. As Table 3.1 shows, the Council on Economic Affairs accounted for just over a half of all such meetings in the two periods for which data is available. In view of the importance of pressing economic issues throughout Reagan's first term, the brisk pace of CCEA activity should not be surprising. However, the relatively low number of meetings held by the remaining six Councils is not so easily explained. Part of the explanation is to be found in the practice of the executive secretaries of several Councils in calling for meetings at Cabinet officer level 'only when an issue is ready or nearly ready for a decision by the President'. In this way it was hoped to minimise the demands imposed by the Council system on hard-pressed Cabinet heads. However, this does not really account for the stark contrast between CCEA and the other six Councils. After all, the demands on CCEA participants were in no way lower than those on participants in other Councils.

Of much greater significance is the fact that (with the noteworthy exception of CCEA) the workloads of the Cabinet Councils were peculiarly low. This was a consequence of the creation and operation of the Council system only after the Reagan administration's economic recovery package of 1981 had been launched. As the prime mover of the recovery package, OMB Director, David Stockman, had taken advantage of significant delays in completing the administration's appointments at sub-Cabinet level in a number of departments to impose budget levels for departmental programmes on a 'top-down' basis at OMB rather than by the more usual 'bottom-up'

Figure 3.1: The Reagan Cabinet Councils

CABINET COUNCIL ON ECONOMIC AFFAIRS

- Secretary of the Treasury ††
- Secretary of State
- Secretary of Commerce
- Secretary of Labor
- Secretary of Transportation
- Director of OMB
- US Trade Representative
- Chairman of CEA
Ex officio members **

CABINET COUNCIL ON COMMERCE AND TRADE

- Secretary of Commerce ††
- Secretary of State
- Secretary of the Treasury
- Attorney General
- Secretary of Agriculture
- Secretary of Labor
- Secretary of Transportation
- Secretary of Energy
- US Trade Representative
- Chairman of CEA
Ex officio members **

CABINET COUNCIL ON NATURAL RESOURCES AND ENVIRONMENT

- Secretary of the Interior ††
- Attorney General
- Secretary of Transportation
- Secretary of Housing & Urban Development
- Secretary of Energy
- Chairman, Council of Environmental Quality
- Chairman of CEA
Ex officio members **

CABINET COUNCIL ON HUMAN RESOURCES

- Secretary of Health & Human Services ††
- Attorney General
- Secretary of Agriculture
- Secretary of Labor
- Secretary of Housing & Urban Development
- Secretary of Education
Ex officio members **

CABINET COUNCIL ON FOOD & AGRICULTURE

- Secretary of Agriculture ††
- Secretary of State
- Secretary of the Interior
- Secretary of Commerce
- Secretary of Transportation
- US Trade Representative
Ex officio members **

CABINET COUNCIL ON LEGAL POLICY

- Attorney General **
- Secretary of State
- Secretary of the Treasury
- Secretary of Commerce
- Secretary of Labor
- Secretary of Health & Human Services
- Secretary of Housing & Urban Development
- Secretary of Transportation
- Director of OMB
- White House Counsel
- Chairman, Administrative Conference of the US
Ex officio members **

CABINET COUNCIL FOR MANAGEMENT AND ADMINISTRATION

- Counselor to the President ††
- Secretary of the Treasury
- Secretary of Defense
- Secretary of Commerce
- Secretary of Health & Human Services # #
- Secretary of Transportation
- Secretary of Energy
- Director of OMB
- Administrator, General Services Administration
- Director, Office of Personnel Management

†† Denotes Council Chairman *pro tempore*

Ex Officio Members

** Vice President, Counselor to the President, W.H. Chief of Staff, Assistant for Policy Development

Vice President, W. H. Chief of Staff, Assistant for Policy Development

Table 3.1:　Cabinet Council meetings

	Total	CCEA	CCCT	CCHR	CCNRE	CCFA	CCLP	CCMA
Feb. 1981–May 1982								
No. of meetings	190	100	31	15	31	10	3	–
No. of agenda Items	398	228	61	22	22	17	4	–
No. of items per meeting	2·1	2·3	2·0	1·5	1·7	1·7	1·0	–
Feb. 1983–May 1984								
No. of meetings	202	95	34	12	23	13	5	20

Sources:　*Strategic Evaluation Memorandum #18, Cabinet Councils and Domestic Affairs Management: an Evaluation* (unpublished White House study prepared by the Office of Planning & Evaluation, 8 June 1982); and data furnished by the Office of Cabinet Affairs, May 1984.

approach from the departments and agencies. In consequence, the domestic Cabinet departments were from the outset effectively 'locked in' by the various budgetary constraints imposed by Stockman. Thereafter, throughout Reagan's first four years, the budget proved to be the main driving force of the administration's approach, with most other domestic policy matters treated in effect as of secondary importance.

The essentially secondary nature of policy issues dealt with by the Cabinet Council process is evidenced by the fact that not only was the budget handled outside the system (with only a few CCEA sessions devoted to budget review work – and these typically only a matter of days before the budget was officially forwarded to Congress), but also such major issues as the abortive 1981 Social Security restructuring and the 1982 New Federalism proposals (see chapter 8, below) had only minimal involvement with the Council system. While it is not a wholly reliable guide, the list of the most frequently occurring topics dealt with by Cabinet Councils in the first fifteen months of the new system set out in Table 3.2 below provides a good indication of the range of issues considered.

Table 3.2:   Most frequently occuring topics in Cabinet Councils, Feburary 1981 – May 1982

Topic	Times on agenda	Council
Thrift industry	22	CCEA
Economic outlook	15	CCEA
Federal credit policy	10	CCEA
International investment policy	8	CCEA
Enterprise zones	8	CCCT
Natural gas decontrol	8	CCNRE
Polish debt crisis	7	CCEA
Tax policy – Economic Recovery Act, 1981	7	CCEA
Clean Air Act	7	CCNRE

Source: Strategic Evaluation Memorandum #18, 1982.

Closely associated with the policy work of the Cabinet Councils was the Office of Policy Development (OPD). As the Reagan administration's successor to the Carter Domestic Policy Staff (DPS) unit (itself the successor to the Nixon-Ford Domestic Council), the OPD operated under the *aegis* of the presidential assistant for domestic affairs who reported to the president through Edwin Meese, as Counsellor to the President (see Figure 3.1). The focus of the OPD was predominantly on the Cabinet Council system, with senior OPD staff members assigned as Council executive secretaries to work with the various chairmen *pro tempore* in coordinating the activities of each of the Councils. Within the Council process, OPD played a major role in the development of policy proposals. For example, the proposal to create enterprise zones to stimulate urban development was developed on the basis of an OPD staff study carried out for the Cabinet Council on Commerce and Trade.

In line with Reagan's determination to downgrade the profile and role of White House staff policy units (particularly in national security and domestic affairs), the OPD was given a relatively low level of staff. Indeed, its 1981 staffing complement of forty-one (including clerical posts) was approximately half the level enjoyed by Eisenstat's DPS unit in the Carter administration. In consequence, the OPD was never in danger of emerging as a strong policy actor in its own right (in contrast to the Carter DPS unit or, more emphatically, to the Nixon Domestic Council under Ehrlichman) (Turner, 1983). The diminished role of the assistant for domestic affairs in the Reagan White House produced clear frustrations within OPD and was responsible for a high rate of staff turnover, both within OPD and at the level of the presidential assistant. Thus Martin Anderson resigned his White House assistant's post in February 1982, having concluded after only a year that the job was not worth having, while his successor, Edwin Harper (who had been Deputy Director of OMB), similarly resigned after a year to return to private life in the Spring of 1983. Adding emphasis to the low status of the presidential assistant's role was the fact that the appointment of Harper's successor, Jack Svahn (who was Undersecretary of Health and Human Services and had served as Commissioner for Social Security), was considerably delayed – leaving the position vacant for several months until September, 1983.

Clearly, both OPD and the Cabinet Councils suffered greatly from the fact that the Reagan agenda had been swiftly cemented into position within the first thirty days of the administration. Thereafter, the Councils and OPD were effectively relegated to policy issues and proposals of essentially secondary importance. This was conceded by the internal White House evaluation of Cabinet Council operations, which concluded in June, 1982:

> The tendency of the budget to dominate policy considerations has been particularly strong in the Reagan administration. As a result, the Cabinet Council role and influence has been less than it would have been with a more balanced approach to the full range of domestic and economic policy concerns (*Strategic Evaluation Memorandum* #18, 1982, 37).

In terms of domestic policy therefore the system of Cabinet Councils failed to fulfil the clear hopes of Meese that it would become the major administration policy vehicle of the Reagan administration.

Table 3.3: President Reagan's attendance at Cabinet Council meetings

Period	Total	CCEA	CCCT	CCHR	CCNRE	CCFA	CCLP	CCMA
Feb. 1981– May 1981	26(190)	7(100)	8(31)	4(15)	5(31)	2(10)	0(3)	–
Jan. 1983– May 1984	53(202)	12(95)	9(34)	7(12)	10(23)	4(13)	4(5)	7(20)

Note:–(Figures in parentheses indicate the total number of meetings held)

Sources: Strategic Evaluation Memorandum #18 (1982) and data furnished by the Office of Cabinet Affairs, May 1984.

Beyond question, the most positive aspect of the Cabinet Council system lay in its capacity for promoting the regular involvement of the president personally with his Cabinet officers. As Table 3.3 indicates, President Reagan participated in a surprisingly large number of sessions, with an average annual attendance at thirty-two Council meetings. This degree of presidential involvement indicates the strength of Reagan's determination to develop and maintain a close working relationship with his various Cabinet officers within the institutional context of the Cabinet. At the same time, however, the fact that Cabinet Councils operated under the *aegis* of the White House was also of some significance: the system regularly pulled Cabinet members into the White House sphere of influence. As Meese has claimed, with the Councils functioning to 'keep agency heads within the White House orbit', the problems associated with presidential appointees 'going native' experienced in past administrations could be considerably reduced (quoted in Kirschten, 1982). In consequence, the new system functioned to develop within the Reagan administration a considerable degree of teamwork and loyalty to the president and his agenda (Newland, 1984).

The Cabinet and Sub-Cabinet appointees

Central to the success of the Reagan agenda was the need to establish presidential control over the operations of the federal establishment. Essentially, the Reagan approach to this was twofold: first, to select Cabinet and sub-Cabinet level appointees on the basis of commitment to broad Reaganite goals; and, second, to adopt personnel management strategies which would not only assert political control over the civil service but which would also work to weaken the scope of independence of action by the 'permanent government' of the federal bureaucracy.

The effort to recruit appointees for the Reagan administration was begun in the summer of 1980, when Edwin Meese brought in E. Pendleton James (a Meese associate who was a professional 'headhunter' for executive business) to establish a Reagan talent-search unit. Begun with a budget of $80,000 drawn from Reagan campaign funds (for which special permission was granted by the Federal Election Commission), the personnel unit operated by James focused tightly on selection criteria which placed commitment and loyalty to Reaganite values and the Reagan agenda above managerial experience or policy expertise. The 'Reagan Revolution' would be effected by a corps of dedicated political appointees willing to assert presidential goals and push for their adherence in the face of anticipated reluctance from a federal bureaucracy committed to the continuance of threatened programmes and services. This was made clear by candidate Reagan in a campaign speech in September, 1980, when he declared:

Crucial to my strategy of spending control will be the appointment to top government positions of men and women who share my economic philosophy. We will have an administration in which the word from the top isn't lost or hidden in the bureaucracy. That voice will be heard because it is the voice of the people (quoted in *New York Times*, 19 Sept. 1980).

In the event, while Reagan's selections for the thirteen Cabinet posts were not reflective of the full range of the American political spectrum neither were they narrowly drawn from the conservative right. Overwhelmingly Republican (the sole Democrat was the neo-conservative Jeane Kirkpatrick, who was appointed as US Ambassador to the United Nations), the Reagan Cabinet was drawn from both the moderate and conservative wings of the Republican Party. Thus Malcolm Baldridge (Commerce), Drew Lewis (Transportation), Donald Regan (Treasury) and Richard Schweiker (Health and Human Services) were all associated with the moderate North-Eastern (Rockefeller) wing of the party. If anything, the conservative right was actually under-represented, with only James Watt (Interior) possessing radical-right credentials. The majority of Cabinet post were filled with mainstream Republican conservatives appointed for diverse reasons: Alexander Haig (State) and Caspar Weinberger (Defense) were appointed both on grounds of commitment to Reaganite values and for their expertise (Haig, as a former General, military commander of NATO and Nixon's White House Chief of Staff, clearly possessed considerable expertise in national security affairs; while Weinberger, as a former OMB Director and Secretary of Health, Education and Welfare, had the managerial experience to deal effectively with the sprawling defence sector whose procurement budgets were in need of tight control). Elsewhere, Reagan appointed: a farmer, John Block, to the Department of Agriculture; a black lawyer, Samuel Pierce, to the Department of Housing and Urban Development (HUD); an education administrator, Terrell Bell, to the Department of Education; a former Governor (and dental surgeon), James Edwards of South Carolina, to the Department of Energy; a lawyer (who was also a close personal friend), William French Smith, as Attorney General at the Justice Department; and a construction industry businessman, Raymond Donovan, to the Department of Labor.

Curiously, Reagan's Cabinet was not much different in character from those of his more recent Republican predecessors; Eisenhower, Nixon and Ford. Indeed, as Barrett accurately observed, 'he wound up with a crew that was overwhelmingly middle-aged, white, male, Christian and Republican' (Barrett, 1983, 71). As Table 3.4 shows, the Reagan Cabinet was comprised largely of outsiders: only two members had held major posts in previous administrations (Haig and Weinberger), a further three had occupied lower-level positions (Bell, Pierce and Watt) and one member had served in both houses of Congress (Schweiker). What the Cabinet predominantly shared was business experience: some seven members had been involved in the business sector for the greater part of their working lives, while a further two (Haig and Weinberger) were corporate executives immediately prior to their appointment to the Reagan administration. This factor had direct significance in an administration committed to market-forces and economic deregulation in the business sector.

While the Cabinet itself was somewhat lacking in prior Washington experience and under-representative of the radical-right, these deficiencies were more than compensated for by the political appointees selected for the broad swathe of sub-Cabinet positions in the various departments and agencies of the federal government. Of 213 such appointees in place in the first few months of the Reagan administration, one study found that a majority (121) had prior experience within the federal government (Havemann, 1981). Moreover, many of these sub-Cabinet posts were occupied by committed radical right conservatives. This point was confirmed in a 1981 study by Calvin Mackenzie, which argued that in many respects the Cabinet presented a misleading guide to the shape of the Reagan administration. In Mackenzie's view,

. . . it was only in the staffing of the operating levels of the subcabinet and the agencies that the political and administrative thrust of this administration was fully revealed. . . . The hostility of many of these appointees on the programs they would administer was a common characteristic of Reagan's choices for second-level positions in the departments and agencies. . . . There was achieved in this second round of

Table 3.4: The Reagan Cabinet, 1981

Department/Position	Name	Age	Ideological position	Occupation	Previous political/public service experience
Agriculture	John Block	45	Moderate Republican	Farmer	Illinois State Director of Agriculture, 1977–81
Commerce	Malcolm Baldridge	58	Moderate/Liberal Republican	Business executive	None
Defense	Caspar W. Weinberger	63	Conservative Republican	Corporate lawyer/ public official	California State legislator 1953–8; California Director of Finance, 1968–70; Chairman, Federal trade Commission, 1970; Dep. Director/Director OMB, 1970–3; HEW Secretary, 1973–5
Education	Terrell H. Bell	59	Conservative Republican	Education Administrator	Commissioner US Office of Education, 1970–1; US Commissioner of Education 1974–6; Utah Commissioner of Higher Education, 1976–81
Energy	James B. Edwards	53	Conservative Republican	Dental surgeon/ public official	South Carolina State legislator, 1972–4; Governor of South Caroline, 1975–8
Health & Human Services (HHS)	Richard R. Schweiker	54	Moderate/Liberal Republican	public official	US House of Reps. 1961–6 US Senate, 1969–80
Housing & Urban Development (HUD)	Samuel R. Pierce Jr	58	Conservative Republican	Lawyer	Asst. to Undersec. of Labour, 1955–7; General Counsel, Treasury Dept., 1970–3
Interior	James G. Watt	42	Radical-Right, Conservative Republican	Lawyer/public official	Dep. Asst. Sec. of Interior 1969–72; Director of Bureau of Outdoor Rec., 1972–5; Commissioner & Vice Chairman, Fed. Power Comm., 1975–7
Justice (Attorney General)	William French Smith	63	Conservative Republican	Lawyer	None
Labour	Raymond J. Donovan	50	Conservative Republican	Construction industry businessman	None
State	Alexander M. Haig	56	Conservative Republican	Retired army general/ business executive	Dep. Asst. to President, 1970–73; W.H. Chief of Staff, 1973–4
Transportation	Andrew L. Lewis	49	Moderate/Liberal Republican	Business executive	Chairman, Republican Finance Comm., 1971–3; Dep. Chairman Rep. Natl. Comm., 1976–80
Treasury	Donald T. Regan	62	Moderate/Liberal Republican	Stockbroking executive	None
US Ambassador to the UN	Jeane J. Kirkpatrick	54	Neo-Conservative Democrat	Political scientist	None

appointments an uncommon degree of ideological consistency and intensity (Mackenzie, 1981).

A key feature of the appointments process directed by Pendleton James (initially in the Reagan Personnel Transition Task Force and subsequently, after Reagan's inauguration, in the White House Office of Personnel Management) was the high degree of centralised control it exercised. Cabinet officers were consulted and involved in the selection of the sub-Cabinet appointees for the departments and agencies under their supervision, but they emphatically did not have a free hand in appointee selection. This contrasted sharply with the principles operated by the Carter personnel selection team which gave to Carter's Cabinet officers the power 'to appoint subordinates of their own choice . . . (and) to set their own priorities for their appointments' (Marchand, 1984, 194). In consequence, whereas the Carter administration came to be characterised by incoherence and contradiction, the Reagan team maintained a high degree of unity of purpose and commitment to the president's goals.

While the personnel selection process was successful in producing an administration which was clearly in tune with the president, it signally failed to meet the appointments timetable it set for itself. Thus the initial deadline for completion of Cabinet selection was set for November, 1980, but in fact the last Cabinet appointee was not publicly announced until 7 January 1981. Similarly, it was intended to have completed the selection of the top 400 sub-Cabinet posts in the departments and agencies by the end of February 1981. However, by May 1981, only 55 per cent of these had been announced, 36 per cent had been officially nominated (for confirmation by the Senate) and 21 per cent had received Senate confirmation. Indeed, many posts still remained unfilled as the administration entered its second year (Johnson, 1982, 8).

Some of the delays in filling positions were a consequence of the normal 'clearance' courtesies afforded to members of the Senate (in cases involving posts considered to be within the general purview of individual Senators). However, this factor does not really account for the unusually high number of delayed appointments. Of greater significance is the fact that the Reagan administration was the first administration required to operate its personnel selection under the provisions of the Ethics in Government Act of 1978. Designed to stop the 'revolving door' practice of individuals moving between departments/agencies and the businesses they dealt with or regulated, this legislation imposed stringent requirements on all presidential appointees in terms of financial disclosure and stock divestiture. In consequence, both the clearance procedures required by the 1978 Act and the difficulties these created for recruitment of appointees willing to undergo the financial disclosures required by it resulted in a severely delayed appointments process. Compounding these problems was the further difficulty of persuading potential administration recruits to accept the relatively low levels of federal pay. These had been eroded considerably in the wake of several past pay-freezes, so that by 1981 they constituted a very real disincentive to acceptance of appointment to federal posts.

The delayed appointments process created significant problems for the various departments and agencies where posts remained unfilled. As previously indicated, OMB Director David Stockman took clear advantage of the situation to impose a 'top-down' approach in determining the shape and funding levels of department and agency programmes. The delays also made it more difficult for appointees to establish direction of and control over department and agency career personnel. Thus there was a paradoxical side to the first year of the Reagan administration: while it was generally credited for the 'fast pace' of its Reaganomics package, this pace of activity masked substantial delays in fully staffing the federal government with Reagan appointees.

A major achievement of the Reagan personnel process to secure appointees committed to Reaganite values was the high level of adherence to the president's policy goals maintained over the course of the administration's first four years. This was confirmed in a set of case studies by Laurence Lynn, which examined the record of success of five Reagan appointees in penetrating and controlling department and agency operations. While the range of agencies covered was wide, and the record of individual achievement was mixed, Lynn concluded that:

> Reagan's practice of appointing like-minded subordinates and of expecting loyal service from them has served him reasonably well. Although his appointees' performances were uneven, on balance all moved the government in directions consistent with his policies. . . . President Reagan helped his cause by choosing appointees who shared his vision and by communicating and implicitly enforcing his sense of purpose among subordinate political executives (Lynn, 1984, 369–70).

Assisting in the maintenance of commitment of administration appointees to the priorities and values of the president was the willingness of Reagan to engage personally with his Cabinet officers on a regular basis. On the formal level of full Cabinet sessions, he met with his Cabinet at an average annual rate of 18 meetings. However, as Table 3.5 clearly shows, the president's sessions with the full Cabinet declined steeply over the four years of his first term. At the same time (as Table 3.3 above indicates), his attendance at Cabinet Council sessions increased suggesting strongly the greater utility of the Council process for communicating presidential values and priorities to Cabinet officers. As for presidential involvement with sub-Cabinet appointees within the administration, Reagan engaged in a commendable effort to meet periodically in the White House with changing groups of assistant secretaries and agency appointees. More systematically, the Cabinet Council system drew into the presidential sphere a considerable number of assistant secretaries involved in the activities of the various Council working groups.

Table 3.5: *Presidential meetings with the full Cabinet*

	1981	1982	1983	1984 (to May 10)
No. of meetings attended	29	21	14	4

Source: Data furnished by the Office of Cabinet Affairs, May 1984.

Controlling the bureaucracy

The second major element in the Reagan approach to establish presidential control over the operations of the federal bureaucracy featured the assertive use of a variety of personnel management strategies. These principally included: reductions in force (RIFs); the downgrading or transfers of senior-level civil servants; the employment of budget-cuts and hiring freezes to reduce the size of the federal work force; the expansion of the non-career Senior Executive Service (SES) to increase the number of political appointees; and, proposals to cut-back sharply federal government activities, including hiving-off tasks to the private sector.

Essentially, the Reagan administration conducted what amounted to a personnel *blitzkrieg* on federal bureaucrats by skilful use of the provisions of the Civil Service Reform Act of 1978. Under this legislation, department and agency heads were given direct authority to hire, promote and fire senior federal employees as well as the power to determine job classification in terms of duties, assignments of duties and work results. Accordingly, the Reagan administration was empowered on a department-by-department basis to reassign or even to downgrade senior, executive-level civil servants who were unsupportive of the administration's goals or priorities or who were simply ineffectual. While the number of senior executive reassignments was relatively low in Reagan's first year (because of a legal prohibition preventing new political appointees from forcibly reassigning career executives within 120 days of assuming office), some 1226 reassignments were made in FY 1982 followed by a further 1100 in FY 1983. Since many of these reassignments involved the geographic relocation of civil servants, the actual numbers reported may understate the full effect of the reassignment approach because many senior personnel left the federal service to avoid adverse moves (Goldenberg, 1984, 397).

More directly, the administration made significant use of reduction in force (RIF) rules governing the termination of civil service positions to bring about the removal or transfer of unsympathetic officials. Under the RIF rules, seniority determines whose job is actually lost, with each RIF consequently involving several personnel who get downgraded one after another until the least senior official in line loses his/her job. Illustrating this process is the following example cited by Richard Nathan:

In the Labor Department, . . . a notice of a reduction in force was sent to the entire staff of the Employment and Training Administration. After the required notice period and elapsed, many staff members were "terminated". The dividing line in seniority for these layoffs was fifteen years of service. Persons with less than fifteen years' service were laid off. Many who stayed on were reduced in grade, with the result that some twenty-year veteran managers were assigned to routine tasks with no substantive authority (Nathan, 1983a, 74).

Over the two year period of FY 1981 and FY 1982, the Office of Personnel Management (OPM) calculated that over 11,000 career bureaucrats throughout the federal government lost their jobs under the administration's RIF actions. Concerning the wider scope of RIF effects, OPM Director Donald Devine commented: 'About three people are affected for every person separated . . . in the RIF, (so) maybe 30,000 might be that status, although they don't necessarily go to a lower grade' (quoted in Kirschten, 1983, 735). Since increased defence spending was a major Reagan priority, the brunt of RIF actions was carried by non-defence departments whose programmes or functions were under hostile scrutiny from the administration (including Health and Human Services, Agriculture and Commerce). An area of particularly assertive RIF activity was environmental policy, with large numbers of personnel cuts imposed at the Interior Department and the Environment Protection Agency (see the discussion in Chapter 10, below).

Besides its RIF and reassignment strategies, the Reagan administration acted to effect reductions in both the size and scope of the federal government. Indeed, within moments of his swearing-in as President in 1981, Reagan signed an order while still in the Capitol building to impose an immediate retroactive federal hiring freeze, and announced plans to reduce the federal bureaucracy (excluding the Department of Defence) by 100,000 posts. In the event, this target was virtually met by September 1983, with OPM estimating that there were then 92,000 fewer federal employees in the non-defence, domestic departments and agencies than in January 1981. Besides personnel reductions achieved in the regulatory sector by its vigorous policy of economic deregulation (see Chapters 5 and 10 below), the administration also sought to increase the contracting-out of services and activities undertaken by federal employees. Accordingly, OMB revised its contracting rules under Circular A-76 to relax the requirements on comparisons between in-house federal costs and private-sector tenders. However, while the contracting-out strategy certainly brings results in terms of reducing or freezing the size of the federal bureaucracy, as Guttman and Willner pointed out in their seminal 1976 study, such hiving-off action may well increase costs without producing many tangible benefits (Gutman and Willner, 1976). Nonetheless, the Reagan administration's determination to privatise many of the operations of the federal government was clearly reflected in the 2478 recommendations submitted by the President's Private Sector Survey on Cost Control (better known as the Grace Commission) in January 1984. While the impact of the Commission's recommendations remains unclear, the total level of savings claimed ($425 billion over a three-year period) for all of its proposed efficiency measures, programme reductions and privatisation initiatives appeared to indicate future federal retrenchment on a very large scale.

Finally, the Reagan administration made the fullest possible use of the provision made by the Civil Service Reform Act of 1978 to permit a maximum of 10 per cent of the Senior Executive Service (SES) positions to be filled by appointive non-career personnel. At the end of December 1981, the Reagan administration had placed 533 non-career appointees in SES posts, a total which rose to 709 (close to the maximum allowed under the 1978 Act) by December 1983. These totals compare with a high of 575 appointees (about two-thirds of the permitted maximum) in the Carter administration (Goldenberg, 1984, 394–5). Beyond these non-career appointive SES posts, however, the Reagan administration was also to make use of a number of Schedule C posts. Established by President Eisenhower in the 1950s, Schedule C posts fall outside normal civil service merit competition rules since Schedule C appointees are presumed to have confidential relationships with the administration's political appointees. By August of 1983, the Reagan administration had a total of 1615 Schedule C appointees, some 11 per cent higher than the Carter administration's previous high of 1466. Under Reagan, therefore, the use of political, non-competitive appointive posts within the civil service was considerably expanded.

Assessment

In broad terms, the approaches and strategies adopted by the Reagan presidency in its first four years proved to be effective. The structural organisation of the EOP (with the exception of the position of the NSC adviser) remained intact and contributed considerably to the maintenance of coherence and collegiality between the White House and the various Cabinet departments and agencies. Again with the exception of the national security/foreign policy area, the administration was remarkably free of internal frictions and disputes. At Cabinet officer level, there were five first-term resignations, see Table 3.6. Of these, only two were fraught with controversy: Secretary of State Haig; and Interior Secretary Watt, whose resignation came as the result of adverse public reaction to his somewhat tasteless humour which was regarded as offensive to various groups. The remaining three resignations came as a consequence of the desire to leave public service to return to the private sector.

The area that did cause the administration problems was that of national security/foreign policy. Reagan's original intention to downgrade the role of the NSC adviser had unfortunate consequences for internal conflict resolution; his initial appointee, Richard Allen, was badly placed institutionally (reporting indirectly to the president through

Table 3.6: Cabinet officer resignations and replacements, 1981–84

Department	Resigner	Date	Replacement
State	Alexander M. Haig	June 1982	George P. Shultz
Energy	James Edwards	Nov. 1982	Donald P. Hodel
Transportation	Andrew L. Lewis	Jan. 1983	Elizabeth Dole
Health & Human Services	Richard S. Schweiker	Jan. 1983	Margaret Heckler
Interior	James Watt	Oct. 1983	William P. Clark

Meese as presidential Counsellor) to act with authority to resolve jurisdictional and policy disputes between Secretary of State Haig and Defence Secretary Weinberger. Allen's resignation, in January 1982, was used to restructure the position: his succcessor, William Clark, was given direct access to the president – thus removing the post from Meese's supervision. While Clark brought a greater measure of authority to bear in dealing with the disputational relationship between Haig and Weinberger (an authority which owed much to Clark's close personal association with the president), matters were not wholly resolved until Haig's own resignation in June 1982. Frustrated by the cross-cutting jurisdictions in the national security area, Haig's problems derived largely from his unfulfilled ambition to become the undisputed 'vicar' of foreign policy in the Reagan administration (see: Haig, 1984). His successor at the State Department, George Shultz, brought a personal style as a facilitator and negotiator which did much to bring a sense of harmony to a considerably troubled area of the administration. Contributing further to the development of harmony and coordination was the appointment of Robert (Bud) McFarlane to the NSC adviser's post in the Autumn of 1983, following the departure of William Clark to take up the Cabinet post of Interior Secretary. Possessing no personal ties to Reagan, McFarlane tended to operate as a 'team-player' and appeared to have little interest in employing his NSC position as a personal power base.

Undoubtedly, one of the administration's greatest achievements was its success in managing and safeguarding the Reagan agenda. In sharp contrast to previous presidents, Reagan was able to maintain amongst his political appointees a high degree of loyalty and adherence to his goals and values. Several factors account for this: the success of the personnel selection process operated by Pendleton James in recruiting a team of appointees committed from the outset to the 'Reagan Revolution'; the efficacy of the Cabinet Council system in pulling both Cabinet officers and their sub-Cabinet department colleagues into the presidential sphere and sustaining a spirit of collegiality and teamwork; and the *blitzkrieg* approach of the various personnel management policies aimed at asserting political dominance over the federal bureaucracy.

There were, however, some costs associated with the administration's assault on the career civil service. While it produced a somewhat submissive bureaucracy, this came at the expense of considerable demoralisation, widespread alienation and an almost complete absence of active support amongst federal employees. Some acknowledgement of these effects was given by OPM Director Donald Devine in the Spring of 1983, with his comment: 'We think there will be some lessening of morale, but we are taking steps to try to minimize it' (quoted in Kirschten, 1983b, 734). The extent to which such remedial action was necessary was revealed in the account provided by *The Washington Post* of the reaction of EPA personnel to the forced resignations, in March 1983, of Administrator Anne Gorsuch and other top Reagan appointees at EPA: 'At EPA's offices in Washington Mall, dozens of career employees found cause for celebration. Downstairs in the shopping mall, Harry's Liquor, Wine and Cheese sold eight cases of champagne and six ounces of Russian caviar to the general counsel's office' (*The Washington Post*, 26 March 1983).

A major feature of the operations of the Reagan administration over its first four years was the intensely *political* dimension built into all of its considerations. As the nationally-elected official presiding over the federal executive establishment, Reagan clearly took the view that the voice of his administration was in effect 'the voice of the people'. Not only was it vital that his agenda be clearly established, it was also essential that his appointees should evidence commitment to its execution and administration. To these ends, the Reagan presidency regarded the administrative sphere of the federal bureaucracy as a vital and legitimate object of political direction. Critics of the Reagan approach have argued that it operated on the basis of an outmoded (and impractical) policy–administration dichotomy, assuming in effect a wall between policy makers and administrators (Campbell, 1984, 412). However, this viewpoint misses the essence of the Reagan strategy, which operated precisely on a contrary perception that no such policy–administration separation should exist. This is evidenced in the importance attached to widening the entry of political appointees into non-career posts at the senior executive level within the administrative layers of the federal bureaucracy.

In conclusion, in its first term the Reagan presidency attempted to implement both a strategic approach (by adoption of a narrowly-focused Reagan policy agenda to which the resources of the presidential office were wholly committed) and a collegial approach (which suited Reagan's personal style and commitment to a Cabinet-centred administration). To these must be added a third element: an administrative approach which, as Richard Nathan noted, sought to implement 'what the electorate frequently says it wants – leadership and change' (Nathan, 1984; 377).

References

Barrett, Lawrence I. (1983). *Gambling with History*: *Ronald Reagan in the White House*, Garden City: Doubleday & Co. Inc.

Campbell, Alan K. (1984). 'No Permanent Change' in L. M. Salamon and M. S. Lund, eds, *The Reagan Presidency and the Governing of America*, Washington, DC: Urban Institute Press

Cronin, Thomas E. (1980). *The State of the Presidency*, 2nd edn, Boston: Little, Brown & Co.

Goldenberg, Edie N. (1984). 'The Permanent Government in an Era of Retrenchment and Redirection' in L. M. Salamon & M. S. Lund, eds, *The Reagan Presidency and the Governing of America*, Washington, DC: Urban Institute Press.

Greenstein, Fred I. (1979). 'Change and Continuity in the Modern Presidency' in A. King, ed., *The New American Political System*, Washington, DC: American Enterprise Institute.

Guttman, Daniel and Willner, Barry (1976). *The Shadow Government*, New York: Pantheon Books.

Haig, Alexander M. (1984). *Caveat: Realism, Reagan and Foreign Policy*, London: Weidenfield & Nicholson.

Hamilton, Gary G. and Biggart, Nicole N. (1984). *Governor Reagan, Governor Brown: Sociology of Executive Power*, New York: Columbia University Press,

Havemann, Joel (1981). 'Inside the Reagan Administration', *National Journal*, 25 Apr., pp. 675–770.

Heclo, Hugh (1983). 'One Executive Branch or Many?' in A. King, ed., *Both Ends of the Avenue: the Presidency, the Executive Branch and Congress in the 1980s*, Washington, DC: American Enterprise Institute.

Heclo, Hugh and Salamon, Lester M., eds (1981). *The illusion of Presidential Government*, Boulder, Colo.: Westview Press.

Heineman, Ben W., Jr and Hessler, Curtis A. (1980). *Memorandum for the President: a Strategic Approach to Domestic Affairs in the 1980s*, New York: Random House.

Hess, Stephen (1976). *Organising the Presidency*, Washington, DC: The Brookings Institution.

Johnson, Willa A. (1982). 'Office of Presidential Personnel' in R. N. Holwill, ed., *The First Year*, Washington, DC: The Heritage Foundation.

Kirschten, Dick (1982). 'Decision Making in the White House: How Well Does It Serve the President?' *National Journal*, 3 Apr., pp. 584–9.

Kirschten, Dick (1983). 'Administration Using Carter-Era Reform to Manipulate the Levers of Government', *National Journal*, 9 Apr., pp. 732–6.

Lynn, Lawrence, Jr (1984). 'The Reagan Administration and the Renitent Bureaucracy' in L. M. Salamon and M. S. Lund, eds, *The Reagan Presidency and the Governing of America*, Washington, DC: Urban Institute Press.

Mackenzie, G. Calvin (1981). 'Cabinet and Subcabinet Personnel Selection in Reagan's First Year: New Variations on Some Not-So-Old Themes', paper delivered at Sept. 1981, meeting of the American Political Science Association.

Marchland, Donald A. (1984). 'Carter and the Bureaucracy' in M. G. Abernathy, D. M. Hill and P. Williams, eds., *The Carter Years: the President and Policy Making*, London: Frances Pinter.

Meltsner, Arnold A., ed. (1981), *Politics and the Oval Office: Towards Presidential Governance*, San Francisco: Institute for Contemporary Studies.

Nathan, Richard P. (1975). *The Plot That Failed: Nixon and the Administrative Presidency*, New York: John Wiley.

Nathan, Richard P. (1983a). 'The Reagan Presidency in Domestic Affairs' in F. I. Greenstein, ed., *The Reagan Presidency: an Early Assessment*, Baltimore: Johns Hopkins University Press.

Nathan, Richard P. (1983b). *The Administrative Presidency*, New York: John Wiley.

Nathan, Richard P. (1984). 'Political Administration is Legitmate' in L. M. Salamon and M. S. Lund, eds, *The Reagan Presidency and the Governing of America*, Washington, DC: Urban Institute Press.

Newland, Chester A. (1984). 'Executive Office Policy Apparatus: Enforcing the Reagan Agenda' in L. M. Salamon and M. S. Lund, eds, *The Reagan Presidency and the Governing of America*, Washington, DC: Urban Institute Press.

Office of Planning and Evaluation (1982). *Strategic Evaluation Memorandum #18, Cabinet Councils and Domestic Affairs Management: an Evaluation*, Washington, DC: The White House, 8 June 1982: unpublished internal report.

Porter, Roger B. (1980). *Presidential Decision Making: the Economic Policy Board*, Cambridge University Press.

Salamon, Lester M. (1981). 'Beyond the Presidential Illusion – Toward a Constitutional Presidency' in H. Heclo and L. M. Salamon, eds, *The*

Illusion of Presidential Government, Boulder, Colo.: Westview Press.

Smith, H., Clymer, A., Silk, L., Lindsay, R. and Burt, R., (1981). *Reagan the Man, the President*, Oxford: Pergamon Press.

Turner, Michael (1983). 'The Domestic Council Under Three Presidents: Nixon, Ford and Carter', *Strathclyde Papers in Government and Politics*, University of Strathclyde.

Watson, Richard A. and Thomas, Norman C. (1983). *The Politics of the Presidency*, New York: John Wiley.

Legislative liaison in the Reagan administration

To be perceived as a successful national leader a contemporary president must be an effective legislative leader. This requires the president to get Congress to enact his agenda of legislative proposals for tackling what he sees as the main problems facing the nation. Although this criteria for judging presidential leadership endures today, the conventional wisdom of recent years argues that political developments which took place within and outside Congress during the late 1960s and the early 1970s have combined to place new and severe constraints upon a president's capacity to exercise effective legislative leadership.

For example, the 91st Congress (1969–70) adopted a series of internal reforms that, along with the Legislative Reorganisation Act of 1970, widely dispersed and decentralised legislative power. This means that the president now has to find the time to court 535 members instead of liaising with only a handful of senior oligarchs. The reform movement also opened up Congress to greater public scrutiny and participation. The publication of members' votes oriented legislators more towards servicing their constituents than to working with the president. Opening Congress' deliberations to greater scrutiny and participation by interest groups means that the president faces a more complex and competitive legislative process. The passage of presidency-curbing legislation in the wake of Vietnam and Watergate placed new statutory constraints upon presidential power in an attempt to restore Congress to its 'proper' place as the 'first branch of government'. At the same time, changes in the political climate made the media and the public more critical of presidential leadership and behaviour. A concurrent decline in the cohesion of American party structures weakened the capacity of these aggregative bodies to unite what the Constitution had separated (King, 1978; Mann and Ornstein, 1981). Taken together, these developments made it very difficult for a 'post-imperial' president to obtain approval from a more assertive, independent Congress for his governing agenda. Indeed, some pessimists regarded the failure of Presidents Ford and Carter to advance their legislative agendas as indicating a need to give serious consideration to adopting constitutional and other reforms to strengthen a now 'imperilled' presidency (Cutler, 1980; Sundquist, 1980).

Set against this background, President Reagan's success in 1981 in gaining speedy congressional approval for his administration's radical budget and tax proposals represents a most impressive achievement. The Reagan administration deliberately sought to overcome the stalemate between both ends of Pennsylvania Avenue in order to both reclaim and recapture the symbolic and effective authority of the presidency following the ineffective presidencies of Ford and Carter. What were the component elements of the Reagan administration's strategy for conducting relations with Congress? What was the overall legislative record of President Reagan in his first term? What lessons regarding the practice of presidential legislative liaison can be learned from Reagan's first term? In seeking to answer these questions it is necessary first to outline the president's legislative strategy and then evaluate his overall legislative record before, finally, assessing the longer-term significance of the Reagan administration's approach to liaison with Congress.

Legislative strategy in the Reagan White House

The 1980 election results sent Ronald Reagan to Washington with a number of immediate political advantages. To begin with, Reagan won the 1980 presidential election in convincing style. The Republican candidate obtained a 9.7% margin in the popular vote over Jimmy Carter that translated into 489 electoral votes to Carter's 49, the third highest electoral vote margin since 1932. The congressional races further gave the president-elect the largest increase in a presidential election year of Senate Republicans since 1868 and of House Republicans since 1920. These results gave the Republicans control of the Senate for the first time since 1954, and narrowed the Democrats' majority to 51 seats – in a split of 243 seats to 192 – in the House. However, these results did not mean that the electorate embraced Reagan's non-centrist policy proposals. Polling analyses attribute Reagan's victory more to a firm rejection of President Carter and his policies than to a political 'realignment' in favour of the Republicans or a 'mandate' for Reagan's campaign promises (Abramson, Aldrich and Rhode, 1983; Pomper *et al.*, 1981; Ranney, 1981; Sandoz and Crabb, 1981). Nonetheless, Reagan's advisers resolved to take quick decisive action, to behave as if the president-elect had won a convincing mandate to implement his campaign promises. In so reasoning, they recognised that, 'Electoral mandates are made, not born' (Pfiffner, 1983, 623), that what an incoming president does during his first few months in office goes a long way to set the tone for the rest of his term. Hence, they decided to capitalise upon the voters' call for 'change' by pursuing a bold, but limited, legislative programme.

In order to inaugurate a 'new beginning' in presidential–congressional relationships, Reagan's advisers devised a legislative strategy that consisted of three main, interrelated ingredients. Firstly, the guiding principle of their approach to Congress consisted of selecting means to control the legislature's agenda. To implement this objective in 1981, the new administration proposed a few, tightly prioritised initiatives. These initiatives were strongly pushed in order to establish an early image of Reagan as a 'winner' with Congress. Secondly, the Reagan administration adopted a system of centralised management of the president's agenda, thereby marshalling the administration's entire resources behind the shot at a 'new beginning'. Finally, the new team adopted a professional approach to presidential legislative liaison that was predicated upon the appointment of experienced 'insiders', wise in the ways of Washington, to the president's White House unit for courting Congress. When taken together, these factors concentrated control over the policy and the political activities of the entire executive branch in the hands of a small 'inner circle' of senior White House aides in order to exploit, counter, and parry the decentralised, fragmented legislative process on Capitol Hill. Let us examine each ingredient in more detail.

Strategic agenda management

In planning its approach to Congress the Reagan team were much influenced by the failure of the Carter administration to exploit the opportunities that exist during the first few months of a new

Congress. This is a time when many of the president's initial legislative proposals succeed because he enjoys a 'political honeymoon' with Congress. This is largely the case because during the early days of the new session the legislature has yet to set its own priorities and agenda and is, thus, receptive to the president's leadership (Light, 1982). However, President Carter failed to exploit his honeymoon period. The Carter administration took too long to develop the president's policy proposals, failed to prioritise them and, for this reason, sent too many. This overloaded Congress and led to inaction on many of the President's proposals. Consequently, Jimmy Carter gained a reputation as an ineffective leader at the start of his term which, despite subsequent successes, endured in the public perception (Davis, 1979; Heineman and Hessler, 1980; Jones, 1981; Wayne, 1978).

To avoid 'Carterism', Reagan's advisers resolved to send Congress a few, highly prioritised legislative proposals as quickly as possible. During the transition period it was decided to limit Reagan's initial legislative agenda exclusively to economic issues. In line with this, work started on a radical proposal to cut federal taxes and a plan to rearrange federal spending priorities by accelerating defence spending and greatly reducing domestic spending, especially on welfare programmes enacted during the 'Great Society' era of expansive government. This narrow focus on the economy was consistent with candidate Reagan's campaign charges that the federal government was, because of its 'excessive' spending and taxes, responsible for America's economic problems, and his claim that the nation's defences were weak. Other campaign positions concerning foreign policy matters and the so-called 'social agenda' issues were put aside to avoid diverting attention from Reagan's bold economic initiatives. In sum, the incoming team believed that a narrow, tightly prioritised legislative agenda would best facilitate control of the congressional calendar.

To enact its legislative agenda, the Reagan administration resolved to 'hit the ground running'. Reagan's advisers were especially sensitive to the importance of political timing. They knew that an incoming president had a limited 'window of opportunity' to exploit, and decided to make the most of Reagan's political honeymoon with Congress. In addition, the new team reasoned that moving quickly would enable them to capitalise effectively upon the disarray among the Democrats, who were smarting from the loss of the White House and the Senate.

To exploit these opportunities, the Reagan administration decided to make strategic use of a split Congress to put the president's legislative agenda on a 'fast track'. This was effected by using Republican control of the Senate to pass speedily the president's budget, domestic policy and defence spending request. The Republican leaders of the Senate were fully involved in this strategy, assisting directly in the choice of policy goals and legislative strategy. Indeed, gaining control of the Senate provided the Reagan administration with the leverage, the motor-power to control much of Congress' agenda in 1981. Control of the Senate also let the administration concentrate its resources upon lobbying the Democratic-controlled House of Representatives. On this point, the Reagan administration only need to maintain unity among the House Republicans and attract just twenty-six defectors from the ranks of the Democrats to gain control of the House. The president's strategists targeted the forty-seven-member strong Conservative Democratic Forum – consisting primarily of members from Southern constituencies in which Reagan ran well – as a very promising source of support. Controlling Congress' agenda complemented this objective because it let the administration choose when to pick its fights in the House (Davidson and Oleszek, 1984; Heclo, 1984; Heclo and Penner, 1983; Ornstein, 1983; Pfiffner, 1983; Salamon and Abramson, 1984; Wayne, 1982).

Thus, the Reagan administration had, in contrast to its predecessors, a deliberate strategy for winning with Congress. In adopting this strategy President Reagan's advisers were gambling that if the president could quickly implement his radical agenda then it was possible that he could both reverse the widespread belief that presidents were increasingly becoming powerless and obtain an early, positive reputation as a leader that would help him weather subsequent vicissitudes.

Centralised agenda management

Because of the high stakes involved in attempting a 'new beginning' in presidential–congressional relationships, the Reagan administration concentrated control over the president's agenda in the White House. In the early days of the administration, a Legislative Strategy Group (LSG) was established to coordinate legislative strategy and policy making for initiatives included on the president's legislative agenda. The LSG soon became the dominant political coalition in the administration, and maintained control over the president's agenda throughout the first term.

The so-called triumvirate of senior White House aides – Edwin Meese, Michael Deaver and James Baker – comprised the core of the LSG. The group's meetings were chaired by James Baker, while Richard Darman – who was Baker's deputy – coordinated the activities of the LSG. President Reagan's chief congressional lobbyist – initially Max Friedersdorf, then Kenneth Duberstein and later M. B. Oglesby, Jr – completed the members from Baker's side of the White House. Craig Fuller, who was responsible to Meese for Cabinet administration, and Michael Deaver completed the list of continuous members of the LSG. A few Cabinet officers and other White House aides also participated in the group's deliberations; David Gergen (the head of the president's Office of Communications), Reagan's National Security Adviser, David Stockman, Treasury Secretary Donald Regan and the head of the Office of Policy and Development were the most frequent participants.

In contrast to the Cabinet, the LSG's meetings were for principals only – substitutes were not accepted – and the paperwork of the group was not circulated to non-members. This was because the LSG was not a 'bureaucratic' operation. Rather was it more of an informal and exclusive body that assembled in Baker's office to force action on any 'hot' issues that might affect the president's agenda.

The White House functions of the core members linked the LSG to all the offices involved in the task of translating Reagan's policy proposals into legislation. Because the group's members managed the policy-making and political operations of the White House, the president's agenda could be readily adapted to changing political forces. Indeed, once a decision had been reached by the group, the core members could easily implement their decision. As one member has stated, 'The beauty of this group is that if the people around the table agree, they represent what's necessary to get anything done in the Reagan White House' (Kirschten, 1981a, 1242).

Centralised management of Reagan's legislative agenda by an informal "committee of the presidency' imparted a high degree of coherence to the administration's dealings with Congress. Centralised decision-making also enabled the administration to blend policy and political considerations in liaising with Congress. This fusion more readily permitted Reagan's strategists to adapt presidential policies to changing political circumstances. This fluid operating style enabled Reagan's advisers flexibly to manoeuvre to take advantage of, or to run from, developments on Capitol Hill. This operating style was well-suited in 1981 to conducting negotiations with the reformed Congress, and also served the administration well in other years (Heclo, 1983).

Professional legislative liaison
President Carter got off to a particularly bad start with Congress because neither he nor the head of his congressional liaison unit fully understood the demands involved in conducting relations with the new, reformed Congress. To begin with, Jimmy Carter campaigned as an anti-Washington 'Mr Clean', a political outsider whose reputation had not been tarnished by the experience of Watergate. By itself, this meant that Carter would be more critically judged by Congress. But once in office, the Democratic president maintained an aloof approach towards Congress. Jimmy Carter refused to involve congressional leaders in the development of his legislative proposals. Instead, Carter appealed above Congress directly to the public for support for his legislative proposals. This 'plebiscitarian' approach often led to the dispatch of legislative initiatives which took Congress by surprise. As a consequence, the president's initiatives frequently failed to gain a place on the congressional calendar. Also, the president's public appeals failed to generate support. In contrast to President Reagan, Jimmy Carter was a poor public speaker. For the most part, the public was confused and uninspired by the president's turgid and technical explanations of his legislative proposals. In short, Carter's style of leadership was ill-suited to conducting successful relations with Congress (Cronin, 1980; Jones, 1985).

To compound the problem, President Carter's congressional liaison staff was initially led and staffed by outsiders to Washington. Their lack of inside knowledge was evidenced in, for example, the failure to exploit the president's honeymoon period. The president's liaison team also lacked status in Carter's administration, which was demonstrated when the congressional liaison unit was accommodated in the Old Executive Office Building instead of in the White House. This visible lack of standing in the councils of the Carter administration soon became known on Capitol Hill, leading members to regard Carter's liaison staff as unable to 'deliver' the president (Davis, 1979; Davis, 1983).

In comparison, Ronald Reagan gave a high priority to establishing good working relations with Congress. Indeed, he began courting

Congress as early as 1977 and visited the Hill frequently during the 1980 campaign and the transition period to seek an end to the 'age of suspicion' in presidential–congressional relations. These meetings fully involved the leaders of congressional Republicans in setting Reagan's legislative strategy. This involvement was very much a two-way affair. For example, it was Senator Peter Domenici, the chairman of the Senate Budget Committee, who first voiced the idea of using the little-known reconciliation budget procedure to package the president's many proposals to cut domestic spending into one comprehensive bill.

President Reagan did not, however, restrict his efforts to liaising only with Republicans. The president's advisers knew that they needed the acquiescence of the Democratic leaders of the House to get the president's agenda to the floor of the lower chamber. Accordingly, the president carefully courted the leaders of the House Democrats. This strategy quickly paid dividends when the Democratic leaders agreed to put the president's legislative proposals on a 'fast track' in the House rather than obstruct their consideration.

When it came to the task of lobbying Capitol Hill, the president willingly enlisted as the 'Chief Salesman' for his policies. The 'Communicator-in-Chief' used his persuasion skills to the full. He delivered a series of televised addresses to the nation which were very effective in promoting a groundswell of support for his legislative proposals. Also in sharp contrast with Carter, President Reagan frequently met with small groups of members and individual congressmen in the Oval Office and at Camp David. These meetings were widely regarded as very successful in gaining support, which contributed greatly to Reagan's string of victories in his first six months in office (Barrett, 1984; Cannon, 1982; Schick, 1982; Wayne, 1982)

To organise these meetings the president needed a legislative liaison team that knew its way around the reformed Congress. During the transition period Ronald Reagan's advisers recruited a strong congressional liaison team. Candidates were required to have substantive experience as presidential or departmental liaison officers in previous Republican administrations. For example, to head his Office of Legislative Affairs, Reagan appointed Max Friedersdorf, who had worked in President Nixon's congressional liaison office and then headed the same office for President Ford.

Friedersdorf was subsequently made chairman of the Federal Election Commission, from where he maintained an up-to-date knowledge of Congress and also the respect of members from both sides of the aisle.

In contrast to the Carter administration, President Reagan's liaison team were accommodated in the prestigious West Wing of the White House, with the overflow located in the East Wing. This decision demonstrated to Congress that Reagan's liaison officers had high status in his administration and could, thus, be treated as reliable, influential go-between in the conduct of presidential–congressional relations. The political intelligence that Reagan's liaison officers gathered on political developments that affected the president's agenda was quickly disseminated in the White House. As a matter of routine coordination, Max Friedersdorf took part in the daily meeting at 8.00 a.m. of senior White House aides and, when legislative matters were to be discussed, the daily meeting of the triumvirate at 8.30 a.m. with President Reagan in the Oval Office. These meetings enabled the administration speedily to assess and respond to political developments in the legislative arena.

At the other end of Pennsylvania Avenue, Friedersdorf's team efficiently functioned as a 'service organisation'. Reagan's liaison officers gave much attention to helping members over problems that could be resolved by the administration. Snags concerning patronage appointments, federal grant applications and requests for tickets for the president's box at the Kennedy Center were readily undertaken to build a good relationship with members, including Democratic congressmen.

The White House liaison team also loosely coordinated the work of departmental liaison officers (which further aided the performance of service work). In general, departmental liaison aides were expected to take the lead on presidential proposals that affected their departments. This practice let the administration pool and, thus, extend its liaison resources. But when the White House mounted a major push, the departmental officers were expected to be good team players and avoid making efforts that would distract attention from the president's initiative (Keller, 1981; Kirschten, 1981b; Wehr, 1981a).

The activities of the White House liaison team were only a part of a broader effort to win support for the president's agenda. The president's liaison officers concentrated upon lobbying Congress. In so doing, they were supported by a series of political outreach units whose job was to solicit support from particular political institutions and interest group networks. These units consisted of an Office of Intergovernmental Affairs, to liaise with state and local governments; an Office of Public Liaison, to gather support from business, industrial, commercial companies and associations; an Office of Political Affairs, to liaise with various organs of the Republican party; and, finally, an Office of Communications, which liaised with a range of media organisations. These various units stroked their target clienteles by holding briefing sessions with the president, Cabinet Secretaries and executive aides in the White House and throughout the country. The prime aim of these meetings was to generate support from all these different sectors for the president's legislative proposals just before key votes in Congress (Wayne, 1982; Wehr, 1981b).

In all, the Reagan administration attached a very high priority to legislative strategy. This was manifested in a professional, disciplined, and strategic approach to lobbying Congress that contrasted sharply with the record of the Carter administration.

The legislative record of the first term

The Reagan administration's legislative strategy led to a planned string of legislative victories in its first six months of office. These successes quickly created a reputation for President Reagan as an effective legislator and national leader. But, this image of effective leadership endured for far longer than did Reagan's mastery of Congress. After mid-1981, the Reagan administration encountered opposition from Congress and other obstacles to presidential leadership. The Reagan White House responded by adopting a defensive legislative strategy to prevent the victories of 1981 from being overturned. This approach to Congress meant that hardly any new legislative initiatives were enacted during the last three years of the first term. In overall terms, the president's initial victories did not establish a lasting 'new beginning' in presidential–congressional rela-tionships, but were followed by conflicts and stalemates which – given the defensive orientation of the administration's legislative strategy – were projected by the Reagan administration as 'victories'.

1981 – The year of the President
In the first year, the Reagan administration moved quickly and effectively to implement its legislative strategy. The president's legislative agenda

was rapidly written into his first annual budget submission and delivered to Congress within only forty-nine days of taking office. This let Reagan take full advantage of his opportunity to set the early legislative agenda of Congress. Packaging the president's agenda into his first budget also permitted the administration to pursue hundreds of across-the-board budget and policy revisions that affected just about every unit of the federal government. Thus, Reagan's narrow agenda was also one that was most comprehensive in its scope. The administration's simplified agenda made Reagan's priorities easily comprehensible to the public, which also facilitated the building of support for the president.

The administration's game-plan divided the president's agenda into three legislative components, which were carefully spaced apart in order both to control the calendar of Congress and to buy time to lobby the House. As planned, the Senate's new leaders quickly moved the first component, when it passed in early April a first congressional budget resolution – which sets Congress' spending and taxing priorities for the next fiscal year (which begins on 1 October) – that endorsed Reagan's fiscal and economic policies.

The president's first legislative victory came on 7 May 1981, when the House approved a first congressional budget resolution that had Reagan's backing. The House Democrats had proposed a resolution which reduced the president's tax and spending cuts and lowered his request for defence spending. In response, the administration took the bold decision to challenge the Democrats' budget on the floor, an action which amounted to a straightforward contest for control of the House. Hence, the administration proposed a substitute measure – known as Gramm-Latta I – that had been worked out with the leaders of the House Republicans and the members of the Conservative Democratic Forum. The plan was supported by a 'Southern Blitz' of forty-five Southern districts held by Democrats to get voters to pressure their Representative to vote with the Reagan administration. President Reagan also gave, shortly after an attempted assassination, a very emotional and effective televised appeal for support. The overall result was a 'blitz lobby' of Capitol Hill that overloaded and closed the telephone exchange with an unprecedented number of calls. This lobby convinced many Democrats to side with the president. In all, 190 Republicans voted for Gramm-Latta I, none voted against it; 63 Democrats broke ranks (Tate, 1981). In so doing, President

Reagan gained the support of both chambers for his budget and economic policies.

The second victory came when the House voted to implement a package of spending cuts that had the support of the administration. The campaign to retrench spending involved rewriting hundreds of laws to lower mandated spending levels. This demand confronted the real possibility that the spending committees, along with their interest group clienteles, which had advocated the spending programmes in the first place, would use the greater autonomy accorded to them by the reformed Congress to protect their pet projects from cuts. To circumvent this danger the administration utilised the reconciliation procedure of the still-evolving congressional budget process. As originally planned by the 1974 Budget Act, reconciliation was intended to be used in mid-September to compel spending committees to comply with the spending levels set by Congress for the annual federal budget. Experience proved that reconciliation came too late to be an effective tool for enforcing Congress' spending targets. This led to reconciliation being moved to the start of the budget process in 1980 to gain more time to cut spending. Early reconciliation provided the administration with a means to package all the president's spending cuts into one omnibus bill, which, as long as the Reagan administration could amass a majority for one vote on the bill on the floor of the Senate and the House, would let the president have his programme of cuts considered as a whole and on his terms, and, thus, let him sidestep resistance from the legislative committees that had initiated the spending programmes (Hogan, 1985; Schick, 1981).

The value of the reconciliation strategy was demonstrated when the House Democrats developed a bill to cut spending by much less than Reagan had proposed. The Democrats sought to protect their bill by bringing it to the floor on a rule which required the bill to be voted in six sections; the rule also prohibited discussion of any substitute measure. The strategy failed because the administration fashioned a majority – by 217 votes to 210 – on 25 June 1981, to overturn the Democrats' rule and substitute their own reconciliation bill. The administration's bill was put to just one vote in order to implement hundreds of reductions in federal spending programmes. The administration's success demonstrated that an inside knowledge of the reformed Congress, especially of the new budget procedures, and a willingness to cultivate contacts with members from both sides of the aisle could pay handsome dividends (LeLoup, 1982).

The third victory came in late July, when the House approved a bill to cut federal taxes that Reagan supported. Once more, the Senate had moved the president's proposal quickly. This time, the Democratic leaders of the House made a determined effort to wrest control of the chamber from Reagan's conservative coalition. Liberal tax concessions were offered by the Democrats to buy support for their bill. The Reagan administration responded in kind. President Reagan made a persuasive television appeal for his bill; the sixty-three Democrats who voted with him on the first budget resolution were personally contacted by the president. Wavering members were offered tax concessions for oil producers, farmers and small businesses in return for supporting the administration. The bidding war was won by the administration, with 48 Democrats joining with 190 Republicans to enact the Economic Recovery Tax Act of 1981 (LeLoup, 1982; Ornstein, 1982; Schick, 1982; Wayne, 1982).

The administration's carefully planned legislative strategy produced a string of victories that provoked very favourable comparisons with Lyndon Johnson's early presidency. The carrot of rapid economic growth undoubtedly led many members to support the president's radical economic policies. But the enactment of the president's economic programme coincided with the beginnings of the severest economic recession since the Great Depression. Most economists outside the administration attributed the recession to Reagan's acceptance of less cuts in spending and much deeper cuts in federal taxes than he had originally proposed. These decisions created an imbalance between federal spending and income. Moreover, this imbalance increased as the president's programme of cuts in federal taxes were implemented each year. The overall result was a federal deficit juggernaut. To finance the deficit, the government needed to borrow money from the credit markets. The Reagan administration's support for tightening the money supply led to a sharp competition for credit between the public and the private sectors, which drove interest rates way beyond the reach of private corporations and consumers. This set off a chain reaction of reduced sales and investment – because neither consumers nor private corporations were, respectively, able or willing to borrow money at high interest rates – that led to economic recession (Palmer and Sawhill, 1982; Schick, 1982).

In an attempt to move the revenue and spending lines of the budget closer together, the administration assembled a second budget for fiscal

1982 that was sent to Congress just before the new fiscal year was about to begin. This emergency budget sought a second round of deep cuts in domestic spending plus some revenue increases to lower the deficit. The plan was a tactical error. Members of Congress had adjourned in early August thinking that their work on the budget had been completed for the session. During the recess, they heard constituents complain about how high interest rates were hurting them. This led members to have second thoughts about supporting the president's economic policies. The 'Fall offensive' was rejected without even a vote; the spending cuts were never formally introduced, and the president's tax rises withdrawn.

Instead, the president sought deep cuts in domestic spending through the annual appropriations process, reasoning that he could use the threat of his veto – which could be sustained by the support of one-third of the members of either chamber of Congress – to impose his views on the federal budget. This decision thoroughly disrupted the annual appropriations process, which became the site of a prolonged battle between the administration and the House Democrats. This led to a stalemate on the passage of the thirteen annual appropriations bills, which, in turn, necessitated the enactment of a continuing resolution bill, a stop-gap measure for financing the work of the federal government. President Reagan criticised a continuing resolution that was passed by the House Democrats as a 'budget-buster' and then vetoed it. This led to the closure of all but 'essential' federal offices on 23 November. President Reagan's aggressive pursuit of spending cuts largely failed; six appropriation bills were passed which exceeded by significant margins the spending levels requested by the president (Hartman, 1982). All in all, President Reagan's mastery over congressional decision-making eroded quickly when the economy moved into severe recession.

1982 – A 'mid-course' correction

A mounting federal deficit, record high interest rates, a deepening economic recession and the mid-term elections fast approaching meant that the administration faced very unfavourable economic and political conditions at the commencement of its second year in office. The Reagan administration responded by changing its legislative strategy. The president refused to listen to those who advised him to cut his defence budget and to revise his programme of tax cuts to lower the deficit. Reagan argued this course would only invite

Congress to further revise his defence and tax policies, thereby
undermining the achievements of 1981. Instead, the president
decided to keep faith with the budget policies initiated in his first
year. In so doing, the president challenged a split Congress to
rewrite, in an election year, his second budget submission. The
administration could then see how Congress responded. This would
let the White House assess whether the president should support or
oppose any budget plan developed by the legislature. But, if a
divided Congress could not develop an independent budget, then
this would satisfy the president because it would mean that the
policies he had initiated in 1981 would be maintained. Thus, instead
of leading Congress, Reagan's legislative strategy in 1982 might
better be called one of 'followership'. In the only change from his
first budget submission, the president's second budget included the
'New Federalism' initiative. This addition was meant to be an
eye-catching proposal to divert attention from the problems of the
federal deficit (Kirschten, 1982a, 1982b)

In stark contrast to 1981, the president's budget was overwhelmingly and quickly rejected by both houses of Congress. But no
consensus emerged in Congress on how to tackle the deficit. The
impasse led to secret negotiations between the administration and
leaders of both chambers of Congress in April. The talks failed, but
were projected by the White House as a public relations victory
because of the president's willingness 'to go the extra mile' and meet
with Speaker O'Neill on Capitol Hill to work out a compromise
budget.

After the talks collapsed, Republican leaders in the Senate took
the initiative. They realised that the recession and the budget deficit
were related in the minds of the voters, and feared if nothing was
done to tackle the deficit then Republican Senators – and Representatives – would fare badly in the 1982 congressional elections. The
Republicans, independent of the president, set about devising their
own budget plan. Their first plan was largely crafted by moderates.
It would raise $125 billion in new taxes over the next three fiscal
years to effect a sizeable drop in the deficit. The moderates also
recognised that they might have to revise the president's programme
of cuts in income taxes to obtain bipartisan support for their budget
plan.

The prospect of placing the president's tax cut programme on the
Senate's agenda quickly forced the president to return to the

negotiating table. This led to hurried negotiations between White House officials and the majority leadership of the Senate. These talks resulted in a fiscal plan that bore the heavy imprint of moderate Republicans in the Senate. The budget left the president's programme of tax cuts alone, but at the price of raising $97 billion in new taxes over the 1983–5 fiscal period. The plan also added $118 billion over the next two budget years, making for a total of $215 billion in new taxes to be levied over the 1983–5 fiscal period. In addition, the budget reduced the president's request for defence spending by around $22 billion over fiscal 1983–5. Domestic spending would be cut by just under $30 billion over the same period, which was significantly less than the president had requested in his second budget submission.

The plan represented a significant reversal of the president's budget policies, and was only supported because the administration believed that Congress – if left alone – might, faced with the pressures generated by the mid-term elections, produce a budget that would be more damaging to the president's policies. The president tried to make the best of a difficult situation by claiming the tax increases to be 'the greatest tax reform in history' and a 'price worth paying for lower interest rates, economic recovery and more jobs'. However, the president's claims were not supported by conservative Republicans in the House of Representatives. They saw the tactically-named Tax Equity and Fiscal Responsibility bill as clearly rejecting the tax policies initiated in 1981, and refused to vote for the proposal. In all, eighty-nine Republicans – all of whom had voted with the president in the budget battles of 1981 – voted against the bill. The tax bill passed on the strength of a bipartisan, largely moderate coalition of 123 Democrats and 103 Republicans, which marked the demise of the president's conservative coalition in the House (Tate, 1982; Kirschten, 1982c).

The Reagan administration incurred further reverses during the second session of the 97th Congress. Just before Congress adjourned for the campaign trail, both chambers voted to override a presidential veto of a supplemental appropriation of $14.2 billion for fiscal 1982. In the last hours of the regular session the president was again defeated in the House on a proposal, which Reagan had campaigned hard for, to amend the Constitution to mandate a balanced budget each year. During the 'lame-duck' session following the mid-term elections, the president had to accept a job creation programme (in the form of a proposal to repair the nations' transport system) that he had initially opposed, rather than risk losing another veto fight with Congress. In the course of the entire session the Reagan administration failed to make progress with many other legislative proposals. These included the defeat of the New Federalism plan, bills to reform the Clean Air and Water acts, various proposals to reform federal regulatory laws and a proposal, which was given much attention by the White House, to recommence the production of chemical weapons.

In general, the Reagan administration ceded the legislative initiative to Congress for the second session of the 97th Congress. This was mainly due to the president's declining influence over the House. The *Congressional Quarterly*'s annual study of presidential support scores shows President Reagan won 55.8 % of the floor votes in 1982 on issues in which he took a clear personal stand in the House. This figure represented a drop of 16.6 % from his impressive achievement in 1981. In addition, the president also lost the support of the conservative coalition in the House. In comparison, President Reagan won 82.4 % of the floor votes on issues in which he took a clear stand in the Senate, which represented a drop of 5.9 percentage points from 1981. But, the 1982 boxscores for the Senate included several votes where the president acquiesced to the Senate's position on major policy issues, and others where the Senate blocked initiatives passed by the House that the administration opposed (Cahodas, 1983; Wehr, 1983a, 1983b). In all, the president both lost control of the House and had to face growing opposition from Republican moderates in the Senate during his second year in office.

1983 – Stalemate

President Reagan faced even more adverse political and economic conditions at the beginning of his third year. The mid-term elections had added twenty-six new Democrats to the House of Representatives. These results tightened the Democrats' grip on the House of Representatives, making it virtually impossible for the president to resurrect the conservative coalition in the House. Although the Republicans retained control of the Senate, many Republicans had been returned by very narrow margins, which made them quite wary of supporting the administration. On the economic front, the recession had pushed unemployment up to around 11 per cent, which was the highest level of unemployment for almost half a century. The federal deficit was projected at around $200 billion for fiscal 1983, which meant that interest rates were still at record high levels.

Rather than change direction, President Reagan opted for consistency in policy leadership by holding fast to the economic policies commenced in 1981. Consequently, the 'followership' strategy was repeated. But, this time the president's third budget submission was based on tough, even pessimistic economic forecasts to discourage any 'easy answers' plan to reduce the deficit. In addition, the president proposed a set of 'standby taxes' – which would be implemented after the upcoming presidential election – if Congress would first enact a package of additional cuts in domestic spending. In contrast to previous years, the administration moved economic issues down the president's agenda, reasoning that progress was unlikely on these issues. In their place, the president's military spending and nuclear arms policies were pushed to the top of his legislative agenda (Reilly, 1983).

President Reagan protected his economic policies from change in 1983 because presidential–congressional relationships on fiscal issues settled into a pattern of stalemate. Budgetary deadlock was encouraged by several factors. To begin with, any plan to reduce annual federal deficits of around $200 billion requires the taking of tough, politically unpopular decisions. When the government is divided between a Republican administration and a split Congress, any plan to tackle the deficit needs bipartisan leadership. This did not happen in 1983 because Congress and the president accentuated rather than compromised their differences on fiscal policies. President Reagan's third budget was rejected by both chambers of Congress, mainly because it was unacceptable in its approach to the deficit. In reply, the president walked away from the budget process when Congress developed a first budget resolution that called for the raising of $73 billion in new taxes to lower the deficit. By detaching himself from further discussions the president effectively stalled any progress on the budget for the rest of the session. This suited the president because it meant that the economic policies he had initiated in the first year remained, with the important exception of the tax increases enacted in 1982, largely intact (Clark and Cohen, 1983).

The president adopted a more varied strategy in pursuit of his military and nuclear arms policies, bending to compromise solutions that suited his interests, and using the Senate as a legislative gatekeeper to block proposals from the House that went contrary to his preferences. For example, when faced with very strong opposition to continuing the controversial MX missile programme the president picked up on a suggestion, made by the late Senator Henry Jackson, to appoint a bipartisan National Commission on Strategic Forces. The panel was set up in late 1982, with the administration and the majority leaderships of both chambers of Congress each appointing a third of the commission's members. The panel's report recommended that the MX missile be deployed, but in smaller numbers than the president had requested, in conjunction with the smaller and less vulnerable Midgetman missile. This compromise gained bipartisan support, and passed Congress in May, 1983 (Kirschten, 1983). In similar vein, the administration and both chambers of Congress worked out a compromise over applying the War Powers Resolution of 1973 to the detachment of US Marines in Lebanon, that largely satisfied the president and the Democrats (Felton, 1983).

When the president could not strike an agreement with the Democrats, the president turned to the Senate to protect his position. For example, when the House voted a defence appropriation that excluded the provision of covert aid to forces fighting the left-wing Sandinist government in Nicaragua, the Senate Republicans extracted a compromise agreement during the conference committee stage on the bill under which $24 million was allocated to the anti-Sandinistas ('contras') on the condition that Congress would later decide whether aid should be continued. The compromise, thus, let Reagan continue his controversial policies towards Central America for another year. This agreement also involved setting a total figure for defence spending that suited Reagan. The Senate further acted as the administration's legislative gatekeeper when it tabled, at the administration's request, a nuclear freeze resolution passed by the House.

1984 – The politics of the campaign trail
With the economy moving into recovery,the administration reasoned that there was little incentive to change course. Consequently, the administration's fourth budget repeated the fiscal policies initiated in the first year. In an attempt to defuse the issue of the deficit, the budget did propose that bipartisan negotiations be held to agree a 'down-payment' for reducing the deficit. The Democrats rejected

the proposal, mainly because they wanted the president to first cut his defence budget.

With a three-way compromise rejected, Reagan agreed a deficit-reduction plan with the Senate Republicans. The plan would reduce the deficit by $150 billion. This would be achieved by making roughly equal cuts in defence spending, domestic spending and by raising some new taxes. But the president stipulated that the defence cuts would have to be made last in order to protect his military defence programme from further cuts by the Democrats. This led to a trial-of-strength between the administration and the House on the issue of the defence budget that lasted for most of the session. In late September, the Democrats settled for a cut of around $20 billion in the president's request for defence spending. The agreement meant that the president had achieved the main goal of his legislative strategy. It also supported Reagan's campaign claim that his administration had strengthened America's defences.

President Reagan, however, lost heavily on his domestic policy initiatives in 1984. The House negated the president's proposals to amend the Constitution to prohibit abortions and to permit school prayers. This meant that President Reagan failed to advance any item on the 'social agenda' during his first term. Congress also rejected the president's proposal to give tax credits to parents who sent their children to private schools. President Reagan's plan to give tax relief to businesses which created new jobs in enterprise zones was also defeated. An administration proposal to lower the minimum wage for teenagers was largely ignored by Congress. The president's requests, made in his State of the Union message, to amend the Constitution to mandate a balanced budget and to empower him to veto specific funds appropriated by Congress, were also rejected.

In general, the politics of the campaign trail sharpened conflicts between both ends of the avenue. As a result, little progress was made on most issues during 1984. Indeed, the president and the 98th Congress left the thorniest problems to the 99th Congress. The MX missile programme, the development of anti-satellite weapons, and the sending of covert aid to anti-government rebels in Nicaragua were left pending. The whole issue of the deficit was further pushed onto the agenda of the 99th Congress. While these decisions did not overturn the president's positions, neither did they confirm them. On major issues, the administration was just about able to use the Senate as its legislative gatekeeper. But this required White House lobbyists to spend much time assembling supportive coalitions. This was the case because nineteen Republican Senators were up for re-election, and were siding more with their constituents than with the administration (Granat, 1984; Pressman, 1984). In all, the 98th Congress rejected every new legislative initiative made by President Reagan, and closed by deciding to resume its battles with the administration in the 99th Congress.

Congressional liaison in the Reagan administration:
an assessment of the first term

When compared with the presidencies of Jimmy Carter and Gerald Ford the Reagan administration was extremely effective in implementing its early legislative priorities. But, as the survey of the administration's overall legislative record indicates, Reagan's rosiest of honeymoons did not produce a lasting 'new beginning' in presidential–congressional relationships. After the first year, the Reagan administration failed to advance any of its new legislative initiatives and had to fight hard to prevent Congress from overturning the achievements of 1981. In overall terms, the president won the opening battle but not the campaign with Congress during his first term in office.

Before considering the reasons why President Reagan did not win the campaign, it is worth remembering that he was the first president since Lyndon Johnson to obtain his initial legislative priorities. In so doing, the Reagan administration initially undermined the conventional wisdom that presidents are becoming increasingly powerless and that America is ungovernable. For these reasons, the administration's victories contributed greatly to the public's perception of Reagan as an effective leader.

These victories were deliberately planned by the administration's legislative strategy. This strategy sought to take quick advantage of good election results to create a few, but bold, legislative initiatives. To do so, the administration decided to pursue a legislative agenda exclusively limited to economic issues. Reagan's strategists believed that implementing his radical proposals for tackling America's economic problems in quick time would demonstrate to the public that the new president was an effective legislative leader. In setting its game-plan the administration worked closely with Republican leaders in Congress. Their main goal was to control the congressional calendar in order to move the president's legislative proposals through Congress by mid-summer. During the transition it was agreed that the Senate would put the president's agenda on a fast track. This decision gave motor-power to the president's proposals. It also let the administration concentrate its resources upon lobbying the Democratic-controlled House of Representatives, directing its efforts to resurrecting the conservative coalition by winning the support of conservative Democrats and maintaining the loyalty of Republican members. Because of its carefully planned legislative strategy the Reagan administration, unlike its immediate predecessors, made the most of its political honeymoon period with Congress.

Centralised management of the president's agenda let the Reagan administration organise its entire resources to counter the decentralised, fragmented legislative process of the reformed Congress. For example, the managers of the president's agenda had the necessary authority to adjust his policy proposals to buy support on Capitol Hill. The programme of spending cuts was revised to suit the different interests of conservative Democrats and liberal Republicans in the House. The president's tax programme was also adjusted to meet the different demands of Republican moderates in the Senate and conservative Democrats in the House. Central management of the president's legislative proposals provided the Reagan administration with the means to make decisions quickly and to adapt policy proposals to changing political circumstances in Congress. This innovation gave the Reagan White House, in contrast to preceding administrations, the capacity for pursuing a flexible approach to Congress. This approach was well-suited to liaising with the new, decentralised Congress and contributed greatly to implementing the president's agenda.

The Reagan administration's early legislative victories further underline the value of appointing experienced hands to the president's team for liaising with Congress. Reagan's liaison aides used their firsthand knowledge of the procedures and the institutional dynamics of the reformed Congress to shape the administration's legislative strategy and tactics. For example, the decisions to 'hit the ground running' with a limited, but tightly prioritised agenda let the administration fully exploit its honeymoon period; the decision to challenge the Democrats' bill of spending cuts on the floor of the House was also based upon good, accurate inside knowledge of

Congress. The president's outreach team effectively supported Reagan's liaison officers. The various field units effectively stroked their target groups to generate, at planned points in the legislative debate, a blitz lobby of Congress in favour of the president's legislative initiatives. This created the impression in the minds of many congressmen that President Reagan had a 'mandate' for his policies, and was not to be resisted.

But after the August recess, the president lost the initiative in liaising with Congress for the rest of his term. This development was a consequence of several factors. In the first place, the president's economic policies did not perform as he had claimed they would. The promise of immediate, rapid economic growth and a balanced budget in 1984, plus a cut in taxes, attracted many members of the House to vote with the new administration. The advent of a deep economic recession and a mounting federal deficit provoked many of the same congressmen to distance themselves from the administration. As such, policy failure led to the collapse of the president's legislative majority in the House. This made it most unlikely that the president would be able again to impose his views on the 97th Congress, and this was underlined by the failure of his fall offensive.

From a related angle, restricting the president's initial legislative agenda to a few, exclusively economic proposals meant that other intiatives, such as the social agenda issues, had to be placed on the backburner. When the economy moved into recession, the administration directed its efforts towards defending the policies initiated in its first six months. The social agenda and other issues were never brought forward to the top of the administration's legislative agenda. As a consequence, the Reagan administration missed an opportunity to implement a range of legislative initiatives during his first term. In overall terms, the president opted for consistency in his governing agenda but at the price of limiting the scope of his legislative achievements.

In similar vein, the decision to limit Reagan's initial legislative agenda to economic issues meant that the president's campaign pledge to overhaul the nations' environmental, product safety, and energy regulations was pursued by administrative means. Legislative proposals to rewrite and terminate a host of federal regulations were subsequently introduced, but they were not enacted because the administration had lost its initial influence over the legislative process. As a consequence, the legislative underpinnings of these regulatory programmes are still intact, which will permit a subsequent administration to overturn the president's deregulation campaign. In sum, the pursuit of a restricted agenda means that the scope of the 'Reagan revolution' will be, in legislative terms, a limited one.

The choice of the annual budget process as the vehicle for implementing the president's agenda further truncated the scope of Reagan's legislative achievements. In 1981, the president only initiated a series of changes in federal spending and tax policies that he anticipated would be sustained in succeeding years by Congress. But when Reagan's economic and fiscal policies failed to realise his promises, the president encountered increasingly stout resistance each year to his attempts to continue his initial budget policies. In overall terms, Congress rejected over half of Reagan's requests for cuts in domestic spending programmes. The president's defence buildup was subjected to growing opposition each year. This resulted in expenditure cuts, with many of them targeted on military programmes – such as the MX missile – that the president had given a high priority. President Reagan further had to accept reverses in his tax policies, most notably in 1982.

In all, the president enjoyed one very good year with Congress, and then confronted familiar barriers to presidential leadership. The legislative record of Reagan's first year clearly indicates to future administrations the great value of adopting a strategic and centralised approach to exploiting the president's honeymoon period with Capitol Hill. Future administrations would also do well to emulate the Reagan administration by appointing seasoned professionals to the president's liaison team. Reagan's legislative strategists carefully planned the victories of 1981 and then adroitly used the Republican Senate to block bills passed by the Democratic-controlled House of Representatives that ran counter to Reagan's preferences. The Reagan White House made the most of the president's initial successes to create an image of Reagan as an effective leader of Congress. This positive appraisal endured despite the fact that the president failed to enact any of his legislative initiatives after his first six months in office. All of which strongly underlines the great importance of setting a favourable perception of presidential leadership during the first months of his term. Indeed, the success of the White House in cultivating this positive image must have contributed greatly to Reagan's re-election.

But, adopting an uncompromising approach to legislative strategy for three years of the first term helped raise obstacles to Reagan's influence in Congress. In pushing ahead with his conservative agenda long after economic and political circumstances had turned against him, President Reagan failed to replace his conservative coalition with a new legislative coalition based on moderates in both parties. As a consequence, Reagan encountered increasing opposition from moderates in his own party, which led to significant revisions in his governing policies. The president's fidelity to his initial legislative proposals also sharpened the differences between his administration and the Democratic-controlled House of Representatives. Because the Reagan administration adopted an adversarial approach towards Congress, no steps were taken to lay the groundwork for a more positive relationship with Congress during the second term. The unwillingness to develop collaborative relationships with key forces in Congress further suggested that the president's legislative agenda would face considerable difficulties during the second term.

References

Abramson, P., Aldrich, J. and Rhode, D. (1983). *Change and Continuity in the 1980 Elections*, Washington, DC: Congressional Quarterly Press.

Barrett, L. (1984). *Gambling With History: Reagan in the White House*, Harrisonburg, Va: R. R. Donnelley and Sons.

Cahodas, N. (1983). 'Presidential Support Study Shows Reagan Rating Fell 10 Percentage Points in 1982', *Congressional Quarterly Weekly Report*, pp. 94–7.

Cannon, L. (1982). *Reagan*, New York: G. P. Putnam.

Clark, T. and Cohen, R. (1983). 'Coming Up Empty Handed', *National Journal*, pp. 2460–9.

Cutler, L. (1980). 'To Form a Government', *Foreign Affairs*, pp. 126–43.

Cronin, T. (1980). *The State of the Presidency*, Boston: Little, Brown & Co.

Davidson, R. and Oleszek, W. (1984). 'Changing the Guard in the US Senate', *Legislative Studies Quarterly*, pp. 635–63.

Davis, E. (1979). 'Legislative Liaison in the Carter Administration', *Political Studies Quarterly*, pp. 286–302.

Davis, E. (1983). 'Congressional Liaison: The People and the Institutions,' in A. King, ed., *Both Ends of the Avenue: the Presidency, the Executive Branch, and Congress in the 1980s*, Washington, DC: American Enterprise Institute, pp. 59–95.

Felton, J. (1983). 'Congress Crafts "War Powers" Compromise', *Congressional Quarterly Weekly Report*, pp. 1963–5.

Granat, D. (1984). '98th Congress Leaves Thorny Legacy for 99th', *Congressional Quarterly Weekly Report*, pp. 2699–731.

Hartman, R. (1982). 'Congress and Budget-Making',·*Political Science Quarterly*, pp. 381–402.

Heclo, H. (1983). 'One Executive Branch or Many?' in A. King, ed., *Both Ends of the Avenue: the Presidency, the Executive Branch, and Congress in the 1980s*, Washington, DC: American Enterprise Institute, pp. 26–58.

Heclo, H. (1984). 'Executive Budget-Making' in G. Mills and J. Palmer, eds, *Federal Budget Policy in the 1980s*, Washington, DC: The Urban Institute Press, pp. 255–91.

Heclo, H. and Penner, R. (1983). 'Fiscal and Political Strategy in the Reagan Administration' in F. Greenstein, ed., *The Reagan Presidency: an Early Assessment*, Baltimore: The Johns Hopkins University Press, pp. 21–47.

Heineman, B., Jr and Hessler, C. (1980). *A Memorandum for the President: a Strategic Approach to Domestic Affairs in the 1980s*, New York: Random House.

Hogan, J. (1985). 'Ten Years After: the US Congressional Budget and Impoundment Control Act of 1974', *Public Administration*, pp. 133–49.

Jones, C. (1981). 'Congress and the Presidency' in T. Mann and N. Ornstein, eds, *The New Congress*, Washington, DC: American Enterprise Institute, pp. 223–49.

Jones, C. (1985). 'Carter and Congress: From the Outside In', *British Journal of Political Science*, pp. 269–98.

Keller, W. (1981). 'Executive Agency Lobbyists Mastering the Difficult Art of "Congressional Liaison"', *Congressional Quarterly Weekly Report*, pp. 2387–92.

King, A., ed. (1978). *The New American Political System*, Washington, DC: American Enterprise Institute.

Kirschten, D. (1981a). 'Reagan's Cabinet Councils May Have Less Influence Than Meets the Eye', *National journal*, pp. 1242–7.

Kirschten, D. (1981b). 'The Pennsylvania Ave. Connection – Making Peace on Capitol Hill', *National Journal*, pp. 384–7.

Kirschten, D. (1982a). 'Fridays at Blair House', *National Journal*, p. 251.

Kirschten, D. (1982b). 'After a Year, the Reagan White House May Be Beginning to Feel the Strain', *National Journal*, pp. 140–4.

Kirschten, D. (1982c). 'Reagan's Legislative Strategy Team Keeps his Record of Victories Intact', *National Journal*, pp. 1127–30.

Kirschten, D. (1983). 'Consensus From Without', *National Journal*, p. 1128.

LeLoup, L. (1982). 'After the Blitz: Reagan and the US Congressional Budget Process,' *Legislative Studies Quarterly*, pp. 321–339.

Light, P. (1982). *The President's Agenda*, Baltimore: The Johns Hopkins University Press.

Mann, T. and Ornstein, N., eds (1981). *The New Congress*, Washington, DC. American Enterprise Institute.

Ornstein, N. (1982). 'Assessing Reagan's First Year,' in N. Ornstein, ed., *President and Congress: Assessing Reagan's First Year*, Washington, DC: American Enterprise Institute, pp. 89–107.

Ornstein, N. (1983). 'The Open Congress Meets the President' in A. King, ed., *Both Ends of the Avenue: the Presidency, the Executive Branch, and the Congress in the 1980s*, Washington, DC: American Enterprise Institute, pp. 185–211.

Palmer, J. and Sawhill, I., eds (1982), *The Reagan Experiment: an Examination of Economic and Social Policies Under the Reagan Administration*, Washington, DC: The Urban Institute Press.

Pfiffner, J. (1983), 'The Carter–Reagan Transition: Hitting the Ground Running', *Presidential Studies Quarterly*, pp. 623–45.

Pomper, G. *et al.* (1981). *The Election of 1980: Reports and Interpretations*, Chatham, NJ: Chatham House.

Pressman. S. (1984). 'White House Lobbyists Find Congress is Less Supportive', *Congressional Quarterly Weekly Report*, pp. 1429–34.

Ranney, A. (1981). *The American Elections of 1980*, Washington, DC: American Enterprise Institute.

Reilly, A. (1983). 'Reagan's Savvy Strategists', *Dun's Business Monthly*, pp. 34–40.

Salamon, L. and Abramson, A. (1984). 'Governance: the Politics of Retrenchment' in J. Palmer and I. Sawhill, eds, *The Reagan Record: An Assessment of America's Changing Domestic Priorities*, Cambridge, Mass: Ballinger Publishing Co., pp. 31–68.

Sandoz, E. and Crabb, C., Jr (1981). *A Tide of Discontent: the 1980 Elections and their meaning*, Washington, DC: Congressional Quarterly Press.

Schick, A. (1981). *Reconciliation and the Congresional Budget Process*, Washington, DC: American Enterprise Institute.

Schick, A. (1982). 'How the Budget Was Won and Lost' in N. Ornstein, ed., *President and Congress: Assessing Reagan's First Year*, Washington, DC: American Enterprise Institute, pp. 14–43.

Sundquist, J. L. (1980). 'The Crisis of Competence in Government' in J. A. Pechman, ed., *Setting National Priorities: Agenda for the 1980's*, Washington, DC: The Brookings Institution, pp. 531–63.

Tate, D. (1981). 'House Provides President A Victory on the 1982 Budget', *Congressional Quarterly Weekly Report*, pp. 783–7.

Tate, D. (1982). 'Budget Battle Erupts on Hill as Compromise Talks Fizzle', *Congressional Quarterly Weekly Report*, pp. 962–72.

Wayne, S. (1978). *The Legislative Presidency*, New York: Harper & Row.

Wayne, S. (1982). 'Congressional Liaison in the Reagan White House: a Preliminary Assessment of the First Year' in N. Ornstein, ed., *President and Congress: Assessing Reagan's First Year*, Washington, DC: American Enterprise Institute, pp. 44–65.

Wehr, E. (1981a). 'Reagan Team on the Hill Getting Members' Praise for Hard Work, Experience', *Congressional Quarterly Weekly Report*, pp. 747–79.

Wehr, E. (1981b). 'Public Liaison chief Dole Reaches to Outside Groups to Sell Reagan's Programs', *Congressional Quarterly Weekly Report*, pp. 975–8.

Wehr, E. (1983a), 'Conservative Success Wanes as Democratic Loyalty Grows', *Congressional Quarterly Weekly Report*, pp. 101–6.

Wehr, E. (1983b). 'Reagan Support Fades in Key Votes of 1982', *Congressional Quarterly Weekly Report*, pp. 117–31.

The Office of Management and Budget and Reaganomics: The rise and decline of a presidential staff agency

During its first fifty years the Bureau of the Budget set and maintained an enviable reputation as a bastion of 'neutral competence' in managing the executive budget and legislative clearance processes, and in undertaking certain programme development, coordination and management functions for the president. This reputation was derived from the recruitment of budget directors and career staffs who were accomplished professionals, people who respected as experts in analysing the work of the many departments and agencies of the executive branch. Throughout Washington's governing community the budget agency was widely perceived as a special institution, one that attracted the best and the brightest and loyally served the president by providing objective advice. The budget agency's prestige changed dramatically when its name, role and style of leadership were altered by President Nixon. The Republican president turned more to his White House domestic affairs office than he did to the renamed Office of Management and Budget (OMB) in making his budget policies. President Nixon used OMB more as a personal staff agency, providing support information for his policy preferences. In line with this, Nixon appointed Republican partisans to head OMB who were loyal to his policy goals, but who were budgetary amateurs. This increase in political control over the budget agency was supplemented by the addition of two layers of politically-appointed Associate Directors to oversee the work of the career staffs. These moves transformed the OMB into a partisan, politicised, and personal agency of the president at the expense of its reputation for neutral competence, and was a development that was continued under the administrations of Presidents Ford and Carter (Berman, 1979; Wayne, 1978).

The politicisation of OMB continued under the Reagan administration, and was developed in several new ways, most visibly in the first year. During the transition the young director of OMB, David Stockman, took the lead in framing Ronald Reagan's budget-oriented governing agenda. This move both displaced the domestic affairs staff of the White House, and made OMB into the administration's central instrument for making Reagan's initial budget, economic and domestic policies. David Stockman also became the leading, most prominent advocate in the administration for Reagan's fiscal, economic and domestic policies. In this new role, Stockman appeared before many press conferences and congressional committees both to defend and to guide the president's legislative proposals through Congress.

The budget agency was also given the new task of overseeing the implementation by federal departments and agencies of Reagan's drive to lighten the burden of federal regulations. Performing this function involved OMB in scrutinising the details of policy making and implememtation by executive departments and agencies, which sharply politicised relationships between them and OMB. In line with the expanded political functions of OMB under the leadership of Ronald Reagan, evidence suggests that OMB's career staffs also had to become much more sensitive to political factors. OMB's career staffs are now expected to undertake quasi-political roles, such as gathering political intelligence from congressional committees and from public interest groups on a range of legislative proposals forwarded by the Reagan administration.

However, the influence of OMB's director within the Reagan administration rose and fell dramatically during the first year. The revelation, in late Autumn, that Stockman privately doubted the policies that he had prominently helped to fashion and implement deeply embarrassed the president and his administration. This disclosure led to a second phase, consisting of a more limited policy-making role within the administration for David Stockman. This diminished role indicates some of the contemporary dangers of politicising executive staff agencies for presidential purposes.

Over-identification with Reagan's economic plan made Stockman and the OMB highly vulnerable to resistance from executive departments and agencies and from Congress, once the president's policies proved to be flawed and inconsistent. Reagan's Cabinet Secretaries had deeply resented the brisk way in which Stockman had cut their department's budget and now provided stiffened opposition to Stockman's budget proposals, particularly his perennial campaign to cut the federal deficit. As a result, Stockman's proposals were rejected and the federal deficit continued to mount. In contrast to the glory days at the start of the administration. Stockman was ultimately superseded as Reagan's lead spokesman, for the wide portfolio of policy areas that he had earlier commanded, by Donald Regan, the Secretary of the Treasury Department.

Excluding OMB's career staff from making Reagan's first budget enabled the administration to write a series of highly optimistic assumptions concerning annual rates of inflation, unemployment and economic growth into the president's first budget. Undoubtedly, many congressmen were attracted by these unusually upbeat economic indicators to vote for the president's economic policies. But when these forecasts were revealed to be hopelessly unrealistic, David Stockman and the budget materials produced by OMB came to be regarded by Congress and the media as deeply lacking in credibility. Fiscal leadership by budgetary amateurs was, thus, revealed to be a risky venture, and provoked a political backlash in Congress that threatened Reagan's initial legislative achievements.

This study of the changing functions and standing of David Stockman and the OMB during Reagan's first term will be divided, for analytic purposes, into three phases, which correspond chronologically with the making, the selling and the unmaking of the administration's initial budget policies. This typology emphasises that OMB continues to be a politicised and personalised agency of the presidency, but further emphasises that OMB now displays this politicisation in new ways. Let us now examine each phase in more detail, beginning with the making of President Reagan's economic plan.

The making of Reaganomics

Reaganomics was a response to the economic problems of the 1970s. During that decade America experienced unprecedented peacetime inflation rates, relatively high levels of unemployment and slow productivity growth rates. In 1980, candidate Reagan keenly argued that Keynesian proposals to tackle these problems had failed because, as he later put it in his inaugural address, they did not recognise that, 'Government is not the solution to our problem;

government is the problem'. In line with this, Ronald Reagan argued that the federal government was an engine of economic disorder, and promised to bring lasting economic growth by switching resources to the private sector.

Although Reagan's campaign speeches were consistent and clear in denouncing the federal government's size, cost and regulatory activities, the press and Jimmy Carter persistently criticised Reagan for being vague on how he was going to implement his political philosophy. In reply, Ronald Reagan delivered a speech in Chicago on 9 September 1980, that was intended to be the definitive campaign statement of his economic policies. In the speech Reagan promised that he would cut deeply both personal and business taxes, sharply increase defence spending, curtail wasteful federal spending, and yet balance the federal budget by fiscal year 1983 (1 October 1982 to 30 September). In unambiguous terms, Reagan stated that government spending would be cut only by 'a comprehensive assault on waste and inefficiency', and emphasised that this would not require drastic cuts in existing government services granted to the American people (Barrett, 1984, 133–4).

Reagan's Chicago speech clearly suggested that the executive budget would be the prime tool for implementing his economic programme. The actual role that a Reagan administration would give to the president's budget agency in making his initial budget proposals was, however, much influenced by David Stockman. This was primarily due to his capacity to provide Reagan's advisers with answers to the problems that they encountered in attempting to translate the Chicago speech into firm budget proposals.

Many of these problems arose because Reagan, unlike many of his predecessors, decided not to downplay his campaign promises once he had defeated Jimmy Carter (Heclo, 1984, 261). Instead, the president-elect directed his inner circle to convert his campaign proposals into hard governing policies. Ronald Reagan's advisers quickly decided to seek to displace Jimmy Carter's outgoing FY 1982 budget submission with one prepared by the incoming administration. In so deciding, they anticipated that they could capitalise upon the president-elect's political momentum to enact rapidly his budget-oriented economic programme, thereby creating a public perception of Reagan as an effective legislative leader in the early months of his term in office.

But Reagan's advisers were stumped over how to slash taxes, increase greatly spending on America's defence forces, and yet balance the budget. This problem, moreover, was also perplexing market analysts on Wall Street. They feared that Reagan's proposals could only increase greatly the size of the federal deficit rather than lead to a balanced budget. In particular, they reasoned that Reagan could not raise sufficient savings from the campaign against wasteful spending to pay for the costs of the defence build-up and the tax cuts, and, thus, enable his administration to balance the budget in only two years' time. In short, they argued that too much was expected from the campaign against waste and abuse in spending. These analysts further believed that the Federal Reserve Board's re-imposition of tight monetary controls following the November elections and Reagan's budget proposals would collide, and provoke a sharp competition between the federal government and the private sector for America's slim reserves of credit. Market analysts anticipated that this clash would sharply inflate interest rates and usher in a recession. This possibility deeply troubled Reagan's advisers because it strongly jeopardised their shot at creating a positive reputation as a leader for Reagan.

It was during this impasse in late November that David Stockman prepared for Representative Jack Kemp, who was to be present at an economic strategy session held by Reagan's advisers, a twenty-three page memorandum. Entitled 'Avoiding a GOP Economic Dunkirk', the document served several functions. From Stockman's viewpoint, the memo was first and foremost a lobbying tool that was intended to persuade Reagan's inner circle that the thirty-four year-old Republican Representative, who had just been elected to a third term, had the qualities to beome Director of OMB. Stockman's candidacy carried the support of Jack Kemp and other supply-siders, plus the Heritage Foundation and other conservative groups. To ensure that the memorandum obtained maximum exposure in promoting Stockman's candidacy, portions of it were leaked simultaneously in the columns of three national newspapers (Blumenthal, 1981).

In policy terms, Stockman's Dunkirk memo depicted a very gloomy picture of the economy during the next year. Stockman argued, in line with Wall Street's analysts, that Reagan's campaign promises were likely to produce deficit budgets, which would clash with tight monetary policies and promote a recession. But, Stockman's assessment of the problems posed by seeking to implement Reagan's Chicago speech also included an answer to these problems. As Stockman put it:

The preeminent danger is that an initial economic package that includes the tax cuts but does not contain *decisive, credible elements* on matters of policy control, future budget authority reduction and a believable plan for curtailing the federal government's massive direct and indirect credit absorption will generate pervasive expectations of a continuing "*Reagan inflation.*" Such a development would almost insure that high interest rates would hang over the economy well into the first year, deadening housing and durable markets and thwarting the industrial spending boom required to promote sustained economic growth (Greider, 1982, 140).

Adopting an extensive package of spending cuts would, Stockman reasoned, enable Reagan to pursue his initial economic policy goals. David Stockman further argued that these cuts should be pursued quickly as part of a comprehensive economic plan that was intended to reverse market expectations. In clear terms Stockman argued:

To prevent early dissolution of the incipient Republican majority only one remedy is available: an initial Administration economic program that is so bold, sweeping and sustained that it totally dominates the Washington agenda during 1981, holds promise of propelling the economy into vigorous expansion and the financial markets into a bullish psychology (Greider, 1982, 150).

The Dunkirk memo was well-received by Reagan and his transition advisers because it offered solutions to the complex economic and political choices that they confronted. Mounting a major attack on domestic spending offered a more credible solution to the tri-sided dilemma of how to cut taxes, increase defence spending and balance the budget than did the earlier dependence on a campaign against waste and abuse in federal spending. Although the assault on domestic spending had not been included in the Chicago speech, it did correspond with Reagan's long-term political philosophy. Stockman's proposal to cut domestic spending was, thus, an enabling amendment to Reagan's Chicago plan that would let the president-elect pursue his programme of cuts in personal and business taxes, plus his proposal to increase defence spending. Furthermore, recommending that the revised economic plan be vigorously and quickly pressed in order to push business expectations and market psychology into a favourable direction dovetailed with the initial choice of legislative strategy for the first year of the Reagan administration.

Stockman was rewarded, in early December, with the appointment he had sought; he was also made a member of Reagan's Cabinet. Ronald Reagan did, however, underline OMB's position as a presidential agency by giving Edwin Harper, OMB's Deputy Director, a concurrent White House post as Assistant to the President, which is a familiar tactic for ensuring the loyalty of executive agencies. OMB's Director and Deputy Director, Associate Director Frederick Khedouri, and Executive Assistant David Gerson (the last two were on the staff of Stockman's congressional office) were all politically experienced, but none of them was a trained economist. These appointments all indicated that the Reagan administration would continue the practice of using OMB as a partisan, personally loyal agency for promoting the president's governing agenda. In contrast, however, to preceding administrations, OMB's leaders were the youngest yet (Blumenthal, 1981; Wyszomirski, 1982).

Although David Stockman was not a trained economist he had acquired an encyclopaedic knowledge of the federal budget and the congressional budget process as a committee aide and then a Representative in the House. His education in budgeting began when he obtained, at the age of twenty-five, the post of director of the research group of the House Republican Conference. In this post, Stockman quickly gained a reputation for being bright and hardworking, and soon mastered the intricacies of House procedures and the federal budget. When he became a Republican Representative in 1976, he aligned himself with conservative study groups and continued his studies of the federal budget. This knowledge was impressively demonstrated in 1979–80 when he and Democratic Congressman Phil Gramm of Texas prepared, using data generated by the congressional budget process, a complete and detailed federal budget proposal to displace President Carter's fiscal 1981 budget submission (Barrett, 1984; Heclo, 1984).

These experiences gave Stockman a base to work from when he took control of preparing Ronald Reagan's first budget in early December. He also had the advantage over other executive departments and agencies of having assembled his governing team early during the transition period. Most importantly, Stockman could call on the work done by OMB's budget examiners in scrubbing departmental and agency bids for budget funds and legislative authority in the course of recently compiling President Carter's outgoing FY 1982 budget request. In a variant of gamekeeper turned poacher, Stockman could use this work to expedite the fashioning and transmission of Reagan's first budget to Congress in time to displace Carter's last budget. These considerable advantages enabled Stockman to take the initiative in executive budgeting.

By early January, Stockman and OMB's career staffs were assembling dozens of position papers on Reagan's first budget and were examining the economic forecasts on which the budget would be based. A government computer, programmed to act as a model of the nation's economy, was instructed to estimate the impact of Reagan's programme of tax cuts and his defence build-up on the federal budget. The computer predicted an immediate string of federal deficits of record size in peacetime, increasing from $82 billion in FY 1982 to $116 in FY 1983. All of which indicated to Stockman that a balanced budget in FY 1983 would be impossible, that the financial markets would panic, sending interest rates up, thus provoking a recession.

Although accounts of what happened next differ in their details, they all agree that the print-out sheet led to a divisive ideological debate between the budget and economic policy-making offices within the Reagan administration. Donald Regan, the Treasury Secretary, argued that the deficit projections meant that the tax cuts should not be introduced until Congress had first cut federal spending, which was intended to make spending and tax cuts more commensurate.

Regan's main subordinates sharply disagreed with the traditional, budget-balancing views of their chief. Norman Ture, the under-secretary for tax policy, and Paul Craig Roberts, the assistant secretary for economic policy, were early prioneers of supply-side economic theories. Ture and Roberts emphatically dismissed Regan's support for spending cuts as favouring a course of action that was unnecessary and, moreover, inconsequential to tackling America's economic problems. They strongly argued that the tax cuts should be quickly moved as the administration's highest priority, rather than play second fiddle to any package of spending cuts. To support their case, they claimed that the tax cuts would immediately increase incentives for people to work and invest their earnings; businesses would also benefit from new depreciation allowances for investing in new plant and equipment to improve the productivity of America's industries, particularly in comparison with competitors in Japan. This, it was anticipated, would increase the domestic and export sales of native industries, and promote sustained economic growth. Increased economic activity would lead to an enlarged pool of earnings to be taxed and, thus, would generate a larger supply of federal revenues. So, the supply-siders argument boiled down to a belief that the tax cuts would quickly create a reflow effect that would wipe out the federal deficit anyway. This view led them to claim that the more quickly the tax cuts were made, the more quickly the budget would be moved into balance. All of which explains why they dismissed spending cuts as 'inconsequential'.

To further complicate matters, the Treasury's under-secretary for monetary policy, Beryl Sprinkel, was a strict monetarist of the Friedman school. He simply wanted the administration to set tight monetary targets and follow them with discipline in order to tackle inflation. But Sprinkel was also known to fear that the tax cuts might stimulate inflation and, thus, undermine the purpose of adopting tight monetary targets.

By comparison with the administration's supply-siders and monetarists, Murry Weidenbaum, Reagan's designated Chairman of his Council of Economic Advisers, had no special theoretical axe to grind. Weidenbaum was, however, disturbed that the participants to the debate wanted to set very positive economic forecasts in order to justify their particular policy objectives. David Stockman was – as the Dunkirk memo evidences – the foremost advocate of cutting spending to accommodate Reagan's programme of tax cuts (Blumenthal, 1981; Barrett, 1984; Gregg and Tate, 1981; Roberts, 1984).

These policy conflicts pitted low-inflation monetarists against high-growth supply-siders, with David Stockman giving priority to adopting spending reductions in order to reduce the impact of the tax cuts on the federal deficit. But because the Reagan administration was seeking to send a full-blown set of budget proposals up to Capitol Hill in time to displace Carter's outgoing budget, there was little opportunity for a protracted, albeit necessary, policy debate within the administration. Consequently, the debate was simply resolved by giving each participant their particular policy objectives. This solution was made possible by compartmentalising the component elements of Reagan's economic plan (Barrett, 1984; Heclo and Penner, 1983). In this 'nobody loses' solution, the supply-siders got their programme of tax cuts and a forecast of high and rapid rates of economic growth, which they claimed would be produced by the tax reductions. The monetarists were appeased by the adoption of tight monetary targets and a forecast of a sharp drop in inflation rates, which they saw as a cause-and-effect relationship. Murray Weidenbaum best described this approach to economic policy-making when he later stated:

It was a forced marriage. The supply-side people insisted on (forecasting) rapid growth in real terms and the monetarists insisted on rapid progress in bringing down inflation. Each of them would go along with a set of numbers as long as their own concern was satisfied.

The monetarists weren't that concerned about growth and·the supply-siders weren't that concerned about inflation (Barrett, 1984, 140).

Because this solution gave each participant their particular policy wishes, the president's economic plan was internally contradictory. The tax cuts embraced a loose fiscal policy, while at the same time the administration was supporting a tight monetary policy. In line with this, the plan endorsed economic growth rates that could not possibly be achieved under a tight monetary regime. The final decisions on the outline of the Reagan administration's economic plan had quickly been devised in a series of high-noon discussions between the heads of the three main economic policy-making offices of the administration. These participants were arguing for their policy preferences and making decisions without detailed briefs from their departmental aides.

David Stockman had successfully used the gloomy deficit projections as a lever to press for vigorous spending reductions. His campaign had begun when he received the bad news from the government computer. He first changed the economic assumptions fed into the computer model to show a swift decline in prices and interest rates and a rapid, historic surge in economic growth. He then informed Reagan, in a two-hour briefing session on the first Wednesday in January, that the federal budget was in 'dire shape'. He stated that Reagan's vague and painless campaign against 'waste, fraud and mismanagement' in federal spending would be insufficient by itself to move the budget into balance. Instead, Stockman informed Reagan that it would be necessary to cut federal spending by around $40 billion in fiscal 1982 to have a shot at a balanced budget. Ronald Reagen agreed to the proposal, but attached certain conditions. To begin with, most of the spending on what Reagan called the 'social safety net' (transfer payments in the form of welfare benefits), which consumed 48 per cent of federal spending, was declared by Reagan to be off-limits to budget reductions. National defence spending, which was scheduled to grow from around 25 per cent to over 30 per cent of total spending, was also exempt. Interest payments on the national debt counted for 10 per cent of federal spending, and could not be forestalled. All of which meant that Stockman had to raise most of his budget cuts from the remaining 17 per cent, which financed the traditional operations of the federal government and a host of federal grant programmes. This broad category included financing the running of the FBI, the Foreign Service and all the other departments and agencies of the federal government, and the payment of grants to state and local governments for such activities as aiding handicapped children or building highways (Greider, 1982, 16–19).

David Stockman had to move very swiftly to make the cuts before Reagan appeared in front of a joint session of Congress on 18 February 1981, to give the details of his economic plan. Because of this tight schedule it would plainly be impossible to go through the normal, time-consuming process of bottom-up budgeting under which OMB requested each spending department and agency to compile and submit its budget bids for consideration, which, once OMB had listed its recommendations, would be followed by an appeals process that saw the thorniest conflicts settled in the Oval Office. Instead, the executive budget process in the early days of the Reagan administration was both dramatically telescoped and centralised under the leadership of David Stockman and the most senior White House aides. Most of the detailed, technical decisions on reducing executive spending were actually taken by David Stockman and his political aides.

A combination of factors facilitated a major centralisation of the executive budget process. OMB's political leaders managed to get off to a quick start because many of the cuts that Stockman had proposed in the FY 1981 budget blueprint that he had earlier co-authored now resurfaced. Stockman also moved quickly because he was particularly eager to make the cuts before the new Cabinet officers were fully familiar with their departments and prepared to defend their turf from budget cuts. In this respect, OMB's director enjoyed the support of Ronald Reagan in seeking to cut departmental spending. The fact that many Cabinet and sub-Cabinet posts were slow to be filled also meant that resistance within the executive branch to spending cuts was reduced, particularly in the earliest days of the administration. Furthermore, those who were eventually appointed to executive positions had to be loyal defenders of Reagan's governing agenda. Centralised budgeting gave Cabinet heads only forty-eight hours to review cuts in their budget. Any protests were heard by a 'budget review group'. This innovation in executive budgeting consisted of James Baker, Edwin Meese, Martin Anderson (Reagan's chief domestic policy adviser), Murray Weidenbaum and Stockman. David Stockman would act as prosecutor; the other members sat as magistrates. In practice, the panel was heavily stacked in Stockman's favour because all the members of the Star Chamber were strong central keepers of

Reagan's governing agenda. Also, Stockman's grasp of the technical details of each department's budget and of the overall budget was unequalled by anyone else in the administration, which gave him a great advantage in driving the executive budget process. This knowledge encouraged him to make decisions independently of the normal scrutiny provided by OMB's budget examiners, who were primarily used to provide backup information (Blumenthal, 1981; Greider, 1982; Heclo, 1984; Newland, 1983; Pfiffner, 1983).

Centralised, high-speed budgeting enabled Stockman to trim around $49 billion from the spending outlays projected in Carter's FY 1981–2 budgets. Even so, Stockman considered these cuts to be insufficient to balance the budget in two years' time. With only a week left before President Reagan was due to address Congress on the details of his first budget, David Stockman sought a last-minute round of additional spending cuts. His proposals were rebuffed. Instead, Martin Anderson convened a meeting on 16 February to consider how to deal with the problem that Stockman had identified. The solution – which was jointly devised by Weidenbaum and Stockman – was found by resort to budgetary sleight-of-hand. This came in the form of the magic asterisk ploy, under which the Reagan administration's first budget incorporated 'unidentified spending reductions' that amounted to around $74 billion over the 1983–4 fiscal years. In essence, the Reagan administration was promising that it would come up with more spending cuts in the future to keep federal deficit spending on a downward track.

This last flurry of frantic budgeting produced a budget document that asked for $197 billion in spending cuts over the fiscal 1982–4 period. These cuts included the magic asterisk savings. Reagan's tax proposal called for revenue cuts of around $300 billion over the 1982–4 fiscal period. To close the gap of approximately $100 billion on paper, the administration wrote in to its first budget a series of heroic assumptions about how positively and quickly America's economy would respond to Reagan's economic programme. Economic growth was projected at just over 5 per cent of real GNP in the three fiscal years 1982 to 1984. Over the same period, inflation rates were projected to fall to around 6 per cent. By comparison, Jimmy Carter's outgoing budget, which was also optimistic in tone, forecast slower growth rates and higher inflation rates. Through adopting these economic assumptions the Reagan administration managed to show on paper a balanced budget for fiscal 1984.

Unemployment was, thus, forecasted to drop to below 7 per cent by 1984 because of the administration's expectation that its programme would result in a quick rebound by the economy (Barrett, 1984; Gregg, 1981; Heclo, 1984).

Selling Reaganomics: winning in Congress, losing on Wall Street

On the morning of 18 February 1981, David Stockman breakfasted with fifteen newspaper reporters at 8 a.m., he then briefed the Cabinet and Republican leaders in Congress on the details of the president's first budget, afterwards held a full-scale press conference, and later spoke to the House Republican Conference. At 9 p.m., after having spent the entire day lobbying for the Reagan administration's first budget, David Stockman sat down with his Cabinet colleagues in the front row and listened to President Reagan present his economic programme to Congress (Blumenthal, 1981, 93).

Stockman continued to play the leading role in pressing Reagan's budget on Capitol Hill. This role was unprecedented and was due to several factors, many of them unique. Unlike his modern predecessors, Stockman not only came from Congress, but he also understood the detailed intricacies of the congressional budget process better than any other department or agency head in the Reagan administration. This knowledge enabled Stockman to become a key member of Reagan's team for determining the administration's legislative strategy on the budget and other issues. Indeed, once it was decided that the budget was going to be the centrepiece of Reagan's initial legislative agenda, David Stockman became the architect responsible for crafting the president's first budget. In this position, he used his insight into congressional procedures in order to obtain bargaining advantages for the administration's budget on Capitol Hill. It was David Stockman who developed the idea of first pursuing the administration's package of spending cuts as a required step to build congressional support for Reagan's tax cuts. Stockman was also fully aware of the advantages to be gained from sidestepping predictable opposition from the congressional committees that had authorised the spending programmes in the first place by packaging the administration's spending cuts into one omnibus bill that was scheduled for implementation through the reconciliation procedure of the congressional budget process, and undertook all the technical and the detailed work necessary to fulfil this plan.

Because Stockman had crafted so much of the administration's first budget, it was to be expected that he took the lead in arguing the administration's case on Capitol Hill. This led to Stockman appearing as the Reagan administration's principal spokesman before a wide range of congressional committees and subcommittees, rather than the heads of the executive departments and agencies affected by a particular proposal. These appearances were supported by the largest pool of budget analysts in the executive branch. This reservoir of specialist assistance helped Stockman keep track of the budgetary impact of a host of decisions made in budget, appropriations and a range of authorising committees and subcommittees in the House and the Senate. This knowledge ensured that Stockman would be at the centre of the administration's decision-making on legislative strategy and tactics, and also enabled Stockman to retain his position as the administration's principal spokesman on budget and related issues.

However, while Reagan's economic plan was moving forward in the legislative arena, Stockman had come to the conclusion that the plan was losing on Wall Street. Market analysts were not appeased by the magic asterisk strategy. They saw it merely as a political gimmick to conceal a string of deficit budgets, and, as Stockman had predicted in his Dunkirk memo, began to raise interest rates. In response, Stockman sought further and deep reductions in spending to lower the deficit. A proposal to reform the ailing Social Security fund was seen as a vehicle for big savings, which President Reagan was persuaded to support. But the proposal was resoundingly defeated by the Senate in mid-May, which led to the establishment of a bipartisan national commission to study and report on the funding of the Social Security system in early 1983 (Storey, 1982).

This decision removed one potential source of big budget savings, but Stockman's attention now switched to the administration's omnibus proposal to retrench federal spending. OMB's budget examiners had discovered that the Democratic leaders of the House of Representatives were taking steps to reduce Reagan's spending cuts by an estimated $48 billion. This prompted Stockman to persuade the White House to substitute its own bill of spending reductions for that of the Democrats. The strategy succeeded, but at a price that Stockman had not anticipated. In order to win votes for its substitute bill, the Reagan administration willingly traded concessions in the form of increased federal spending on a variety of programmes. These trades lowered the overall cuts to a figure that was costed at $35.1 billion for FY 1982 in the Omnibus Reconciliation Act of 1981, which was some $6 billion less than Reagan had requested. However, this initial costing has been challenged as greatly overestimating the actual amount of cuts in federal spending. Subsequent estimates lowered the total of cuts to only $31.6 billion, and this figure was lowered by some analysts to only $12–15 billion (Palmer and Mills, 1982, 79).

David Stockman next targeted the president's proposal to lower federal revenues in a continuing attempt to recalibrate the administration's fiscal policies. A number of conservative Republicans in the Senate shared Stockman's fears that the president's economic plan would increase the deficit and held out for reductions in Reagan's programme of tax cuts. As a result, the cuts in personal income taxes were reduced from a total of 30 per cent spread over a three-year period to 25 per cent, and depreciation and other tax allowances for private corporations and businesses were trimmed. These changes lowered the projected loss in federal revenues to around $280 billion over the fiscal period 1982–4. However, tax lobbyists responded to these revisions by provoking a tax auction between the administration and the Democratic leaders of the House of Representatives. In effect, the tax lobbyists won the bidding war because they pressured the administration to outbid the Democrats, which resulted in an historic loss in federal revenues. The single most important decision came in the enactment of a provision to permanently insure taxpayers against the future effects of inflation by indexing the personal income tax structure. This means that from 1985 personal exemptions would be adjusted automatically for changes in the annual inflation rate. As a consequence individual taxpayers would not be pushed by inflation into higher income tax brackets, which would thereby lower federal revenues. Business corporation benefited from the enactment of more generous tax allowances. All in all the Economic Recovery Tax Act of 1981 reduced federal revenues over the 1981 to 1987 fiscal period by an amount of money that was estimated at $963 billion by OMB; the Congressional Budget Office forecast a loss of $1041 billion in federal revenues over the same fiscal period (Hulton and O'Neill, 1982, 113; Wehr, 1981).

President Reagan's legislative victories had been bought at the cost of a long-term loss of fiscal discipline. The Omnibus Reconciliation Act

gave the Reagan administration significantly less spending reductions than it had initially proposed, while the Economic Recovery
Tax Act led to a much larger loss of revenues than Reagan had
requested. This led to a yawning gap between federal revenues and
spending, which provoked the very clash between fiscal and
monetary policy that Stockman had feared. Wall Street responded
by raising interest rates to over 20 per cent during mid-summer,
which started a recession that proved to be the most severe and
protracted one since the Great Depression (Ellwood, 1982; Heclo
and Penner, 1983; Palmer and Mills, 1982; Schick, 1982).

The unmaking of Reaganomics

David Stockman saw the onset of recession as providing him with a
good opportunity to cut the defence budget and to revise Reagan's
tax programme. He had been very disappointed in January when
Reagan had exempted defence spending from reductions because he
felt that the Pentagon budget was bloated. In line with this,
Stockman believed that defence spending was driven more by the
demands of private contractors than by the needs of a national
defence programme. In giving the Pentagon what he called a 'blank
check' he believed that a chance had been lost to show the public
that the 'Reagan Revolution' was committed to attacking 'powerful
clients with weak claims' on the federal purse (Greider, 1982, 13). In
essence, Stockman believed that reducing the defence budget would
indicate to liberal critics that the administration was concerned with
issues of equity in its campaign against federal spending. Much the
same concerns motivated his desire to lower the cost of the president's tax cuts. Stockman's plan to alter the president's economic
strategy received the support of Reagan's senior White House
advisers. Their support was motivated by political rather than
economic reasons. Reagan's advisers feared that a recession would
damage the chances of doing well enough in the mid-term elections
to consolidate and extend Republican influence in Congress, and
therefore got behind Stockman's drive to revise the administration's
fiscal policies. The plan failed, however, to persuade the most
influential remaining advocate of Reaganomics within the administration – President Reagan. The president claimed he remained
optimistic that the economy would respond speedily and positively
to his economic strategy and, thus, would not be pressured into

altering course. Instead, he directed Stockman to compile a proposal that would once again cut domestic spending programmes in order to lower the deficit. The fall ofensive was ill-received by Congress, and resulted in only limited savings, which were insufficient to make a sizeable dent in the ever-mounting federal deficit (Hartman, 1982).

Stockman's intense frustrations over his inability to convince the administration to give top priority to reducing the deficit became public knowledge with the publication in mid-November 1982 of an article in the *Atlantic Monthly*. The article was a public relations disaster for several reasons. Stockman's statement that supply-side theories were nothing more than a 'Trojan horse' for traditional, Republican trickle-down economic policies – under which federal tax cuts put much more money into the pockets of the well-to-do, which, as the theory goes, lead to a chain of economic actions that eventually benefit the poor – further damaged the residual credibility of Reaganomics. Stockman's criticism of supply-siders as having a naive, nonpolitical view of the economy and being possessed of a 'happy vision' of being able to move overnight to a 'world of growth and no inflation with no pain' made him the scapegoat of the year for conservative supply-siders.

But perhaps the most damage to the administration was done by Stockman's statements that it did not really know what it was doing when the president's economic plan was formulated. Stockman confessed:

None of us really understands what's going on with all these numbers. . . . You've got so many different budgets out and so many different baselines and such complexity now in the interactive parts of the budget between policy action and the economic environment and all the internal mysteries of the budget, and there are a lot of them. People are getting from A to B and it's not clear how they are getting there (Greider, 1982, 33).

The furore that followed the publication of the article led to the public humiliation of Stockman, which included an interview with Reagan that Stockman colourfully likened to a 'trip to the woodshed' after dinner. Although his services were retained, his standing and role within the administration were much diminished during the remainder of the first term. Donald Regan, the Treasury Secretary, speedily displaced Stockman as the principle spokesman for and architect of the president's budget and economic policies. Regan's pre-eminence was partly due to the fact that he was a long-term confidante of the president, and also because he shared Reagan's opposition to changing course on fiscal policies. As the chairman of the Cabinet Council on Economic Affairs and as a key member of the White House legislative strategy group, Regan was well-placed to block any proposal made by Stockman to change the administration's fiscal policies. David Stockman did try to get the administration to raise new taxes in Reagan's second budget submission, but was roundly rebuffed (Tate, 1982). The most vivid illustration of Stockman's diminished influence over executive budgeting came in early 1983, when his proposals to make deep spending cuts in the budgets of executive departments and agencies were successfully and speedily resisted in four meetings of the budget review group (Kirschten, 1983).

Although he was repeatedly rebuffed in his quest to put tackling the deficit at the top of the administration's agenda, Stockman did manage to effect some significant changes in budget management. During his office the president's budget was progressively broadened in its scope to include credit spending, off-budget spending, entitlements spending and cost-of-living adjustments that preceding administrations had considered to be uncontrollable sources of federal spending. In line with these improvements in budget accounting, the Stockman era also led to a greater awareness of the importance of federal tax expenditures, both as a means for distributing benefits and as an option to be taken increasingly into account when seeking to reduce the deficit. Although these reforms in budget accounting were pursued by Stockman to direct attention to areas where spending reductions could be considered, they did produce a federal budget that now provides a more comprehensive picture of the forces that drive spending (Hartman, 1984; Heclo, 1984). However, Stockman's most pronounced failure in budget management lay in his almost complete inability to get to grips with the defence budget, which was because the defence budget continued to be protected by the president from spending reductions. (Stubbing, 1984). Nonetheless, new accounting procedures were established that can be more fully applied to defence and other areas of expenditure by any succeeding administration.

The influence of OMB and its director on the executive branch was not, however, restricted to budget making during Reagan's first term. Expanding upon procedures begun by Gerald Ford and elaborated upon by Jimmy Carter, Ronald Reagan established a new

Office of Information and Regulatory Affairs (OIRA) to implement his campaign promise to lighten the burden of federal regulation. This new unit was organised to exercise central authority and oversight over all new regulations proposed by. executive departments and agencies for inclusion in the *Federal Register*. This innovation meant that OMB was empowered to scrutinise the details of policy implementation throughout the entire executive branch, and included the power to reject proposed regulations. To serve as Reagan's key-line agency in the campaign against federal regulations, OIRA expanded to include ninety staff, and also serviced the work of the president's Task Force on Regulatory Relief (Eads and Fix, 1982; Newland, 1983).

The administration's deregulation campaign generated much controversy, but led to few substantive policy changes. The Report of the Task Force on Regulatory Relief, which was published in August 1983, claimed that one-time savings for American consumers and businesses of $15 to $17 billion and annually recurring savings of $13 to $14 billion had been obtained from actions taken by the Reagan administration to reduce the burden of federal regulation. But these figures have been challenged as overestimating the actual savings by about two-thirds of the total amount claimed (Quick, 1984, 309). The effectiveness of OIRA's actions has also been contested. Critics charge that OMB, from which OIRA's staff were recruited, does not have the substantive expertise and experience to act as an effective overlord of policy implementation by all the departments and agencies of the executive branch. Nonetheless, the administration heavily relied upon administrative discretion as its preferred policy instrument. This took the form of cutting the budgets and staff of regulatory agencies, usually with the active support of the political executive of the affected agency. In the case of the Environmental Protection Agency (EPA), its budget was cut by more than 50 per cent and its staffing levels were reduced by nearly 30 per cent over the fiscal period 1980–84. However, the administration's actions secured, even on its own terms, mixed results in the area of environmental policy. The administration succeeded in reducing noise control and sewage regulations, but failed to achieve its goal of improving basic research, monitoring, enforcement and analytical capabilities. The way in which these changes were clumsily pursued by Reagan's inexperienced political appointees provoked a political backlash in Congress, which eventually led to the appointment in 1983 of a new team to head EPA. The areas of energy, natural resource and agricultural regulation similarly generated much controversy but little substantive progress. The adoption of a purely administrative route to deregulation also resulted in many of the administration's decisions – especially in the regulation of natural resources and the environment – being successfully challenged in the federal courts. Furthermore, the failure of the administration to obtain major legislative changes in regulatory laws means that subsequent administrations can reverse policies more easily. All in all, the administration achieved few fundamental changes (Eads and Fix, 1982; Portney, 1984).

Implementing the administration's deregulation and other policies had involved OMB's career staffs in performing an expanding range of quasi-political roles. Career staff were pushed in the Stockman era into much more intimate contact with the political world of congressional accounting and negotiations. A group of bill-trackers were now continuously involved in covering the meetings of many congressional committees to track the progress of budgetary decisions. This required cultivating supportive relationships with minority and majority staffs, and with a range of public interest groups. The materials obtained were fed into a computerised Central Budget Management System, which enabled Stockman to keep abreast of the budgetary impact of congressional decisions. These new roles have involved OMB's career staff more in supplying information than in developing objective, professional and substantive analyses of the spending programmes themselves, which was the traditional strength of OMB's career staff. Indeed, Hugh Heclo concluded, after a series of interviews with OMB officials, that David Stockman ran 'OMB much like a congressional office rather than an executive institution'. Under this approach, David Stockman and his small circle of personal assistants developed the ideas and budget strategies to be employed in negotiations with outsiders. 'The remainder of the organisation is called upon for quick responses to help the front office do what it has decided to do' (Heclo, 1984, 279). The careerists were now required to provide a steady stream of data, without knowing how it was to be used. As a consequence, the amount of time and the importance devoted to learning about and analysing the substance of policy was diminished, which many observers have feared is threatening to deeply undermine the traditional, institutional capacities and strength of

OMB (Heclo, 1984; Newland, 1983; Tomkin, 1985; Wyszomirski, 1982).

The experience of the first term of the Reagan administration indicates that these fears are well-founded. Excluding the professional staffs of OMB enabled the administration to impose highly partisan, flawed and inconsistent policies and improbably optimistic economic assumptions on its first budget. The centralisation of executive budgeting under the political executive facilitated high-speed budgeting, but came at the expense of a loss of fiscal discipline.

Reaganomics and the federal budget: the record of the first term

Overall, President Reagan succeeded handsomely in his intention to lower federal taxes; he also succeeded in obtaining a sharp acceleration in the amount of money spent on national defence. President Reagan failed to achieve the initial reductions that he sought in non-defence spending, but he managed to lessen significantly the total amount spent on non-defence programmes. However, the Reagan administration failed to produce a balanced budget in fiscal 1983. Instead, the 1983 fiscal budget produced a record peacetime deficit of $208 billion, with even larger deficits forecast for later on in this decade. The major developments in each of these areas can be briefly summarised as follows:

Revenues

The federal tax burden increased from 18.5 % of gross national product (GNP) at the end of the Eisenhower administration (Mills, 1984, 110) to 21.6 % of GNP in fiscal 1982, as indicated in Table 5.1. The Reagan administration succeeded during its first term in dramatically reducing this trend towards increasing the total of federal revenues. The provisions of the Economic Recovery Tax Act were largely responsible for quickly reducing federal revenues to 18.6 % of GNP in FY 1984.

Defence spending

The defence budget fell from 9.1% of GNP during the Vietnam era to around 5.2 % of GNP during the mid-1970s, before picking up to around 6 % of GNP at the end of the Carter presidency (Mills, 1984, 110). Although Congress trimmed President Reagan's requests for defence spending during the second half of his first term, the president succeeded both in increasing the rate of defence spending each year and in building in additional growth – for weapon programmes that are in the spending pipeline – on defence spending for the rest of the decade (see Table 5.1). This increase raised

Table 5.1: Budget projections under 1985 and 1981 policies (by FY, as % of GNP)

	1982	1983	1984	1985	1986	1987	1988	1989	1990
Under 1985 policies									
National defence	6·1	6·5	6·4	6·5	7·0	7·2	7·4	7·6	6·8
Non-defence Programmes	15·0	15·4	14·1	14·4	13·5	13·3	13·1	12·9	13·6
Net interest	2·8	2·8	3·1	3·4	3·6	3·9	3·9	4·1	3·5
Unified budget outlays	23·9	24·7	23·5	24·3	23·9	24·1	24·3	24·4	24·6
Revenues	20·3	18·6	18·6	19·1	19·0	19·1	19·3	19·3	19·4
Deficit(-) or surplus	-3·6	-6·1	-4·9	-5·3	-5·0	-5·0	-5·0	-5·1	-5·2
Under 1981 policies									
National defence	6·0	6·0	5·7	5·6	5·8	5·8	5·8	5·9	5·9
Non-defence programmes	16·3	16·9	15·4	15·4	15·1	15·0	14·8	14·6	14·4
Net interest	2·8	2·7	2·9	2·9	2·7	2·5	2·4	2·2	1·9
Unified budget outlays	25·1	25·6	24·0	23·9	23·6	23·3	23·0	22·7	22·3
Revenues	21·6	21·0	21·4	22·0	22·1	22·4	22·7	22·9	23·5
Deficit(-) or surplus	-3·5	-4·7	-2·6	-1·9	-1·5	-0·9	-0·4	0·2	1·2

Source: Congressional Budget Office, *The Economic and Budget Outlook: Fiscal Years 1986–1990* (Feb. 1985) p. 152.

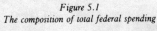

Figure 5.1
The composition of total federal spending

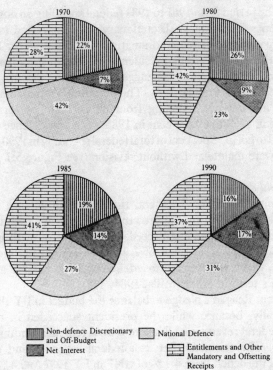

Source: Congressional Budget Office, *The Economic and Budget Outlook: Fiscal years 1986–1990* (Feb. 1985) p. 56.

defence spending from 23 per cent of total federal spending in FY
1980 to 27 per cent of total spending in FY 1985. Moreover, this
increase in defence spending was forecast to continue. The Congressional Budget Office forecast, in February 1985, that the defence
budget would consume 31 per cent of total federal spending in FY
1990 if current policies were maintained (see Figure 5.1).

Non-defence spending
During the period from 1961 to 1981 federal spending on non-defence
programmes (non-defence discretionary, off-budget and mandatory
transfer payments) increased dramatically, accounting for 16.3 % of
GNP at the end of Carter's presidency. Although President Reagan
sought deeper reductions, he managed to lower non-defence spending
to 14.1 % of GNP in fiscal 1984. The president's retrenchment drive
lowered non-defence spending from 68 per cent of total federal
spending in 1980 to 60 per cent in 1985, with non-defence spending
projected to fall to 53 per cent of total federal spending in 1990 if current
policies were maintained without revision (see Figure 5.1).

The federal deficit
Throughout the Nixon-Ford era, the decline in defence spending
was more than offset by the growth of non-defence spending. The
overall growth in spending exceeded the rate of growth in federal
revenues, leading to a deficit of 2.9 % of GNP during the Nixon–
Ford era, which was lowered to a deficit of 2.7 % of GNP at the end
of Carter's term in office (Mills, 1984, 115).

President Reagan's pledge to balance the budget in FY 1983 failed
dramatically, because while the president succeeded in massively
cutting federal revenues he failed to reduce federal spending propor-
tionately. The mismatch between federal revenues and spending
increased the deficit from 4.1 % of GNP in FY 1982 to 6.4 % of GNP
in fiscal 1983, with the deficit projected at above 5 % of GNP for the
rest of the decade. In dollar terms, the federal deficit grew from $79
billion in FY 1981, to $208 billion in FY 1983, with even higher
deficits projected for the rest of the decade (see Table 5.2). One
immediate by-product of the deficit was to increase interest payments on the national debt from 9 per cent of total federal spending
in 1980 to 14 per cent in 1983, with interest payments projected at 17
per cent of total federal spending in 1985. As a consequence, interest
payments on the national debt have become the fastest-growing part

Table 5.2: Federal deficits, fiscal 1981–90

	$ billions	% of GNP
Actual		
1981	79	2·7
1982	128	4·1
1983	208	6·4
1984	185	5·2
Projected		
1985	214	5·6
1986	215	5·2
1987	233	5·2
1988	249	5·1
1989	272	5·2
1990	296	5·3

Source: Gregory B. Mills, "The Budget: a Failure of Discipline," in John L. Palmer and Isabel V. Sawhill eds, *The Reagan Record: an Assessment of America's Changing Domestic Priorities* (1984) p. 108; Congressional Budget Office, *The Economic and Budget Outlook: Fiscal Years 1986–1990* (Feb. 1985) p. xiv.

of the federal budget since the inauguration of President Reagan (see Figure 5.1). Another way to illustrate the magnitude of the recent increase in the size of the national debt is by noting that the debt doubled from $900 billion in 1980 to twice that amount in 1985 (Pascal, 1985, vii).

Conclusion

President Reagan's first term produced a radical rearrangement of the spending priorities of the federal budget and established a long-term imbalance between federal revenues and spending. The president's insistence on staying the course with his initial policy proposals was one of the key factors that contributed to the growth of the federal deficit. Any attempts to tackle the deficit needed to face the fact that, because of the altered composition of the federal budget, sizeable deficit reductions could only be obtained by the politically tough combination of raising taxes and cutting defence spending. This is the case because interest payments cannot be altered, and because there is growing resistance on the part of both parties in Congress to President

Reagan's proposals to increase defence spending and to lower the deficit by embarking on further cuts in non-defence spending. This analysis suggests therefore that the areas in which President Reagan fulfilled his initial objectives during the first term are the very ones that will be most at risk in the second term.

From a related angle, the second Reagan administration would do well to take steps to restore OMB's reputation for hard-headed policy analysis. Placing more value upon OMB's traditional strengths would better enable any administration to cost accurately and analyse the substance of any new plan to deal with the deficit. Recent experience, however, suggests that OMB will only be influential to the extent that its recommendations dovetail with the wishes of the president and his most trusted advisers. This suggests that an OMB that is not politically responsive to the Oval Office can only lead to the persistence of policy proposals that do not serve the best interests of the president or society as a whole.

References

Barrett, L. (1984). *Gambling With History: Reagan in the White House*, Harrisonburg: R. R. Donnelley and Sons.
Berman, L. (1979). *The Office of Management and Budget and the Presidency, 1921–1979*, Princeton University Press.
Blumenthal, S. (1981). 'David Stockman: The President's Cutting-Edge', *The New York Times Sunday Magazine*, 15 Mar, pp. 24–94.
Eads, G. and Fix, M. (1982). 'Regulatory Policy' in J. L. Palmer and I. Sawhill, eds, *The Reagan Experiment: An Examination of Economic and Social Policies under the Reagan Administration*, Washington, DC: The Urban Institute Press, pp. 129–53.
Ellwood, J. ed. (1982) *Reductions in US Domestic Spending*, New Brunswick, NJ: Transaction Books.
Gregg, G. (1981). '"Let Us Act Together", Reagan Exhorts Congress,' *Congressional Quarterly Weekly Report*, pp. 331–5.
Gregg, G. and Tate, D. (1981). 'Reagan Economic Officials put Differences Behind Them', *Congressional Quarterly Weekly Report*, pp. 259–61.
Greider, W. (1982). *The Education of David Stockman and Other Americans*, New York: E. P. Dutton.
Hartman, R. (1982). 'Congress and Budget-Making', *Political Science Quarterly*, pp. 381–402.
Hartman, R. (1984). 'Issues in Budget Accounting' in G. B. Mills and J. L. Palmer, eds, *Federal Budget Policy in the 1980s*, Washington, DC: The Urban Institute Press, pp. 423–47.
Heclo, H. (1984). 'Executive Budget Making' in G. B. Mills and J. L. Palmer, eds, *Federal Budget Policy in the 1980s*, Washington, DC: The Urban Institute Press, pp. 255–91.
Heclo, H. and Penner, R. G. (1983). 'Fiscal and Political Strategy in the Reagan Administration' in F. Greenstein, ed., *The Reagan Presidency: an early*

Assessment, Baltimore, The John Hopkins University Press, pp. 21–47.

Hulton, J. and O'Neill, J. A. (1982). 'Tax Policy' in J. L. Palmer and I. Sawhill, eds, *The Reagan Experiment: an Examination of Economic and Social Policies under the Reagan Administration*, Washington, DC: The Urban Institute Press, pp. 97–128.

Kirschten, D. (1983). 'Dealing the Cards – Only the Beginning of a Lengthy Game of Budgetary Poker', *National Journal*, pp. 111–3.

Mills. G. B. (1984). 'The Budget: a Failure of Discipline' in J. L. Palmer and I. Sawhill, eds, *The Reagan Record: An Assessment of America's Changing Domestic Priorities*, Cambridge, Mass: Ballinger Publishing Co., pp. 107–39.

Newland, C. A. (1983). 'The Reagan Presidency: Limited Government and Political Administration', *Public Administration Review*, pp. 1–21.

Palmer, J. L. and Mills, G. B. (1982). 'Budget Policy' in J. L. Palmer and I. Sawhill, eds, *The Reagan Experiment: an Examination of Economic and Social Policies Under the Reagan Administration*, Washington, DC: The Urban Institute Press, pp. 59–95.

Pascal, G. (1985). *The Trillion Dollar Budget: How To Stop the Bankrupting of America*, Seattle: The University of Washington Press.

Pfiffner, J. (1983). 'The Carter-Reagan Transition: Hitting the Ground Running', *Presidential Studies Quarterly*, pp. 623–45.

Portney, P. R. (1984). 'Natural Resources and the Environment' in J. L. Palmer and I. Sawhill, eds, *The Reagan Record: an Assessment of America's Changing Domestic Priorities*, Cambridge, Mass: Ballinger Publishing Company, pp. 287–316.

Quick, P. (1984). 'Businesses: Reagan's Industrial Policy' in J. L. Palmer and I. Sawhill, eds, *The Reagan Record: an Assessment of America's Changing Domestic Priorities*, Cambridge, Mass: Ballinger Publishing Company, pp. 287–316.

Roberts, P. C. (1984). *The Supply-Side Revolution: an Insider's Account of Policy-Making in Washington*, Cambridge, Mass: Harvard University Press.

Schick, A. (1982). 'How the Budget Was Won and Lost' in N. Ornstein, ed., *President and Congress: Assessing Reagan's First Year*, Washington, DC: American Enterprise Institute, pp. 14–43.

Storey, J. R. (1982). 'Income Security' in J. L. Palmer and I. Sawhill, eds, *The Reagan Experiment: an Examination of Economic and Social Policies Under the Reagan Administration*, Washington, DC: The Urban Institute Press, pp. 361–92.

Stubbing, R. (1984). 'The Defence Budget' in G. E. Mills and J. L. Palmer, eds. *Federal Budget Policy in the 1980s*. Washington, DC: The Urban Institute Press, pp. 81–110.

Tate, D. (1982). 'Congress Ponders Strategy for Assault on Budget Deficit', *Congressional Quarterly Weekly Report*, pp. 303–4.

Tomkin, L. (1985). 'Playing Politics in OMB: Civil Servants Join the Game', *Presidential Studies Quarterly*, pp. 158–70.

Wayne, S. (1978). *The Legislative Presidency*, New York: Harper & Row.

Wehr, E. (1981). 'White House Lobbying Apparatus Produces Impressive Tax Vote Victory', *Congressional Quarterly Weekly Report*, pp. 1372–3.

Wyszomirski, M. (1982). 'The De-Institutionalisation of Presidential Staff Agencies', *Public Administration Review*. pp. 448–58.

Part 3

The Reagan presidency and the policy process

Foreign policy and the Reagan administration

The Reagan administration came into office in January 1981 determined to reverse what it saw as a gradual decline of US strength and influence on the world stage: a decline set in motion in the wake of Vietnam and Watergate. The administration's approach involved a massive increase in defence spending as a means of signalling clearly to the Soviet Union Reagan's resolve to confront Soviet expansion and adventurism. This drive to increase military spending was to be coupled with an uncompromising posture on a variety of fronts: with the Soviet Union (over Poland and Afghanistan); in Central America (especially over El Salvador and Nicaragua); with European allies; and, in defence of US positions, at the United Nations. Thus hard rhetoric, combined with a vigorous strengthening of American military capabilities, would evidence to the world the administration's determination to restore respect for the US regardless of possible offence to both allies and adversaries alike in the achievement of that goal.

Reagan's approach

While Ronald Reagan entered the White House with more experience as a political chief executive than any US president since Franklin D. Roosevelt, in one significant respect he was as inexperienced as most of his Oval Office predecessors: he lacked knowledge and expertise in foreign affairs. However, this did not mean that he brought no foreign policy agenda into office with him. On the contrary, throughout the presidential campaigns of both 1976 and 1980 Reagan had outlined the major elements of his basic approach to foreign affairs (Smith *et al.*, 1980; Valis, 1981).

Essentially, Reagan's approach was premissed on his life-long conviction that the Soviet Union seeks world domination and therefore must be resisted on all fronts. Invoking Roosevelt's Second World War view that the US 'must be the great arsenal of democracy,' Reagan campaigned on the necessity of building up a powerful nuclear arsenal as a deterrent to the Soviet Union. In his dealings with the Soviet leadership, Reagan promised an approach based on firmness and consistency. In a post-election interview with *The Sunday Times* on 9 November 1980, he declared:

I believe that in the Soviet Union right now there is an element of confusion about the vacillation of our recent foreign policy, the threats and then the backdowns. . . . I honestly believe that the Soviet Union would prefer consistency. That you can be firmer with them, make it clear that you would not be pushed around, and they would know what to expect. . . . I believe that they would be happier with someone – even though it was someone who is firmer, someone who opposed some of the things they did – who let them know what they were dealing with.

As an essential component of this firmness of approach, Reagan also argued the need for US support of countries opposed to communism – regardless of whether or not they themselves were governed by authoritarian regimes. He therefore rejected Carter's policy of withholding American aid to anti-Marxist authoritarian regimes (particularly in Central America) whose record on human rights was deemed to be unacceptable. The Reagan policy on human rights would be pursued through 'quiet diplomacy' to encourage the development of justice and liberty in such countries, while at the same time ensuring the provision of aid for their resistence to communist insurgency.

Reagan's broad approach to Europe, the Middle East, Africa and Asia was also framed in the context of the confrontation with world communism. A strong supporter of NATO, he put a high priority on the creation of 'genuine dialogue' with America's European allies. However, his hard-line approach to the Soviet-bloc in the course of the 1980 campaign appeared problematic for some European allies (notably France and West Germany), who preferred the continuation of the Carter policy of *détente* with Moscow. On the Middle East, Reagan indicated a pro-Israel stance. In a campaign speech in April 1980, he declared that 'Israel, a stable democracy sharing our own values, serves as a vital strategic asset with its highly trained and experienced military forces, and is a deterrent to Soviet expansion in that part of the world.' Equally compelling, for similar strategic reasons, was support for South Africa – while employing 'quiet diplomacy' to press for reform of the Pretoria government's apartheid policy. Finally, Reagan emphasised his support for Taiwan with hints during the campaign that he would move to re-establish 'official' relations with the Taiwanese government; a position that was promptly denounced by the People's Republic of China.

It would be easy to dismiss Reagan's starkly simple approach to foreign affairs as the straightforward product of his lack of experience and expertise in this field. However, such a dismissal ignores the hard fact that his general outlook, based as it was on traditional values, tended to view the complexities of the modern world in simple terms. His position was clearly stated in the course of the 1980 campaign with his observation to American voters that 'for many years now, you and I have been shushed like children and told there are no simple answers to complex problems that are beyond our comprehension. Well, the truth is that there are simple answers – just no easy answers'.

Relations with the Soviet Union

Dominating the foreign policy of the Reagan administration in the first term was the president's personal perception of the threat posed by the Soviet Union. At his first press conference in January 1981, Reagan made clear his belief that the Soviet goal was world domination, and commented further that Soviet leaders 'reserve unto themselves the right to commit any crime, to lie, to cheat, in order to attain that, and that is moral not immoral (for them)'. As a consequence, the decline in US–Soviet relations that followed the Soviet invasion of Afghanistan in December 1979 appeared certain to continue under the new administration.

While taking a hard rhetorical line, the administration's initial actions in its dealing with the Soviet Union were appreciably softer. Within weeks of taking office, the administration gave approval to the sale of pipeline technology to the USSR for construction of the Siberian pipeline. In April 1981, within two weeks of leaving hospital following the Hinckley assassination attempt, Reagan fulfilled a campaign pledge given to American farmers and announced the lifting of the embargo on US grain sales to the Soviet Union imposed by Carter following the invasion of Afghanistan. Of greater significance was the disclosure made by Secretary of State Haig at the NATO foreign ministers' meeting on 4 May 1981, that Reagan had indicated to Brezhnev his willingness to begin arms limitation talks on intermediate-range missiles in Europe as part of mutual and balanced force reduction regotiations.

Overshadowing the administration's relations with the Soviet Union throughout its first year in office, was the situation of unrest inside Poland (following the breakdown in relations between Solidarity and the Polish government) that ultimately led to imposition of martial law on 13 December 1981. As early as April, the administration considered the possibility of a trade embargo on the USSR in the event of Soviet moves against Poland. Reagan's approach to the Polish situation was conditioned by two separate factors: first, by his evident desire to see further liberalisation within Soviet bloc satellites; and, second, by his recognition of the importance in domestic US politics of the Polish–American vote that supported him against Carter in 1980. Indeed, this latter factor was a vital consideration in the authorisation of a $30 million grant to Poland in late November to help overcome severe food shortages.

Following the Polish declaration of martial law, Reagan announced in a televised address on 23 December the imposition of economic sanctions against the Polish government and warned of further action unless 'the rights of the Polish people to free speech and association' were restored. Reagan blamed the Soviet Union for the Polish military takeover and warned: 'If the outrages in Poland do not cease, we cannot and will not conduct business as usual with the perpetrators and those who aid and abet them.' This was followed on 29 December by direct economic sanctions against the USSR, including: suspension of export licences for US electronic, oil and gas equipment, suspension of a new maritime accord and of US flights by the Soviet airline, Aeroflot. Significantly, a fresh embargo on US grain sales was not imposed.

Reagan's determination to deal firmly with the USSR over Poland was carried further by extending his 29 December sanctions policy to include equipment for the Siberian pipeline supplied by overseas US subsidiaries and by foreign firms manufacturing under US licences. This extended policy adversely affected several major European allies (in particular, Britain, West Germany, France and

Italy) who had negotiated supply and credit contracts with the Soviet Union, and who immediately denounced Reagan's approach as an infringement of their national sovereignty. Pointing to the absence of a US grain embargo, the West Europeans were unimpressed by the American argument that the grain was being purchased by the Soviets with hard currency whereas the pipeline was financed by means of credits advanced by western nations on favourable terms to the USSR (Joffe, 1983).

Unmoved by outraged responses from his allies, Reagan continued his sanctions policy in an effort to force the lifting of martial law and the release of political prisoners in Poland. Finally, after ten months of mounting acrimony, Reagan reached a settlement with the West Europeans, Canada and Japan in late November 1982. Under this agreement, pipeline sanctions would be lifted on condition that Western nations would not 'engage in trade arrangements which contribute to the military or strategic advantage of the USSR or serve to preferentially aid the heavily militarized Soviet economy.' The agreement also provided for greater controls on the Western sale of strategic items to the Soviets and for harmonization of credit policies in East–West trade. However, Reagan's immediate goal remained unfulfilled, with martial law continuing in Poland into the summer of 1983 (Destler, 1983, 148–51).

Reagan's hard-line stance against the Soviet Union was underscored by his refusal in November 1982 to attend Brezhnev's funeral. With this refusal, he passed up the opportunity of an early personal meeting with Yuri Andropov, who had succeeded Brezhnev as Party Secretary. In March 1983, Reagan went much further by denouncing the Soviet Union in his celebrated 'evil empire' speech to the US National Association of Evangelicals. In this speech he declared: 'Let us beware that while they preach the supremacy of the state . . . and predict its eventual domination of all peoples of the earth, they are the focus of evil in the modern world.'

Yet, despite this hard-line rhetoric, in the Autumn of 1983 there appeared to be encouraging signs of some rapprochement. On 18 August, Soviet leader Yuri Andropov met with a delegation of US Senators in the Kremlin (his last public appearance prior to his death 6 months later). Further, on 25 August, the US and the USSR signed a new five-year grain purchase agreement.

But prospects of further relaxation were quickly dashed by the Soviet shooting down of Korean Air Lines Flight 007 on 1 September, killing all 269 persons aboard – including US Congressman Larry McDonald. While Reagan excoriated the Soviet Union on 5 September for a 'barbaric act' in firing on a civilian airliner, nonetheless he avoided making any dramatic response in retaliation. However, the Soviet action had the immediate effect of cancelling an imminent meeting between Secretary of State Shultz and Soviet Foreign Minister Gromyko.

Relations between the two superpowers were further soured by the Soviet response to the implementation of NATO's 1979 dual-track decision (itself a response to the initial Soviet deployment of SS-20 missiles targeted on Western Europe). Confronted by the arrival in Western Europe of the first Cruise missiles on 14 November and by the vote in the West German Bundestag on 22 November to approve the installation of Pershing missiles, the Soviet Union withdrew from all arms negotiation talks with the US. Thus the USSR pulled out of three separate sets of negotiations: on 23 November, from the Intermediate Nuclear Force (INF) talks at Geneva; on 8 December, from the Strategic Arms Reductions Talks (START); and, on 15 December, out of conventional arms talks at Vienna.

Faced with an almost total breakdown in relations with the Soviet Union, Ronald Reagan began 1984 with a much more conciliatory approach. On 16 January he declared:

We must and will engage the Soviets in a dialogue . . . to promote peace in the troubled regions of the world, reduce the level of arms and build a constructive working relationship. . . . 1984 is a year of opportunities for peace. But . . . we must do more to find areas of mutual interest and then build on them.

Despite the failure to elicit any positive response to this overture, Reagan reiterated his commitment to seeking constructive dialogue some six months later in a speech on 27 June:

I don't think there is anything we are encouraging the Soviet leaders to do that is not as much in their interest as it is in ours. If they are as committed to peace as they say, they should join us and work with us. If they sincerely want to reduce arms, there's no excuse for refusing to talk. And if they sincerely want to deal with us as equals, they shouldn't try to avoid frank discussion of real problems.

It would be easy to dismiss Reagan's recast image as a conciliator in 1984 as simply the product of election year politics. Indeed, the immediate response both in the USSR and the US was to denounce his 16 January overture as 'election-year propaganda' (Tass, the official Soviet press agency) and as an election year move 'trying to deal with the politics of a problem instead of the problem itself' (Mondale). Certainly it was the case that Reagan's previously harsh rhetoric created a widespread impression both in the US and Western Europe that he was more interested in confrontation than constructive dialogue – an impression which held dangers for an incumbent president running for re-election. But it would be a mistake to view Reagan's approach in 1984 as simply a departure from previous positions which was dictated by electoral politics. Without dismissing the importance of the electoral factor, there was also the view of the Reagan administration that the president had consistently followed a position of 'peace through strength' and that it was the rebuilding of US military strength which made possible the endeavour to engage the Soviet Union in meaningful dialogue.

In any case, in 1984 the major barriers to negotiations between the US and the USSR were largely domestic: in the USSR, the death of Andropov on 9 February; and, in the US, the Presidential Election. In the Soviet Union, Andropov's death was preceded by uncertainty at the top which was translated into negative responses during his long period of illness. This continued with his successor, Konstantin Chernenko, whose grasp of leadership was weak and who followed a hard-line position *vis-à-vis* the US set by Gromyko. The immediate prospects for positive responses to Reagan's overtures for dialogue were therefore understandably bleak, and certainly not helped by his second refusal in fifteen months to attend the funeral of a Soviet leader. In any event, the new Soviet leadership was faced with the prospect of the US Presidential Election. Clearly, it would not suit Soviet interests to engage in initiatives which might assist the re-election of Ronald Reagan.

In these circumstances, it came as a surprise when the Soviet Union offered on 28 June to meet with the US at Vienna in September to open negotiations on banning anti-satellite weapons. Although National Security Adviser Robert McFarlane indicated that the US would set 'no preconditions', nonetheless it was clear that the Reagan administration desired a broader agenda and wished to take up the question of other (stalled) arms negotiations once the Vienna talks began. The Soviet response was to insist that there be no linked discussions at Vienna. Consequently, the long period of limbo in US-Soviet relations appeared unlikely to be broken – at least until after the November election.

Reagan policy on Central America

Ronald Reagan's inauguration in 1981 came amidst a period of considerable turmoil in Central America and the wider Caribbean Basin area. In Nicaragua, the Cuban-backed Sandinistas had overthrown the five-generation Somoza dynasty and this success encouraged left-wing guerrillas with Soviet, Cuban and Sandinistan assistance to threaten the governments of El Salvador and Guatemala. These threats in turn posed difficulties for neighbouring Honduras and Costa Rica, while Grenada and Suriname experienced the throes of *coup d'états* (Falcoff, 1980).

The problems of the Central American countries guaranteed that the Reagan administration would focus attention on the area, given its strategic importance to the security of the US. Approximately 50 per cent of US foreign trade (including oil supplies) passes through the Panama Canal and the Caribbean Sea. Of equal significance was the awareness that, in the event of a European crisis, 50 per cent of American supplies for NATO operations would pass Cuba which was now host to a Soviet combat brigade with air and submarine bases capable of servicing Soviet air and naval forces.

Two other considerations prompted the Reagan administration to focus on Central America's problems. The first of these concerned the long-standing American claim to the western hemisphere as its sphere of influence. This claim dates back to the Monroe Doctrine of 1823, proclaiming that the United States would not allow outside powers to interfere in the affairs of Central and South America. This Doctrine was supplemented in 1904 by the Roosevelt Corollary, under which President Theodore Roosevelt reserved the right of the US to interfere in Latin America in instances of 'Chronic wrongdoing or an impotence which result in a general loosening of the ties of civilized society'. These declarations provided the basis of considerable past American intervention, with US troops deployed in Central America on twenty occaions between 1889 and 1920 and other more recent cases of involvement in the internal affairs of individual countries (Schulzinger, 1984, *passim*). The second focusing factor was Reagan's own intense commitment to opposing the spread of communism. Given the clear involvement of Soviet- and Cuban-backed left-wing insurgents in Central America, it was inevitable that his administration would develop a counter-strategy to deal with them.

El Salvador became an area of priority treatment for the incoming Reagan administration when leftist guerrillas mounted a 'final offensive' to seize power during the final weeks of the Carter administration. Reversing his previous policy of withholding military aid because of civil rights violations, Carter had resumed military assistance to El Salvador and announced the despatch of nineteen military advisers to help the moderate Duarte-led junta combat the guerrillas. Judging the Carter level of assistance to be inadequate, Reagan moved within a month of taking office to increase military aid from $10 million to $35 million and the number of US military advisers from 19 to 54 by the Spring of 1981. The president also promised economic aid for El Salvador totalling $131 million over 2 years.

From the outset, it was clear that the administration intended to treat El Salvador as a major test-case of its resolve to confront communist expansion. At his second news conference, on 6 March 1981, Reagan declared:

It isn't just El Salvador. What we're doing in going to the aid of a government that asked that aid of a neighbouring country . . . is (to) try to halt the infiltration of the Americas by terrorists and by outside interference and those who aren't just aiming at El Salvador but, I think, are aiming at the whole Central and possibly later South America, and I'm sure eventually North America.

Regan's support for El Salvador brought into stark relief a major shift in US policy. Under Carter, relations betwen the US and individual governments in Central and Latin America were conditioned by each government's human rights record and by its commitment to the development of acceptable social policy. Thus the Carter administration sought to break with the past American record of support for (or, at least, tolerance of) authoritarian dictatorships which were repressive in character and constituted a major obstacle to social and economic development. Under Carter, economic and military assistance were made conditional on acceptable progress on each government's human rights records. By this means, Carter sought to reduce social inequities and thus to end the social and political unrest so characteristic of these authoritarian societies (Brzezinski, 1983; Stoessinger, 1979).

Carter's approach was heavily criticised by the Reagan administration for its assumption that social and political unrest were simply the product of social and economic inequities. Missing from the Carter assessment, it was argued, was any recognition of the disruptive role of the Soviet Union and its Caribbean ally, Cuba, in creating and fostering such unrest in Central and Latin America in order to install marxist regimes wherever possible. As a consequence, the Carter policy of withholding US military aid for human rights violations was viewed as a policy which unwittingly rendered affected contries more vulnerable to Soviet/Cuban-backed insurgents – as in El Salvador in January 1981.

Reagan's initial policy statements concerning his support for the moderate Duarte-led junta government in El Salvador were couched totally in terms of an East–West confrontation, and as such were open to strong criticisms that they appeared to ignore the internal needs and interests of El Salvador itself (McMahan, 1984, 103–18). However, the administration countered such criticisms (somewhat belatedly) with the point that its aid package included economic assistance amounting to $131 million over two years to help El Salvador to develop as a more liberal, democratic society. Given the horrendous death toll from the on-going conflict within El Salvador between right- and left-wing groups, this administration argument appeared at first sight to be wholly disingenuous. However, underlying it was a further critical element of Reagan's Central America policy, namely: the distinction between right-wing authoritarian and left-wing totalitarian dictatorships developed by Jeane Kirkpatrick, US Ambassador to the UN.

In Kirkpatrick's analysis, right-wing dictatorships (historically, the most widespread form of government in Central and Latin America) are basically authoritarian systems based upon economic oligarchy, political despotism and military repression to varying degrees. They posess, however, (in their private sector economies and in their non-totalitarian character) the basis for developing pluralist groups and institutions capable of liberalisation and progress towards democracy. In contrast, left-wing dictatorships are essentially totalitarian in character and are based on a command economy and a self-appointed élitist vanguard imposed by guerrilla war. Kirkpatrick's assessment was that, faced with a choice between these two contrasting forms of dictatorship, the US has little alternative to supporting the right-wing (given its possibilities for democratisation) while at the same time acting as a force for liberalisation (Kirkpatrick, 1982, 23–52).

In El Salvador, the US chose to support a moderate junta government pledged to potentially wide-reaching reforms. Under the Basic Law of March 1980, an extensive land reform programme was planned which would go some way to a restructuring of Salvadoran society. By 1982, approximately 30 per cent of agricultural land had been transferred to 210,000 formerly landless peasant families, with about 50 per cent of total agricultural acreage remaining in the hands of small owner–operator families. Elections were also planned for a Constituent Assembly in March 1982 – with further general elections to follow under the terms of a new constitution to be drawn up by the Constituent Assembly. Accordingly, the Reagan administration was able to point to tangible signs of progress in its goal of democratising and reforming Salvadoran society.

Meanwhile, concerns raised in Congress about human rights in El Salvador and the on-going activities of various left- and right-wing 'death squads' had resulted in legislation to ensure Congressional oversight of the administration's policy (Spanier and Uslaner, 1985, 89–90). In consequence, the Reagan administration was confronted by the International Security and Development Cooperation Act of 1981. Under this, to secure Congressional approval of military aid funding for El Savador, the administration was required to certify at 180-day intervals that the Salvadoran government was:

1. Making a concerted and significant effort to comply with internationally recognised human rights;

2. Achieving substantial control over . . .its own armed forces;

3. Making continued progress in implementing essential economic and political reforms, including the land reform programme; and

4. Committed to the holding of elections at an early date.

In the event, neither the Reagan administration nor Congress was totally satisfied with the actual record of progress achieved in all of the above areas, although some reductions were made in the appalling death totals arising from the internal warring between leftist and rightist groups. In 1980 the slaughter had totalled over 10,000 deaths, but by 1981 these had been reduced to 5300 and were further cut to some 2600 in 1982. However, Congress broadly (if reluctantly) accepted the regular certification reports submitted subsequently by the administration stating that 'the statutory criteria for certification are met', and military aid was continued.

The elections for the El Salvadoran Constituent Assembly in March 1982 brought decidedly mixed results for the administration. While some 74 per cent of the electorate voted despite guerrilla threats (thus giving a measure of legitimacy to the elected Assembly), the outcome of the elections was less desirable. The largest single party in the new Assembly was the Christian Democrats, led by moderate centrist Jose Napoleon Duarte. However, the Assembly was dominated by a coalition of the right, led by Roberto d'Aubuisson of the Nationalist Republican Alliance (ARENA). For the Reagan administration, the formation of a government led by d'Aubuisson was bad news. Not only was he widely associated with the right-wing death squads, he was also openly hostile to the reforms sponsored by the Duarte-led junta government. However, by means of the considerable leverage of its military and economic assistance programmes, the Reagan administration succeeded in pressuring d'Aubuisson to continue the agrarian reforms, to establish a Salvadoran Human Rights Commission and to proceed with the drafting of a new constitution.

The new Salvadoran constitution developed by the Constituent Assembly was approved in December 1983, and presidential elections were scheduled for the spring of 1984. When the elections for the presidency were held on a run-off basis in March and May 1984, Reagan's policy was considerably boosted by the victory of Duarte over d'Aubuisson. This came as welcome news for the administration, and was instrumental in persuading the US House of Representatives to vote narrowly by 212 to 208 in favour of a substantial economic and military aid package for El Salvador. Beyond that, the Reagan administration was hopeful that, under Duarte's leadership, the Salvadoran government would speed up the land reform programme and crack down hard on the death squads of both the right and the left.

Although El Salvador was initially the focal point of Reagan's Central American policy, the scope of the administration's action widened with its charges that anti-government guerrillas in El Salvador were being supplied by the leftist Sandinista regime in Nicaragua with arms financed by the Soviet Union and Cuba. In order to cut off the arms supply lines (which ran through Honduras, thus threatening to destabilise the Honduran government), Reagan gave approval in December 1981 for covert CIA operations to finance and supply counter-revolutionaries (contras) fighting against the Sandinistas inside Nicaragua and from bases in Honduras.

Initially, the covert CIA action was financed at $19.5 million to support a force of 500 contras. A year later, in December 1982, *Time* magazine reported intelligence sources as indicating a massive expansion in the CIA operations, with approximately 200 CIA personnel operating in Honduras, the air-shipment of arms from Panama on a fortnightly basis and an increase in the contra force to approximately 4500. This expansion of CIA activities prompted the US Congress to pass the Boland Amendment in December 1982, proscribing US aid for guerrilla groups that had 'the purpose of overthrowing the government of Nicaragua or provoking a military exchange between Nicaragua and Honduras'. While the Reagan administration had no such plans, the contras financed by CIA funds extravagantly claimed that the overthrow of the Sandinista regime was exactly what they had in view.

Despite the administration's protestations that the Boland Amendment applied to the intentions of the US government and not the contras, in the House of Representatives both the Foreign Affairs Committee and the Intelligence Committee voted to cut-off the covert funding for the contras. On 28 July 1983, these committee actions were emphatically supported by a House Floor vote of 228 to 195 to end such funding. However, the Republican-controlled Senate declined to follow suit, and the covert funding was continued.

By the Spring of 1984, the mood of the Senate shifted considerably with disclosures about CIA involvement in the contras' mining of Nicaraguan harbours. This changed mood came principally from the Senate's outrage over the inadequate briefing given to the Senate Intelligence Committee by the CIA about its covert action in support of the contras. This led to a Senate vote (by a margin of 84 to 12) on 10 April to condemn the CIA involvement and to cut off funding for any future mining. The House quickly moved two days later to pass a similar resolution. While the immediate outcome produced little more than embarrassment for the administration, the longer-term implications were more serious. The shifting Senate mood on Reagan support for the contra operations in Nicaragua continued to harden against the president, and in July the Senate voted by a devastating margin of 88 to 1 to support the House of Representatives in cutting off all further funding for the contras.

It was clear in 1983 and 1984 that the shape of Reagan's Central America policy was in flux. Evidence of a 'two-track' approach to dealing with Nicaragua increasingly emerged as the administration balanced up its hard-line policy of pressuring the Sandinista government (by supporting the contras' struggle) with more conciliatory diplomatic efforts. Largely inspired by Secretary of State Shultz, the diplomatic side of the 'two-track' approach was geared to finding ways of engaging in negotiations with the Sandinistas.

The principal focus of the Shultz initiative to develop a diplomatic strategy was the Contadora proposals to establish a negotiating process to end the flow of arms and military personnel in the Central

America region. Developed in January 1983, the proposals advanced by the Contadora group of countries (Mexico, Venezuela, Columbia and Panama) set out twenty-one objectives which principally included: democratisation; arms control measures; the cessation of support for subversion; and, gradual withdrawal of foreign military and security advisers.

The Reagan administration gave strong support to the Contadora objectives and moved in September to pressure Nicaragua to accept them. The response from the Sandinistas was both swift and surprising. Within a month, they presented the US with four draft treaties which sought to address American concerns by endorsing the Contadora objectives, including: the halting of arms purchases; reducing the size of the Nicaraguan army; ending support for regional revolutionary movements; and, holding elections in Nicaragua.

The Sandinista government's draft treaties were received coldly by the Reagan administration which characterised them as 'cosmetic' and incapable of necessary verification as required by Contadora guidelines. Yet, while rejecting the draft treaties, the administration indicated its willingness to continue discussion by referring them to the Contadora group for further reworking.

Despite the subsequent failure of the Contadora process to generate further movement by the Sandinistas towards a position acceptable to Washington, Shultz persisted with his diplomatic initiative. In June 1984, he made a surprise personal visit to Nicaragua to meet with Sandinista leader, Daniel Ortega. This was followed up in early July by a series of direct talks between US Special Envoy Harry Shlaudeman and Nicaraguan Deputy Foreign Minister Victor Tinoco. In these discussions, the US pressed for four main concessions on the Nicaraguan side: the ending of Nicaragua's ties with the USSR and Cuba and removal of 3500 foreign military advisers; reductions in Nicaragua's massively expanded military capability; cessation of Nicaraguan support for left-wing guerrillas in El Salvador; and, the full implementation of earlier Sandinistan pledges on political pluralism (to reverse the movement towards a one-party state). On the US side, the administration offered financial and other assistance – in particular, aid to replace funding lost by the cutting of ties with Soviet-bloc countries. However, the Shlaudeman–Tinoco talks failed to develop any substantive results, and they simply dragged on through the last months of Reagan's first term before being terminated by the administration as 'fruitless' in January 1985.

Ever-present in the Reagan administration's Central America policy was the risk of domestic division within the US. In a nation still scarred from the internal divisiveness of the Vietnam War trauma, the administration faced considerable problems in attempting to reassure the American public that its policy objectives were geared to the social and economic needs of Central America – as well as to the region's military needs. To that end, the President had unveiled his 'Caribbean Basin Initiative' in February 1982, proposing an emergency economic aid programme totalling $350 million to selected countries (but principally including El Salvador, Jamaica, the Dominican Republic and Honduras).

The problem with Reagan's Caribbean Basin Initiative was that by itself it was insufficient to impact critically on the economic problems of the region. This was recognised within a year, with key Reagan advisers (notably Kirkpatrick) counselling the President to develop an aid programme on the lines of the US Marshall Plan in post-war Europe. Prompted by this advice and by the need to combat growing domestic criticism that he was committed to a military solution in Central America, Reagan responded in July 1983 by establishing a National Bi-Partisan Commission on Central America under the chairmanship of Henry Kissinger. The central task of the Commission was to produce recommendations 'on what (the US) must do in the years ahead to meet the underlying problems of peace, poverty, democracy and dictatorship in the region'.

When it reported back to the President some six months later, the Commission proposed the 'Marshall Plan' approach advocated by Kirkpatrick. In essence the Commission recommended: an economic aid package totalling some $8 billion over the period FY 1985–89; an immediate supplemental economic assistance package of $400 million for FY 1984; a development aid package of $336 million in FY 1984–85 for population, nutrition, education, agriculture, rural development and housing programmes administered by the Agency for International Development. Also recommended was the creation of a development organisation for the region, the Central American Development Organisation (CADO), to be established by Central American countries to disburse approximately 25 per cent of US assistance aid for the region. Participation by individual states in CADO would be based on human rights progress, 'building democracy', and on 'encouraging equitable economic growth through policy reforms'.

The Kissinger Commission recommendations were immediately endorsed by the President who submitted them to Congress in February 1984, as an administration-backed bill, the 'Central America Democracy, Peace and Development Initiative Act of 1984'. Yet, in spite of its far-reaching significance, the bill languished in Congress – a victim of Election Year politics. Ronald Reagan had other ideas, however. In what many considered to be his most impressive TV performance as president, he spoke directly to the American people on 8 May in an address on the problems of Central America. While he was unlikely to prod an uncooperative Congress into any action on his proposals in advance of the November election, his points were made directly to the electorate:

The National Bipartisan Commission on Central America has done its work. Our administration has done its work. We now await action by the Congress. . . . The simple questions are: Will we support freedom in this hemisphere or not? Will we defend our vital interests in this hemisphere or not? Will we stop the spread of communism in this hemisphere or not? Will we act while there is still time?

Lebanon

Beyond question, the most public foreign policy disaster of Reagan's first term came in Lebanon in 1983 and 1984. Here, the president's persistence in maintaining a US Marine Corps peace-keeping force in Lebanon, long after its utility had gone, highlighted confusion and contradictions over the administration's policy goals.

Initially, the US sent in a Marine force of 800 on 25 August 1982, which operated in Beirut harbour to supervise the withdrawal from Lebanon of Yasir Arafat's PLO forces, and which was withdrawn by 10 September. Some ten days later, the US Marines were returned to Lebanon as part of a larger multinational force (including French, Italian and – later – British units). This return followed the assassination of President-Elect Bashir Gemayel, the entry of Israeli troops into West Beirut, and the massacre of hundreds of Palestinian civilians by Christian Phalangist militiamen in the Sabra and Shatila refugee camps. Announcing the dispatch of 1600 US Marines on 20 September, President Reagan stated that they were returning 'with the mission of enabling the Lebanese government to restore full sovereignty over its capital, the essential precondition for extending its control over the entire country'.

The problem with this announcement was that the Lebanese government to which the US was now committed was itself only one of several factions in a highly divided country. Moreover, this in turn was compounded by the Reagan administration's backing of an ill-fated agreement of 17 May 1983 between Lebanon and Israel, which called for withdrawal of Israeli troops and for future accommodations between the two countries. Secretary of State Shultz, whose shuttle diplomacy produced the 17 May accord, incorrectly assumed that Syria would also be a party to the agreement in order to get withdrawal of both Israeli and Syrian forces from Lebanon. Syria refused, however, and in consequence Lebanese Moslem attitudes towards the US hardened into hostility.

By September 1983, US support for the beleagured Lebanese government became overtly activist with US warships shelling in support of the Lebanese army against Syrian-backed Lebanese opposition. A major casualty of this increased level of involvement was the US Marine force based at Beirut airport. On 23 October this was the object of attack when a truck loaded with explosives was driven into their base headquarters killing 220 marines.

Speaking on 25 October, in the aftermath of the killing of US Marines in Beirut and the successful US invasion in Grenada, President Reagan asked: 'Can the US . . . stand by and see the Middle East incorporated into the Soviet bloc?' Answering his own question, he affirmed that 'we have vital interests in Lebanon' and that the effort to secure withdrawal of Israeli and Syrian forces was 'central to our credibility on a global scale'. Thus Reagan effectively put US credibility on the line, maintaining that the struggle within Lebanon was part of a larger East–West conflict, without really clearly defining what 'vital interests' were actually at stake.

On a gradual and seemingly inevitable basis, the Lebanese army crumbled under constant pressure from opposition Druze and Amal forces. By 5 February 1984, with the resignation of his Cabinet, President Amin Gemayel's government stood bereft of authority and in control of little more than some sectors of Beirut. Under severe pressure (notably from the US Congress) to withdraw the US Marine force, Reagan refused to consider such 'surrender' and declared that there was no reason for the US 'to turn our backs on our friends and cut and run'. He therefore announced on 7 February that the US would increase its assistance, employing US ships and planes to attack forces opposing the Gemayel government. However, the increasing pressures on Gemayel from Syria forced Lebanon some two weeks later to scrap the 17 May accord with Israel. This came in the wake of contradictory American statements about the US position. On 17 February, while Shultz declared that 'we continue to support the 17 May agreement', Reagan was telling reporters: 'We're not a party to (the agreement) so there's no way we should have a position one way or the other.'

The inevitable withdrawal of the US Marine force from its role of protecting Beirut's airport came on 26 February amidst a sense of utter failure. As one observer bitingly observed: 'The Marines spent a total of 533 days in Beirut, suffered 240 deaths and more than 130 wounded and accomplished virtually nothing. . . . The Reagan administration turned Lebanon into a test of strength it never had to be' (Friedman, 1984).

For the Reagan administration, the pull-out from the Lebanon represented a major foreign policy disaster whose roots lay in a series of mistakes and miscalculation. It was firstly a mistake to regard the Lebanese government as anything other than one faction among many in a hopelessly divided state. Secondly, it was a miscalculation to assume that Syria would be part of the 17 May accord. Finally, it was mistaken strategically to have elevated US involvement into maintenance of 'vital interests' as part of a global East–West conflict. The consequence was to produce what *Newsweek* on 27 February 1984 termed 'easily the worst US foreign policy débâcle since the Iranian crisis'.

Grenada

The sharp and decisive military action taken by the US (at the request of, and in concert with, some six Caribbean states) in Grenada on 25 October 1983 stood in stark contrast with US military ineffectiveness in Lebanon. Indeed, the two areas of operation – Grenada and Lebanon – were momentarily interwined as the truck bomb attack on US Marines at Beirut airport came in the final hours of consultation and planning of the Grenada invasion.

Grenada had been of concern to the United States over the increasingly close ties forged with Cuba and Soviet-bloc countries by the government of Maurice Bishop and the radical New Jewel (Joint Endeavour for Welfare, Education and Liberation) Movement (NJM). On seizing power from the authoritarian government of Sir Eric Gairy in March 1979, the Bishop regime had suspended the

Constitution and announced its replacement by a series of 'People's Laws'. Although the Bishop government was granted recognition by the US and retained Grenadan membership of the British Commonwealth, its growing reliance on Cuba for arms, military advisers and other aid had prompted the Carter administration to suspend all official contact with Grenada.

President Reagan continued this Carter policy, but in turn became increasingly concerned about the security implications posed for the US by construction of a 9000-foot airstrip at Port Salines with Cuban assistance (which was considered by the US to be unnecessary for merely domestic purposes). When completed, the airstrip would present the possibility of Cuban/Soviet MIG-23s operating from Cuba and Grenada to enjoy overlapping ranges covering the entire Caribbean. Since 50 per cent of US sea trade and oil imports pass through the Caribbean, and because strategic planning required the US Navy to have free movement from ports on the Gulf of Mexico, vital US interests were thus considered to be at risk.

The invasion of Grenada was triggered by the disintegration of the NJM government following the killing on 19 October 1983 of Bishop, three Cabinet ministers and other leaders by a more radical NJM faction. Alarmed by this turn of events, by arrests and by rumours of continuing killings, the Organisation of Eastern Caribbean States (OECS) voted on 21 October to request the US, Barbados and Jamaica to participate in joint intervention to restore stability in Grenada. The formal request for US assistance dated 23 October cited: 'The current anarchic conditions, the serious violations of human rights and bloodshed . . . and the consequent threat to the peace and security of the (Caribbean) region created by the vacuum of authority in Grenada.'

The combined security intervention was launched on 25 October with a force comprising 1900 US Marines and Army rangers and 300 military and police forces from 6 Caribbean countries. At the end of a week of action against Cubans and Grenadan NJM supporters, the US and Caribbean forces had secured the island. The official toll of US casualties was 18 dead and 116 wounded while Grenadan casualties were 45 dead (including 21 from accidental US bombing of a mental hospital) and 337 wounded, and Cuban casualties numbered 24. Some 638 Cubans were taken prisoner and 5 warehouses of arms and documents impounded. Hostilities ended on 2 November, with Cuban, Soviet-bloc and other personnel returned to their own countries. US forces were withdrawn from early November, with the alst combat troops leaving on 15 December. A contingent of 300 US military personnel remained to provide police, medical and support personnel.

The Regan administration argued that US participation in the Grenadan action was based on three considerations. First was the need to protect the safety of 1000 US citizens whose lives were considered to be endangered 'by the breakdown of law and order, by a shoot-on-sight curfew, and by an unpredictable internal power struggle'. Second, there was the OECS request for US assistance. Third, there was a confidential appeal from the Grenadan Governor-General, Sir Paul Scoon (then under house-arrest), to OECS and other regional states to restore order on the island.

The considerations listed by the administration are all important in providing a variety of justifications for US action. The first – to protect US citizens – constitutes a basis for the president taking military action under the terms of the War Powers Act of 1973. This Act was passed by Congress over the veto of President Nixon to ensure against presidents using their constitutional powers as Commander-in-Chief of the US armed forces unilaterally to commit the US in undeclared war (the power to declare war is the constitutional prerogative of the Congress.) Thus the Act requires that the President, in taking military action, must first consult with Congress and then must withdraw US forces from conflict within 60–90 days unless specifically authorised by Congress (Javits, 1973; Holt, 1978). In the case of his Grenada action, while he did not directly invoke the 1973 Act nonetheless Reagan briefed Congressional leaders of his plans ahead of the invasion. He therefore met a key provision of the Act. However, both Houses of Congress insisted on applying the terms of the Act and refused to authorise action beyond sixty days. Consequently, the US combat contingent was subsequently withdrawn within the required period.

As for the second and third considerations – the requests for assistance from OECS and the Grenadan Governor-General – these provided the Reagan administration with a legal basis under international law for US action. Indeed, the administration gave great weight to Sir Paul Scoon's appeal for aid. In the absence of any other government authority after the murder of Maurice Bishop, he became – as the Queen's representative – the sole remaining source of governmental legitimacy in Grenada. Finally, an invitation by a lawful governmental authority is a valid legal basis for foreign states to provide requested assistance.

While it was widely supported by the Grenadan people, the US action in Grenada was broadly condemned by the international political community. Although much of this condemnation was predictable, the Reagan administration was surprised and dismayed by the hostile response from Western Europe. This came at a time when the administration was seeking support from its European allies for its Middle East policy and for the deployment of Cruise and Pershing II missiles in Europe. In particular, the refusal of the Thatcher government to support (much less to join with) the US was a personal disappointment for the president. However, from the standpoint of the administration, the positive side of the Grenadan action (besides the overwhelming public support it received from Grenadans) was that it signalled to the world that the US could take firm and decisive military action. It also served notice on the other states in the western hemisphere (in particular Cuba and Nicaragua) that the Monroe Doctrine was alive and well.

Reagan and Foreign Policy: an assessment

Surprisingly for a politician dedicated to a 'new beginning' in foreign and domestic policy, Ronald Reagan did not endeavour in his first term to recast totally American foreign policy of the post-war period. Thus he retained US membership and participation in the United Nations (only withdrawing from UNESCO in 1984 as a protest against its policies and spending priorities), continued the US foreign aid programme and maintained official US involvement with the World Bank and other international organisations.

Yet, at the same time, the president clearly set his face against the modernist impulses which have increasingly shaped the character of American foreign policy in the post-war era and which are manifested in the growing emphasis on multilateralism, transnationalism and interdependence. Indeed, such impulses were condemned by the Reagan administration as the major contributors to the decline of US power and influence; with multilateralism and interdependence both perceived as antithetical to American autonomy. This is broadly in line with the conclusions of E. L. Morse, who has argued:

The major problem for foreign policy that stems from interdependence is that of the autonomy of . . . decision making. Interdependence, by definition, makes governments increasingly dependent upon actions taken by other governments for the achievement of both domestic and foreign policy goals.

Related to the problem of national autonomy is a second problem associated with the increased vulnerability of modernized societies to the actions of others under inderdependent conditions (Morse, 1976).

While not attempting to turn the clock back entirely, Reagan's foreign policy sought to reassert traditionalist concerns with sovereignty, national interest, power and security against modernist preoccupations with transnationalism, international bodies and a reduced concern for national interest stemming from interdependence. Consequently, at the outset the Reagan administration assigned priority to policy instruments which would reflect traditionalist concerns and thus engaged in the rebuilding of US military strength, foreign military aid, foreign arms sales, and covert action. Such instruments were also mandated to deal with the second of the president's policy priorities: confronting the expansionist tendencies of the Soviet Union in its desire to widen the frontiers of communism. Both sets of priorities intermeshed with the the the over-arching Reagan goal of reversing the decline of US power and influence and re-establishing America's pre-eminence in the world. As Haig summarised the position: 'The United States . . . must behave like a superpower' (Haig, 1984, 26).

Beyond question, Reagan's most evident (and controversial) area of achievement was his strengthening of US military capabilities by means of a massively expanded defence budget (see the discussion in Chapter 7, below). This basis of increasing strength gave a hard edge to the administration's dealings with the Soviet Union, exemplified by the prompt imposition of US economic sanctions following the declaration of martial law in Poland. The administration's firmness of purpose and action were also underscored by the successful military intervention in 1983 to restore democracy in Grenada, by the efforts to maintain a non-Marxist governent in El Salvador while promoting democratisation and reform of Salvadoran society, and by unwavering support (including military aid and covert CIA assistance) for the contras' struggle against the Sandinistas in Nicaragua. While the administration's objective *vis-à-vis* the Soviet Union was to re-establish at least superpower parity, its policy actions in the Caribbean and Central America went further than parity in attempting to restore US leadership over the region. In both cases, however, the administration sought above all to reassert the primacy of American strategic interests.

At the same time, it is also clear that considerable confusion and contradictions were present in Reagan policy, The débâcle in Lebanon with the peace-keeping US Marine force in 1983–4 evidenced dubiety and internal dispute concerning the administration's policy goals. Equally striking was the contradiction inherent in the Siberian pipeline sanctions imposed on the USSR in the wake of Polish martial law: these American-imposed sanctions required European allies to break off from pipeline contracts which involved American corporate subsidiaries or US commercial licences, yet at the same time the Reagan administration continued with its US–USSR grain sales. Moreover, even as the administrtion proceeded with its action against martial law in Poland, it maintained its refusal to consider the imposition of economic sanctions against the repressive system of apartheid in South Africa.

Much of the dismay and irritation experienced by US friends and foes alike stemmed from the efforts of the Reagan administration to re-establish American pre-eminence and autonomy in decision making and action in international relations. At bottom, the problem was that to many the erosion of US world hegemony appeared irreversible (Kaldor, 1979; Calleo, 1982). Moreover, it was a reality that seemed to be confirmed by Jimmy Carter's acceptance of the modernist perspective with his hopes of a new international system which would comprise 'a new world-wide mosaic of global, regional, and bilateral relations'. It is true that, in his final year in office, Carter disavowed this perspective and began taking action to reverse defence cuts, rebuild the CIA and treat the world as a highly fragmented and dangerous place in which the issue of global security should be dominant (Moore, 1984). However, by that time, the world view of the US as a power in decline was set. This perspective of US decline significantly gained ground in Western Europe, in particular within the European Community where member states increasingly engaged in the modernist approaches of transnationalism and interdependence. This posed particular problems for the US–European relationship. As Michael Smith has pointed out: 'Much of the apparatus of American hegemony is still in place, but it operates in a rather creaky manner if at all. . . . The "transmission belts" of Amerian influence on the affairs of Western Europe are not in good repair it seems . . .' (Smith, 1984, 97).

It came as a considerable shock, therefore, that the Reagan administration should attempt to reclaim a past style of assertive international leadership. West European leaders, who were still trying to recover from the administration's pre-emptive actions in employing sanctions against martial law in Poland, were in consequence visibly stunned on being informed by Vice-President Bush on his 1982 European tour: 'I'm sorry. The United States is the leader of the Free World, and under this administration we are beginning to act like it' (Quoted in Watt, 1984; see also Kahler, 1983).

With the American public, Reagan's foreign policy assertiveness enjoyed considerable support. Opinion polls conducted by Gallup at the mid-point and the end of his first term in office produced the following responses to the question: 'Do you think the following problems have gotten much better, somewhat better, somewhat worse or much worse as a result of Reagan policies?'

	June 1982			February 1985		
	Better	Worse	Same	Better	Worse	Same
Defence	54%	13%	26%	62%	10%	20%
Respect for US	35%	39%	19%	44%	30%	18%
Chances for peace	24%	44%	26%	35%	29%	30%

Thus, on the vital Reagan issues of military strength and restoration of America's world position, the president carried the public with him. Moreover, his landslide re-election in November 1984 appeared to provide emphatic confirmation of this.

There were, however, some doubts in the public mind about specific aspects of Reagan's foreign policy record. In a CBS News/ *New York Times* poll conducted in October 1984 (just four weeks before the election), the public thought:

	For %	Against %
More should be done by the US to achieve a nuclear arms agreement with the USSR	54	36
An immediate, verifiable testing and production freeze on nuclear weapons should be effected.	78	18

The US should not provide military
assistance to the people (contras) trying to overthrow
the pro-Soviet government of Nicaragua.   44   30

Consequently, the public verdict on Reagan's first term, foreign policy record was somewhat mixed. Clearly there was considerable support for his emphasis on US military strength and world stature, but there was also a demand for greater efforts in diplomacy and arms control.

On Capitol Hill, the Reagan administration's relations with Congress were also somewhat mixed. Initially, the president enjoyed considerable success in securing approval for the multi-year expansion of the defence budget; but, as his term progressed, Congress began to question and oppose specific defence requests. Congress was concerned from the outset about the administration's policy concerning the Caribbean and Central America. As noted earlier, administration support for El Salvador and for the contras' struggle against the Sandinista regime in Nicaragua came under critical congressional scrutiny. No action was taken on the administration's requested $8 billion economic aid package which was recommended by the Kissinger Commission. Moreover, funding for the contras was finally cut off. Ever jealous of its exclusive constitutional powers, Congress invoked the provisions of the War Powers Act to require Reagan's military action in Grenada to be halted within the stipulated 60 day time limit. Thus the administration obtained support for the means of carrying through the main thrust of its policy goals, but found Congress increasingly critical of actions that held the potential for escalating conflict (Spanier and Uslaner, 1985 *passim*).

Finally, it should be asked whether the foreign policy record of Ronald Reagan's first term was sufficiently novel, coherent and distinctive enough to merit the label 'The Reagan Doctrine'? Rejecting this proposition have been the many critics of the administration who contend that Reagan policy was not novel, coherent or distinctive. Indeed, far from constituting any kind of 'new beginning,' many have discussed Reagan's foreign policy as constituting nothing more than a backward step into the bleak world of cold-war combativeness (Bennett, 1982; McMahan, 1984). A similar theme has been sounded by Schulzinger who characterised Reagan policy as 'the diplomacy of nostalgia' (Schulzinger, 1984, 339–47).

John Spanier has offered a slightly different perspective in arguing that American foreign policy essentially displays no real discontinuities and no real 'new beginnings' or 'backward steps'. In his view, the post-war policy goal of the US has been the containment of Soviet military power on a global scale. Arguing that even *détente* should be viewed as containment in a different guise, he contends that: 'From Truman to Reagan, American foreign policy has displayed a remarkable continuity, despite frequent four-year changes of administration, . . . changes of parties in power, and the erosion of the original cold war consensus' (Spanier, 1985, 305).

Against these critics are the proponents of Reagan policy who argue that Reagan as President managed to transform the policy agenda and stamp his personal imprint on American foreign policy to a remarkable degree. This line of argument has been most forcefully expressed by Jeane Kirkpatrick who contended in 1981 that the 'Reagan phenomenon' 'was a watershed event in American politics which signalled the end of one major post-war period and the beginning of a new one' (Kirkpatrick, 1983, 28). Four years later, Kirkpatrick's assessment was that 'the Reagan phenomenon' should more accurately now be termed 'the Reagan Doctrine'. In arguing this, she focused on the interaction of the President's strong commitment to the idea of freedom and the challenges to freedom from the Soviet Union's growing military strength, expansionism and influence on western concepts and values. It is in the response to these challenges that she has located the following key elements of the Reagan Doctrine:

- The rebuilding of US defences and the development of new defence systems;
- The willingness to confront the expansion of Soviet power and influence, and the affirmation of American solidarity with peoples struggling to prevent their incorporation into the Soviet empire or to regain their freedom;
- The reassertion of the moral superiority of liberal democratic institutions and pluralist society (Kirkpatrick, 1985).

Clearly, no consensus is possible here between the competing claims of 'new beginning,' 'continuity,' and 'backward steps.' Nevertheless, it is beyond dispute that Reagan's determined efforts succeeded in restoring a heightened profile to US foreign policy. His vigorous reassertion of traditionalist concerns of national interest, power, security and autonomy recast American policy to such a degree that the label, the 'Reagan Doctrine', as Kirkpatrick has proposed it, is merited. Less evident was the extent to which this 'doctrine' would be capable of coherent and consistent application in Reagan's second term.

References

Bennett, Roy (1982). 'Reagan's Foreign Policy: the First Period' in A. Gastner, C. Greer and F. Reissman, eds, *What Reagan Is Doing to Us*, New York: Harper & Row.

Brzezinski, Zbigniew (1983). *Power and Principle: Memoirs of the National Security Advisor, 1979–1981*, London: Weidenfeld & Nicolson.

Calleo, D. (1982). *The Imperious Economy*, Cambridge, Mass.: Harvard University Press.

Chomsky, N., Steele, J. and Gittings, J. (1984). *Superpowers in Collision: the New Cold War of the 1980s*, 2nd edn., Harmondsworth: Penguin.

Destler, I. M. (1983). 'The Evolution of Reagan Foreign Policy' in F. I. Greenstein, ed., *The Reagan Presidency: an Early Assessment*, Baltimore: The Johns Hopkins University Press.

Falcoff, Mark (1980). 'Latin America' in P. Duignan and A. Rabushka, eds, *The United States in the 1980s*, London: Croom Helm.

Friedman, Thomas L. (1984). 'American's Failure in Lebanon'; *New York Times Magazine*, 4 Apr. 1984.

Haig, Alexander M., Jr (1984). *Caveat: Realism, Reagan, and Foreign Policy*, London: Weidenfeld and Nicolson.

Holt, Pat M. (1978). *The War Powers Resolution*, Washington, DC: American Enterprise Institute.

Javits, Jacob K. (1973). *Who Makes War: the President versus Congress*, New York: William Morrow.

Joffe, Joseph (1983). 'Europe and America: the Politics of Resentment (Cont'd),' *Foreign Affairs*, pp. 569–90.

Kahler, M. (1983). 'The United States and Western Europe: the Diplomatic Consequences of President Reagan' in K. Oye *et al*, eds, *Eagle Defiant: the United States Foreign Policy in the 1980s*, Boston: Little, Brown & Co, pp. 273–309.

Kaldor M. (1979). *The Disintegrating West*, Harmondsworth: Penguin.

Kirkpatrick, Jeane J. (1982). *Dictatorship and Double Standaards*, New York: Simon and Schuster.

Kirkpatrick, Jeane J. (1983). *The Reagan Phenomenon*, Washington, DC: American Enterprise Institute.

Kirkpatrick, Jeane J. (1985). *The Reagan Doctrine and US Foreign Policy*, Washington, DC: The Heritage Foundation

McMahan, Jeff (1984). *Reagan and the World: Imperial Policy in the New Cold War*, London: Pluto Press.

Moore, Raymond A. (1984). 'The Carter Presidency and Foreign Policy' in M. G. Abernathy, D. M. Hill and P. Williams, eds, *The Carter Years: Presidency and Policy Making*, London: Frances Pinter, pp. 54–83.

Morse, Edward L. (1976). *Modernisation and the Transformation of International Relations*, New York: Macmillan Free Press.

Schulzinger, Robert D. (1984). *American Diplomacy in the Twentieth Century*, New York: Oxford University Press.

Smith, H., Clymer, A., Silk, L., Lindsay, R. and Burt R. (1981). *Reagan the man, the President*, Oxford: Pergamon Press.

Smith, Michael (1984). *Western Europe and the United States: the Uncertain Alliance*, London: G. Allen & Unwin.

Spanier, John (1985). *American Foreign Policy Since World War II*, 10th edn, New York: Holt, Rhinehart & Winston.

Spanier, John and Uslaner, Eric M. (1985). *American Foreign Policy Making and the Democratic Dilemmas*, 4th edn, New York: Holt, Rhinehart and Winston.

Stoessinger, John (1979). *Crusaders and Pragmatists: Movers of Modern American Foreign Policy*, New York: W. W. Norton & Co.

Valis, Wayne (ed.) (1981). *The Future Under President Reagan*, Westport, Conn.: Arlington House Publishers,

Watt, David (1984). 'As a European Saw It', *Foreign Affairs*, pp. 521–32.

7 *Michael Turner*

Defence policy and arms control: the Reagan record

Defence policy has been the critical component of the Reagan administration's determined efforts to restore American influence and leadership in world affairs. The unprecedented peacetime build-up of US military capabilities pursued by the administration throughout its first four years in office was employed as a major means of signalling renewed US vigour and firmness of purpose in international relations. The impetus for a massive programme of defence modernisation and expansion came from analysis by the Reagan team that American defences had fallen dangerously behind those of the Soviet Union, in terms of both overall effectiveness and technical development.

Tied inextricably to its expanding defence programme was the administration's policy on arms control. The position adopted by President Reagan from the outset focused on the necessity of impressing on the Soviet Union the determination of the US to match Soviet defence spending across the board and system by system. The clear message was that, regardless of the resources expended on defence, no advantage over the US could be gained. In effect, the Reagan view was that successful negotiations on arms reductions could be concluded with the Soviet Union only from a position of American strength. Accordingly, arms control was made an integral part of Reagan defence policy.

US defence deficiencies and the Reagan critique

At the heart of the Reagan critique of the US defence programme inherited from previous administrations was the relative decline of American defence spending and capability compared to the increased levels of spending on, and increased effectiveness of, Soviet defence systems. Yet, while much of Reagan's 1980 election campaign criticism was directed at the Carter administration's policy record, the fact was that the relative American decline had much earlier beginnings and can first be located in the policy actions of the Nixon administration.

Major reductions in defence spending were effected by President Nixon as a direct product of his policy of pursuing regional security in world affairs by turning over peace-keeping responsibilities to US allies and friendly states (under the so-called 'Nixon Doctrine'). Moreover, as a consequence of the Nixon policy of *détente* and arms limitation agreements with the Soviet Union, further cuts were made in US conventional forces (to levels below those of 1964). Similarly, little or no improvements were made in American strategic forces –other than to equip US ballistic missiles with multiple warheads (i.e. multiple independent re-entry vehicles – MIRVs) (Huntington, 1983, 86). These reductions in defence spending were also a product of the growing antipathy to American involvement in Vietnam, with Congress reflecting public concerns by cutting some $40 billion from defence requests submitted in the early- and mid-1970s.

As the Ford administration quickly realised, while US defence spending had been decreasing the problem was that spending on defence by the Soviet Union was on the increase (by 3–4 per cent annually in real terms from the mid-1960s onwards). Furthermore, the USSR had worked to strengthen considerably its conventional forces in Eastern Europe and on the Chinese border, had developed significantly its air and sea power capabilities, and had developed and deployed new generations of strategic and intermediate missiles. In consequence, the Ford administration responded with a new strategy featuring three major priorities: first, the modernisation of US strategic forces; second, the strengthening of NATO's conventional forces and modernisation of theatre nuclear forces in Europe; and, finally, the urgent development of new force capabilities to defend western interests in the sensitive oil-producing area around the Persian Gulf.

To implement his administration's new strategic concerns, President Ford proposed in 1975 a five-year programme to raise the level of US defence spending by 40 per cent in real terms over the period, FY 1976–80. Included in Ford's programme were the following major proposals:

1. the annual construction of 32 ships, to produce a 540-ship navy by the mid-1980s;
2. the procurement of a new force of 244 B-1 strategic bombers;
3. the deployment of the MX missile by 1983;
4. the production of three Trident submarines every 2 years;
5. the annual purchase of 500 tactical and attack aircraft and of over 2000 tank and other tracked combat vehicles (McCoy and Kraemer, 1981, 92).

Ford's programme to revamp Amerian defence was, however, largely blunted by his successor, Jimmy Carter, whose first two years in office were characterised by a somewhat sanguine belief in the sufficiency of existing defence capabilities. While comitted to a 3 per cent increase in defence spending (in line with the agreement reached by all NATO members in the spring of 1977), the Carter administration effectively negated this by internal disputation over the base against which the increase should be calculated. In the event, Carter cut back considerably the Ford programme with reductions in projected defence spending which totalled some $40 billion between FY 1978 and FY 1980. In achieving this, he cut the planned shipbuilding programme in half, cancelled the B-1 bomber, delayed the MX missile programme by four years, cut the projected production rate of Trident submarines by a third, and reduced planned purchases of tactical aircraft and tanks by 20 per cent. Moreover, while his own administration had proposed the creation of a Rapid Deployment Force (RDF) to deal with sudden conflicts outside the NATO area (with special focus on the third of Ford's strategy priorities–defence of western interests in the Persian Gulf), the fact was that Carter provided little or no funding for RDF in the period, FY 1978–80.

The Carter approach to defence was put into reverse, however, by a series of unconnected events in 1979: first, the fall of the Shah of Iran gave sudden urgency to the RDF concept; second, the Soviet invasion of Afghanistan revived public pressures on the administration to 'get tough' with the Soviet Union (and, at the same time, significantly altered Carter's own perception of Soviet leaders); and, finally, there was the NATO decision in December to match the Soviet deployment of SS-20 missiles in Eastern Europe with delayed deployment of Cruise and Pershing II missiles on a 'dual track' basis in Western Europe. Publicly announcing the Carter administration's changed view, Defense Secretary Harold Brown declared in the spring of 1980, in his *Annual Defense Report for FY 1981*, that 'the defense program must be substantially increased over the next five years, and . . . we must begin the effort now'. Accordingly, Carter submitted to Congress a defence budget for FY 1981 that sought to increase defence spending by 5 per cent in real terms over his budget request for FY 1980, and he projected increases for defence totalling 22 per ent over the 5-year period, FY 1981–5.

In terms of specific defence programmes, Carter moved to reverse his position, most notably on the MX missile, by announcing in the Summer of 1979 his decision to deploy MX missiles on a mobile basis in Nevada and Utah. This decision was significant for its acceptance of the arguments (made most vociferously, but by no means exclusively, by the American right), on the increasing vulnerability of the American Minuteman III ICBM force to the new generation of missiles deployed by the Soviet Union – the SS-18 and the SS-19 missiles (Brzezinski, 1983, 332–7). Steps were also taken in March 1980, to develop the RDF, following the President's declaration in his State of the Union Address on 23 January that any attempt by an outside force to gain control of the Persian Gulf would be treated as an attack on the United States.

More significantly, the Carter administration now accepted that US defence doctrine and progammes were becoming increasingly inferior to growing Soviet capability. Indeed, Brzezinski (as Carter's national security adviser) concluded that the Soviet Union was 'reaching out for a genuine nuclear-war fighting capability, through its command, communications, control and intelligence structures (C^3I), hardening of key command sites, etc., and was on the professional military level articulating a doctrine to that effect' (Brzezinski, 1983, 455). The result was a new strategic doctrine set out in Presidential Directive 59 which Carter signed in July 1980. In essence, PD 59 placed greater targeting emphasis on military targets and war-supporting Soviet industries. C^3I was to be given greater priority and broadened to provide control of both strategic and general purpose forces in the event of protracted conflict. Thus, by stressing its intentions to minimise the vulnerability of its own command, comunications, control and intelligence structures and to employ them to make US strategic targeting more flexible, the Carter administration sought to tighten the doctrine of deterrence. The message sent to the Soviet Union was clear: the US would guarantee that nuclear war was unwinnable.

Accordingly, Carter's final year in office evidenced a major U-turn on defence and produced a tougher response to Soviet military developments. However, for candidate Ronald Reagan this was much too little and too late as he unremittingly attacked Carter on defence throughout the 1980 campaign. Thus he denounced the Carter administration's dealings with the Soviet Union as 'bordering on appeasement', and cited in evidence Carter's cancellation of the B-1 bomber and his delays or postponements of the Cruise missile programme, the MX missile and the Trident submarine. In contrast, Reagan declared in a campaign policy statement issued in January 1980: 'I favor development of the neutron warhead for US theatre forces, including ballistic missiles, Cruise missiles, artillery and bombs' (sic).

Some indication of the lines of defence policy thinking within the Reagan campaign team was provided by two sets of policy analyses. In the first of these, William Van Cleave (Reagan's chief defence adviser in the 1980 campaign) advocated the need to counter the 'substantial disparity in favor of the USSR in the ability to fight, survive, win, and recover from nuclear war'. To deal with the increasing vulnerability of US strategic forces he proposed a series of 'quick fixes', including: deployment of the MX missiles; production of the B-1 bomber; deployment of more air-launched Cruise missiles (ALCMs); and, protection of key military installations (e.g. missile silos) by construction of an antiballistic missile (ABM) system (Van Cleave, 1980). Throughout the 1980 campaign, Van Cleave pressed for all of these proposals to be included in the defence agenda of a Reagan administration.

The second major indicator of Reagan defence thinking came in a confidential paper prepared for Richard Allen, who was Reagan's campaign adviser on national security matters. Titled, 'Strategic Guidance', this paper also warned of the growing imbalance between the US and the USSR and set out remedial proposals. Included amongst these were the need to consider ways of protecting the civilian population from nuclear attack, possibly by building an ABM system, and the redirection of US strategic deterrence to switch from population centres to military and political targets within the Soviet Union. The paper also counselled that, while the US would at times require the assistance of its allies in deterring Soviet actions, 'the availability of allied support should not constrain American action in defense of its interests' (Smith *et al.*, 1981, 87–8).

Other study groups similarly advised the Reagan campaign of the urgent need to rebuild American defence capabilities. A Republican task force headed by retired General Edward Rowny argued in the Summer of 1980 that the US would need 200 additional warships, 5 new army divisions and some 9 additional tactical air squadrons. Quantifying US defence needs in dollar terms, the Commitee on the Present Danger (which had earlier convinced President Ford of the necessity for an immediate US response to the growing Soviet military capability) indicated to Reagan in 1979 that the defence budget would need to be increased by $200 billion (over a 5-year period) beyond the Carter administration's defence spending projections.

Accordingly, as he prepared to succeed Carter to the presidency in January 1981, Ronald Reagan's position on defence was relatively clear: much more was needed in order to match the USSR in terms of both its nuclear and non-nuclear capabilities. His campaign pronouncements gave every indication that he was prepared to commit the necessary resources to that end, despite his equally clear commitment to reduce the overall size of the federal budget.

The Reagan defence programme

As previously indicated, it was the conviction of the incoming Reagan administration that defence spending was a case for 'special treatment.' It was certainly the case that the defence share of the US federal budget had declined dramatically over a 20-year period from a 46 per cent share in FY 1962 to a projected 26 per cent share in FY 1982. In the same period, the USSR had steadily increased its defence budget to an annual level that reached (US) $275 billion in 1982 or approximately 14% of Soviet GNP (compared to the US defence share which was projected to be 5.6 % of GNP in FY 1982). The net result in the view of many analysts was to tip the military balance between the two superpowers in favour of the USSR (Iklé, 1980; Hoeber and Douglas, 1980).

It was to redress this perceived imbalance that the Reagan administration moved immediately to increase defence spending. On 10 March 1981, the President submitted to Congress his proposed revisions to the Carter defence budgets. For FY 1981, Reagan requested approval for a $6.8 billion supplement in defence budget authority, while for FY 1982 he sought an increase of $26.3 billion in defence budget authority over the Carter administration's requested total of $200.3 billion. For the five-year period, FY 1982–6, he asked Congress to approve defence budget authority totalling $1460 billion, which represented an increase of 14.4 % over the five-year total requested by Carter. Amongst the additions in the Reagan defence requests were funds for a new strategic bomber, acceleration of the shipbuilding programme and increased production targets for combat aircraft.

Early critics of the Reagan administration's requested revisions to the FY 1981 and 1982 defence budgets focused on both the levels of funding requested and the content of defence spending plans. Thus James Fallows, in arguing that mere money could not be equated with a strategy, bitingly observed: 'The most important theme of President Reagan's proposals for defence has little to do with strategy or concepts, but rather with sheer quantities: the budget stands for *more*' (Fallows, 1981). Concerning the content of the Reagan proposals, others charged that the new President's revisions to the Carter budgets merely comprised the spending preferences of the military service chiefs rather than those of the incoming Defence Secretary, Caspar Weinberger. Thus it was argued that, instead of a Reagan defence programme, Congress had been presented with spending requests which reflected the actions of the service chiefs and their staffs working to obtain the reinstatement of favoured priority items which had previously been deleted (Kaufmann, 1981). In a similar vein, the Heritage Foundation's analysis of Reagan's first year defence proposals argued: 'The administration has limited itself to modest increases in the underfunded Carter program and a few praiseworthy advances in procurement reform.' Critical of the administration's failure to deal with the vital problem of strategic vulnerability, the Heritage assessment complained about the absence of any 'articulated policy framework or Reagan posture statement' (Green, 1982).

Regarding these criticisms, it should be noted that every incoming administration is faced with the problem of being seen to be continuing with the policies and programmes of its immediate predecessor over its first year in office. This is particularly the case with defence, where the necessarily long lead-times of defence procurement programmes constrain the shaping of budget plans for several years ahead. Accordingly, it would have been surprising had Reagan's defence budget proposals revising Carter's FY 1981 and

1982 budget requests not followed in large measure the programmes and policies of the departed Carter administration. Notwithstanding this point, Defence Secretary Weinberger conceded (with surprising candour) the validity of the criticism that the Reagan defence requests submitted in March 1981 had failed to set out any new defence strategy. In a major address in June 1981, on 'The Defence Policy of the Reagan Administration', he argued that 'we knew little was to be gained by an early enunciation of some elaborate "conceptual structure", (or) a full-fledged Reagan strategy'. His view was that such 'grand strategy' concepts had proved to be problematic in the past because they 'prejudged and oversimplified reality: they put blinkers on our vision' (Weinberger, 1981).

In its second year, the Reagan administration moved to develop a more distinctive defence programme. Echoing the criticisms that the defence proposals of the administration's first year had amounted to little more than 'a collection of departmental policies', NSC Adviser William Clark launched in the spring of 1982 an interagency study to produce an 'integrated strategy for preserving our national security' (Clark, 1982). The resultant product was a National Security Decision Directive (NSDD) on military strategy which was approved by the President in May 1985. This NSDD document, together with the various components of the massive five-year defence programme outlined in the administration's FY 1983 defence budget, the *Annual Defense Report for FY 1983* submitted to Congress by defence Secretary Weinberger in February 1982, and the FY 1984–8 Defense Guidance Plan (disclosed by the *New York Times* on 30 May 1982), set out the basic elements of the Reagan strategy. In essence, this focused on four major priorities: pursuit of 'economic warfare' against the USSR; modernisation of US strategic nuclear forces; arms development as a precursor of arms control; and the capability to deal with Soviet actions in terms of 'prolonged war' and 'horizontal escalation'.

The first of these priorities, 'economic warfare', sought to displace the policy of economic diplomacy employed by previous administrations to influence Soviet behaviour by a more direct, aggressive approach aimed at weakening Soviet strength. This new policy would entail a much harder line to deny economic credits, to apply more stringent economic controls on technology exports (both legal and illegal) to the USSR by tightening the operations of the Co-ordinating Committee for Multilateral Exports Controls

(COCOM), and to develop other proposals likely to increase the economic burdens of the Soviet Union. The second major area of focus was US strategic force modernisation. Given the increasing vulnerability of US strategic capability to the new generations of weapons systems developed by the USSR, it came as no surprise that William Clark should affirm that modernisation would be given 'first priority in our efforts to rebuild the military capabilities of the United States'. The third strategic priority concerned the linkage of arms development to the issue of arms control. Essentially here it was argued by the administration that arms control agreements with the Soviet Union should be pursued from a position of US strength rather than weakness. The Reagan policy thus effectively incorporated the notion of 'bargaining chips' into its weapons procurement programme.

As for the fourth of the administrtion's strategic priorities, this focused on the concepts of 'prolonged war' and 'horizontal escalation'. The need to develop the capability to fight a conventional war of a prolonged duration was considered vital in maintaining effective deterrence, and indicated, according to Weinberger, that the administration 'had abandoned the dangerous fallacy of a "short war"'. US policy therefore no longer assumed that conventional war would be brief or would quickly escalate to the nuclear level. As for 'horizontal escalation', this was a somewhat controversial strategy developed by the administration for deterring Soviet attacks against US interests by threatening simultaneous retaliation elsewhere against equally vital and vulnerable Soviet interests. Thus Clark argued that the US needed to develop 'a capability for counter-offensive on other fronts' (Clark, 1982; Halloran, 1982; Huntington, 1983, 90–104).

The FY 1983 defence budget submitted to Congress by the president in February 1982 contained many of the key programme and procurement elements needed for the Reagan military strategy. However, perhaps the most arresting aspect of the president's defence request was its size: it sought to effect increases in defence spending at an annual rate of 7.4% in real terms over the five-year period, FY 1983–7. In dollar terms, as Table 7.1 indicates, the projected total for defence budget authority requested over this period would amount to nearly $1700 billion. Relative to the total US economy, defence spending over the period FY 1983–7 was projected to average out at an annual rate of 6.9% of GNP (with a peak level of 7.3% in FY 1986 and 1987). This projected average can be contrasted with the 5.4 average percentage annual share of GNP taken by defence in the period FY 1978–82, but was still lower than the 10 per cent average for defence in the years immediately after the Korean war.

Table 7.1:   US defence budget authority requests ($billion)

FY 1983	Reagan request	263·0
FY 1984	Reagan projection	291·0
FY 1985	Reagan projection	338·0
FY 1986	Reagan projection	374·9
FY 1987	Reagan projection	408·4

Source: Budget of the US Government for FY 1983 (1982, Washington, DC).

With its FY 1983 defence budget proposals, the administration sought first to strengthen the conventional/non-nuclear capabilities of the US military. To achieve this, three key policy goals were affirmed: first, the basic commitment through NATO to confront any Soviet threat to Western Europe; second, the need to protect oil supplies and sea-lanes in the Persian Gulf from both Soviet and non-Soviet threats; and, third, the need to counter threats to US interests in Central and Latin America. To meet these conventional force needs, purchases of new equipment were to be accelerated beyond the rates envisaged by the Carter administration's defence plans, thus producing 29 per cent more M-1 tanks, 24 per cent more fighting vehicles and 25 per cent more anti-tank helicopters. Beyond this, the procurement of additional fighter and attack aircraft (together with the modernisation of divisional equipment) was to be speeded up. Finally, the administration aimed to achieve the goal of a 600-ship US navy (to include provision of 2 nuclear-powered aircraft carriers at $7 billion), which would reflect a substantial increase over the 496-ship total inherited from Carter.

Within its conventional force programme, the Reagan administration established two clear priorities: the provision of an operational Rapid Deployment Force (RDF); and development of its new policy of 'horizontal escalation'. For the RDF, the administration made provision for the assignment of five army divisions, marine amphibious forces, tactical air and bomber force wings, three naval carrier battle groups and sought to procure a new 'family' of light armoured vehicles (capable of use by both the army and the Marine Corps). As for implementation of the strategy of 'horizontal escalation', this was to be largely the responsibility of the US Navy. This gave rise to criticism that the administration's policy appeared to advocate withdrawal to the seas and thus opening up the possible land domination of Eurasia by the Soviet Union.

On nuclear weapons policy, the Reagan administration sought with its FY 1983 defence requests to restore 'essential equivalence' with the Soviet Union. This entailed the dualism of approach alluded to earlier: on the one hand, building up the US nuclear arsenal and the substantial modernisation of strategic systems; while, on the other hand, seeking agreement on arms control measures with the USSR. Since the basic Reagan view was that the Soviet leadership only respected strength, it followed that the arms imbalance in favour of the Soviet Union must first be remedied.

In large measure, the administration's strategic weapons approach was shaped by the basic principles of diversity, flexibility and endurance. The diversity principle has been effected in US strategic policy by maintaining a 'triad' of launch systems, comprising land-based missiles, submarine-based ballistic missiles and intercontinental bombers. By means of this triad of launch systems, the US has endeavoured to minimise vulnerability that otherwise might arise from a single Soviet technological breakthrough. The second principle, flexibility, is invoked to ensure the availability of a sufficient range of weapons capability to cover a variety of Soviet targets under different 'limited' scenarios. Finally, the endurance principle requires weapons systems which will survive Soviet attack and be capable of flexible deployment.

To achieve its central goal of restoring 'essential equivalence,' and to implement the principles of diversity, flexibility and endurance, the Reagan administration's FY 1983 defence budget included the following major strategic systems requests:

– Funding for two different strategic bombers: first, for the production of 100 B-1B bombers (at an estimated cost of over $29 billion); and, second, for the development of an advanced technology 'Stealth' bomber (for deployment in the 1990s);
– The installation of air-launched Cruise missiles (ALCMs) on B-52 bombers (a proposal later cancelled by the administration);
– The production and deployment of 100 MX (Peacekeeper) intercontinental ballistic missiles (ICBMs);
– The production of one Trident submarine a year (to a fleet total of 20 submarines), and the development and production of the more advanced Trident II (D-5) submarine-launched ballistic missiles (SLBMs);
– The installation of sea-launched Cruise missiles (SLCMs) on attack submarines (CBO, 1982; Huntington, 1983).

In essence, the defence proposals presented in the FY 1983 budget set out the core of the Reagan defence programme for the remainder of the president's first term. While Congress involved itself with some trimming of the Reagan defence budgets for FY 1983, 1984 and 1985, and the administration itself made some slight downward adjustments to take account of growing public concern about the increasing federal budget deficit, the growth pattern established for defence by the FY 1983 five-year projections remained largely intact. Thus, Reagan's defence budget for FY 1986 (in fact the final defence budget prepared in his first term, but presented in February 1985, at the start of his second term) requested budget authority of $322.2 billion. Athough this was some $52.7 billion less than the figure of $374.9 billion projected in 1982 for FY 1986, much of this decrease could be accounted for by lowered estimates for inflation, cost-of-living adjustments (COLA) on pensions and military pay increases. Overall, however, the clear trend in defence spending was still upwards (CBO, 1985).

Yet, the Reagan administration found itself assailed by critics on the right who complained that while the issue of modernisation had been addressed, not enough had been done to deal with the problem as a matter of urgency; the 'quick fixes' approach advocated by Van Cleave had not been adopted. By holding over considerable elements of its defence modernisation programme on a phased basis into the 1990s (as with the 'Stealth' bomber, deployment of a completed fleet of Trident submarines and the Trident II (D-5) SLBMs), the administration had not moved sufficiently to close the 'window of vulnerability' created by the Soviet Union's programme of new developments begun in the 1960s (CBO, 1982; Green, 1982; Cohen, 1985).

The MX missile controversy

The MX missile was widely regarded as a vital element in the modernisation of US strategic forces because it would provide a comparable capability to that of the new generation SS-18 and SS-19 missiles deployed by the Soviet Union. Like the SS-18 and SS-19, which respectively carry ten and six independently targetable warheads (or, multiple independent re-entry vehicles – MIRVs), the MX was a MIRVed missile which would carry ten warheads. However, the new and vital feature of this generation of ballistic missiles lay in their extremely accurate targeting which made possible nuclear strikes at missile silos and other military targets rather than population centres.

For the US, the problem was that the land-based component of its strategic triad, the Minuteman III missiles installed in 1000 fixed underground silos, were now highly vulnerable to a first-strike of SS-18 and SS-19 missiles. While it was the case that the two remaining US triad components (strategic bombers and submarine-launched ballistic missiles ([SLBMs]) would provide a second-strike, retaliatory capability, there was serious doubt about whether it could be employed in such circumstances. After all, the argument ran, if a US President were to be confronted by a Soviet threat to employ a third-strike (counter-retaliatory) at American cities, could he do so in the knowledge that he would be committing the US to national suicide? In such circumstances, the US would be open to nuclear blackmail.

The basic problem with Reagan's FY 1983 budget request for 100 MX missiles was that it negated the very feature which made the MX a solution to the problem of Minuteman III vulnerability. As indicated earlier, the Carter administration had proposed deploying 200 MX missiles on a mobile basis designed to conceal the location of each individual missile at any given moment. However, by rejecting this plan and proposing instead to install 100 MX missiles in hardened, fixed-position, existing Minuteman III silos, Reagan would ensure that the MX was as vulnerable to first-strike attack as the missile it replaced. This flaw was quickly seized on by critics of both the left and the right who argued that the administration's proposal made no strategic sense. Worse, in the view of many, was the real possibility that such a vulnerable mode of deployment would encourage the US to employ the MX as a first-strike weapon against the Soviet Union. It was contended that the vulnerability of a fixed-position, silo-based MX system to the SS-18 and SS-19 missiles would tempt the US in a time of extreme tension and crisis to launch a pre-emptive strike against Soviet military targets rather than to simply await a Soviet first-strike. Consequently, critics argued that the proposed Reagan MX deployment plan would promote a 'launch on warning' situation (Green, 1982; McMahan, 1984).

The damage done by these criticisms to Reagan's MX proposal was considerable. Congress refused to endorse it and indicated that any MX funding would be contingent on submission by the administration of an acceptable, alternative MX deployment mode which was significantly less vulnerable. However, while the president did respond with a revised submission by the stipulated deadline of 1 December 1982, his new proposal proved to be just as unacceptable. Essentially, what was proposed was a 'dense pack' plan to place all 100 MX missiles within an area of 20 square miles. The untested theory on which 'dense pack' was based held that the explosions produced by a first wave of incoming Soviet missiles would work to destroy subsequent waves, thus leaving MX missiles located in silos not directly hit completely unscathed. However, Congress found this a highly dubious proposition and refused to grant MX funding for FY 1983. Again the administration was asked to reconsider deployment modes and to report back with a further proposal by a deadline of 1 March 1983 (later extended to April).

Concerned that a further setback could well prove fatal to the deployment of the MX in *any* kind of basing mode, Reagan adroitly moved on 3 January 1983 to resolve the issue by setting up a Presidential Commission on Strategic Forces which would investigate possible solutions and produce a recommendation which Congress could be persuaded to accept. Under the chairmanship of Brent Scowcroft (Kissinger's successor as NSC Adviser in the Ford White House), and with a bipartisan membership which included four former Defense Secretaries and two former Secretaries of State, the Commission's recommendations in April 1983 were scarcely less controversial than the president's own proposals earlier rejected by the Congress.

Accepting the need to match the Soviet Union's deployment of its SS-18 and SS-19 missiles with a comparable American counterforce, the Scowcroft Commission simply side-stepped the vulnerability issue and proposed that the MX missile should be deployed in specially-hardened, existing Minuteman III silos. In view of the scale of the criticism that had greeted Reagan's identical plan, this was an astonishing recommendation. However, the Commission also proceeded to argue that the MX be deployed only on an interim basis and that it should be replaced in the early 1990s by a much smaller, single-warhead missile. Because of its relatively small size, this replacement missile (instantly dubbed the 'Midgetman') would be capable of deployment by means of mobile launchers and thus less vulnerable to pre-emptive strike. Nonetheless, until its actual deployment in the 1990s, the vulnerability problems faced by the land-based component of the US strategic triad would remain.

In making these recommendations, the Scowcroft Commission focused on the terrible implications of first-strike and 'launch on warning' scenarios inherent in the deployment of the new generation of super-accurate, MIRVed ballistic missiles. With non-MIRVed missiles, the Commission contended, such dangers would be considerably lessened and the more stable balance enjoyed in the earlier period of single-warhead missiles in the 1960s could be restored. To achieve such a position, it would of course be necessary for each side to adopt a common policy of installing only non-MIRVed warheads in their new generation of ballistic missiles. To persuade the Soviet Union to agree to this, the Commission further proposed employing the MX as a 'bargaining chip' in arms negotiations by holding out the prospect of its withdrawal (either wholly or in part) by the US in return for similar Soviet moves with regard to the SS-18 and SS-19 missiles.

Surprisingly, in view of its rejection of an identical MX deployment plan previously submitted by the administration, Congress gave its approval to the recomended deployment of the MX in hardened, Minuteman III silos and voted in May 1983 to fund production of 21 MX missiles in FY 1984. However, to obtain this Congressional support, the president had to give assurances to members of both Houses that he would implement fully the Scowcroft recommendations. Thus he agreed to develop and deploy a single-warhead 'Midgetman' missile to replace the MX and to engage in arms control negotiations with the Soviet Union holding out the MX as a bargaining chip. As a further concession to secure MX approval, Reagan also agreed to incorporate the concept of 'build-down' into the US negotiating position. Proposed in early 1983 by Republican Senator William Cohen, the notion of 'build-down' involved a simple 'two-for-one' rule for long-range strategic missiles under which two older warheads would be withdrawn for every new warhead deployed. Thus the administration managed to obtain FY 1984 funding for the production of 21 of the 40 MX missiles requested. Reagan's success, however, came not because of the persuasiveness in Congress of the strategic arguments for MX deployment, but rather from the Congressional perception of the utility of the MX as useful bargaining leverage (on both the administration and the Soviet leadership) to spur meaningful arms negotiations (CBO, 1984; Spanier and Uslaner, 1985, 217–25).

The administration's goal of deploying 100 MX missiles was still very much at risk in 1984, when the president included in his FY 1985 defence budget a request for a further forty missiles. Employing the wider stage proffered by the 1984 elections, Congressional opponents of the MX were able to mobilise against the MX missile system. To that end, they employed broader concerns about the growing federal budget deficit, the ever-rising level of defence spending, and the stalled arms negotiations with the USSR (the product of the Soviet withdrawal from arms control negotiations in November and December 1983, following deployment of Cruise and Pershing II missiles by NATO in Western Europe as a counter to the Soviet Union's SS-20 missiles). The eventual outcome of fiercely contested votes in both houses (with MX funding surviving by a mere six votes in the House and by the tie-breaking vote of Vice President Bush in the Senate) was highly fraught for the president. He was given qualified authorisation of $2.5 billion for MX funding (to include the production of a further 21 missiles). However, the qualifications imposed on the release of the bulk of this funding posed severe difficulties for him.

Essentially, the Congress had voted to grant immediate release of $1 billion for MX research and development but withheld the remaining $1.5 billion for production of 21 missiles contingent on the state of play of US arms negotiations with the Soviet Union. Under a complex arrangement, Congress decided to subject the release of the $1.5 billion for MX production to two votes in the House and Senate in March 1985. Implicit in this arrangement was the prospect that if the Soviet Union resumed arms negotiations with the US by that time, then the MX funding would remain withheld. Thus the role of the MX as a bargaining chip was significantly changed; it was held out by Congress as an incentive to the Soviet Union to return to the arms talks, but, in doing so, Congress could deny to the Reagan administration future use of the same chip. The future of MX production was now tied not simply to a legislative veto (with both houses of Congress to vote in March 1983 on release of production funding), it was also the subject of a possible Soviet veto. By returning to the stalled arms talks with the US by the spring of 1984, the Soviet Union could trigger Congressional action to withhold MX production funds (Towell, 1984b: Gordon, 1984b).

In the event, agreement was reached with the Soviet Union in January 1985 to begin a new round of arms control talks to be held in

Geneva. Following this, in March, the president was successful in persuading both houses of Congress to vote for release of the $1.5 billion of funding for production of the further 21 MX missiles that had been withheld. His argument to Congress was simple: 'production and deployment (of the MX) is closely related to our chances of achieving significant reductions in nuclear arsenals in Geneva'. Thus the bargaining chip concept had been well and truly stood on its head, with the administration now employing arms control prospects as a chip to secure Congressional funding for MX deployment! Meanwhile, the 'window of vulnerability' which underlay the urgent need for the MX missile at the outset remained to be closed.

Reagan and arms control

At first sight, there is an inherent contradiction in the Reagan administration's dual policy of massively rebuilding America's military capability while at the same time working to secure arms reduction agreements with the Soviet Union. Indeed, critics of this dual approach focused on its contradictory nature to dismiss the president's stated commitment to arms control as 'an exercise in public relations' (McMahan, 1984, 48–69). Countering this view, the administration argued that its duality of approach possessed an inner logic and consistency in line with Reagan's conviction that effective arms negotiations with the Soviet Union could only be conducted from a position of US strength and not of weakness.

In his 1980 campaign, Reagan took strong issue with Carter on his administration's SALT II treaty provisions, arguing that these were profoundly flawed and significantly advantageous to the USSR by locking the US into long-term strategic inferiority. Amongst its major shortcomings, in the Reagan analysis, was firstly the fact that SALT II basically counted missile launchers and did not limit the number of warheads allowed to each side; thus the Soviet Union could significantly increase the number of its ballistic missile warheads within the terms of the treaty. Secondly, SALT II codified a unilateral Soviet right to maintain some 300 heavy ICBMs. Third, while no limits had been set on Soviet deployment of its new intermediate nuclear force (INF) weapon, the SS-20 missile, a SALT II protocool restricted deployment of the new American INF Cruise missiles until after 31 December 1981. Yet, while he rejected the unratified SALT II agreement, Reagan adopted a position of seeking to move beyond SALT II in a new round of arms talks with the Soviet Union. In a *Sunday Times* interview on 9 November 1980 (only days after his victory over Carter), he stated his view that 'We could take what is useful out of SALT II, and tell (the USSR) that we are not going to ratify the treaty the way it is and then make it plain that we are ready to sit down to legitimate negotiations'.

As one of its first actions in office, the Reagan administration commenced in January 1981 a major review of US security and arms control policy. While this did not produce immediate initiatives for negotiation with the Soviet Union, the review did develop four key objectives to guide development of arms control proposals. The first of these was the attainment of security: arms control should not be viewed as an end in itself but rather a means of increasing the security of the US and its allies while reducing the risk of war. Second, arms control should produce militarily significant arms reductions. Thus the number and destructive power of nuclear systems should be reduced and not merely capped at high levels. Third, arms control should aim at achieving equality. Reductions on both sides must therefore be carried out under equal ceilings for similar types of forces in order to secure balance, deterrence and stability. Finally, arms control should make provision for effective verifiability: without some effective means of verifying that arms control measures have been implemented, neither side would confidently make substantial reductions in military forces which were fundmental to its national security (Burt, 1982).

It was not until November 1981 that the administration announced its first arms control initiative, with the president proposing a 'zero-zero' approach to the Soviet ˙Union for intermediate-range nuclear force (INF) reductions. Under this approach, Reagan offered to cancel the planned deployment in Western Europe of 464 ground-launched Cruise missiles (GLCMs) and 108 Pershing II missiles in return for Soviet withdrawal of its deployment of SS-20, SS-4 and SS-5 missiles. This initiative was followed up six months later with the announcement in May 1982 of the president's Strategic Arms Reduction Talks (START) proposal, which sought to effect a two-phased approach to achieving reductions in strategic weapons. In phase one, it was proposed to reduce the total number of ballistic missile warheads by a third. Thus both the US and the USSR would be left with about 5000 warheads each, of which not more than half (2500 warheads) would be deployed on land-based, intercontinental ballistic missiles (ICBMs). At the same time, the total of deployed ICBMs would be limited to 850 missiles for each side. In phase two, additional constraints, including imposing equal limits of ICBM throw-weights, would be introduced. Here, the objective would be to move towards systems with less destructive power (i.e. lower throw-weight) to promote greater stability in the nuclear balance between the two sides.

With his INF 'zero-zero' and START proposals, Reagan indicated his desire to move away from the mere 'limitation' approach of the SALT I and SALT II agreements in order to pursue arms reductions. Moreover, the focus of the START initiative was on warheads and throw-weight, and was therefore concerned with a more meaningful measure of each side's strategic capability than would be provided by counting only launch missiles (the basic unit of measurement in SALT I and SALT II). At the same time, Reaan's proposals also evidenced his administration's opposition to the proposals of the growing freeze movement in the US, which sought to bring in a comprehensive freeze to halt the development of new strategic weapons and to stave off the acquisition of effective first-strike capability by either side (Kennedy and Hatfield, 1982). Basically, the view of the administration on the freeze proposal was that it would merely lock-in the significant strategic weapons advantage possessed by the Soviet Union which Reagan was pledged to remove (Garfinkle, 1984).

The INF negotiations between the US and the USSR began in Geneva in November 1981, with little immediate prospects for success. On the Soviet side, there was total rejection of Reagan's 'zero-zero' proposition: the Soviet Union took the view that it was being asked in effect to give something for nothing, to withdraw *deployed* SS-20, SS-5 and SS-4 missiles in return for the non-deployment of Cruise and Pershing II missiles not yet in place. The counter-offer from the Soviet Union was equally unacceptable to the US negotiators: essentially, the USSR contended that because there was already parity in INF capability the planned deployment of Cruise and Pershing II missiles would imbalance the situation. Agreement was briefly achieved between the American and Soviet negotiators at Geneva on the so-called 'walk in the woods' proposals in July 1982. Under the terms of this unofficial 'agreement', Soviet SS-20 missiles would be cut back from 240 to 75 missiles (with a total of 225 warheads) and the US would deploy only 300 of the planned total of 464 Cruise missiles and no Pershing II missiles. However, neither government in Washington or Moscow was prepared to accept this formula, and the 'agreement' was dismissed by both as unauthorised.

In December 1982, the new Soviet leader Yuri Andropov proposed a revised INF formula which offered to cut back the number of deployed SS-20s to match the total of 144 submarine-launched ballistic missiles (SLBMs) deployed separately by Britain (64 SLBMs) and France (80 SLBMs), with no US deployment of Cruise or Pershing II missiles. However, this proposal was not only unacceptable to the Reagan administration, it was also rejected out of hand by both Britain and France, who regarded their respective SLBM forces as defensive and strategic and not at all comparable to the Soviet SS-20. In March and September 1983, Reagan announced modifications to the US negotiating position. Declaring that his 'zero-zero' option was still the optimal position, the president nonetheless offered to reduce the planned deployment of Cruise and Pershing II missiles to a level equal to that of the total global deployment of SS-20s. However, the INF negotiations were abruptly halted on 23 November, when the Soviet Union pulled out in protest against the arrival in Britain and Germany respectively of the first Cruise and Pershing II missiles.

In the separate START negotiations which commenced at Geneva in June 1982, the Reagan administration put forward the president's two-phased approach to achieve deep cuts in both ICBM launchers and warheads. However, this met with a wholly negative response from the Soviet Union, largely because the bulk of its ICBM force was land-based. This would therefore impose greater adjustment burdens on the USSR than on the US, since the greater portion of the American ICBM force was submarine-based. The counter-proposal from the Soviet side sought to establish a less rigid pattern of system reductions (certainly less demanding on its land-based ICBMs) and a higher ceiling on launchers and warheads.

Following the recommendations of the Scowcroft Commission in April 1983, to shift away from MIRVed ballistic missiles to single-warhead missiles as a means of lessening the risk of first-strike and 'launch on warning' situations, the Reagan administration submitted new proposals for START discussion. In June, the president announced a relaxation of his previously proposed limit of 850 deployed ICBMs in order that both the US and the USSR could have the option of restructuring their respective strategic forces with smaller and less vulnerable non-MIRVed ICBMs. In October, he announced that the US was incorporating into its proposals the concept of a mutual, guaranteed build-down to withdraw older strategic weapons as newer ones were deployed. However, as with the INF negotiations, the START talks broke down at the end of the fifth round of discussions on 8 December 1983, when the Soviet Union declined to set any resumption date in protest against the NATO INF deployments in Western Europe.

Arms control negotiations might well have remained in a state of limbo following the Soviet withdrawals from the INF and START talks at Geneva in November and December 1983, but for a speech made several months earlier by Ronald Reagan on 23 March 1983. At first, not much attention was given to what the president said, but the concept that he introduced came to capture the central stage of strategic thinking and ultimately prompted the return of the Soviet Union to arms control negotiations. In his 23 March speech, the president announced in a televised address:

Consistent with the obligations of the ABM (antiballistic missile) Treaty and recognizing the need for closer consultation with our allies, I'm taking an important first step. I am directing a comprehensive and intensive effort to define a long-range research and development program to begin to achieve our ultimate goal of eliminating the threat posed by strategic nuclear missiles. This could pave the way for arms control measure to eliminate the weapons themselves. We seek neither military superiority nor political advantage. Our only purpose – one all people share – is to search for ways to reduce the danger of nuclear war.

Essentially, what Reagan had set out in his speech was the core of the concept which became known as the Strategic Defence Initiative (SDI) (more popularly referred to as 'Star Wars'). As it was subsequently developed by the administration, SDI became a major programme focused on advanced defensive technologies with the aim of providing a better basis for deterring aggression, improving stability and strengthening the security of the US and its allies. Employing highly advanced new technologies, SDI was geared to developing the possibility of a system of layered defence against ICBM attack. With such a system, ICBMs could be destroyed at different stages of their flight:
1. Some missiles could be destroyed shortly after launch, and with them the warheads would also be destroyed in their unarmed launch state.
2. Missiles surviving the launch stage could be destroyed at the point when warheads are about to be released and dispersed.
3. Released warheads travelling through space on target trajectories would offer the next defensive attack point.

4. Finally, warheads that survived the outer defensive layers would be destroyed in the terminal stage of their ballistic flight.

Under the SDI programme, a number of different technologies were considered for development, including 'direct-energy' weapons (e.g. lasers) and 'kinetic energy' weapons (e.g. satellite-launched guided missiles) (Weinrod, 1985, 3–36). The research and development budget projected by the administration in February 1984 for the five-year period, FY 1985–9, totalled in excess of $43 billion (with approximately half of this total, $21.5 billion, earmarked for the final year, FY 1989). However, not all of this funding reflected research and development which was begun as a result of Reagan's 23 March speech: indeed, of the $1.8 billion requested for FY 1985, only $250 million represented new funding requests subsequent to the president's speech. More spectacularly, over half of the $21.5 billion projected for FY 1989 was in process prior to the SDI announcement (Towell, 1984a; Stares, 1985).

If the SDI research and development programme is vast in budget terms, its strategic significance could make costs pale in comparison. In the first place, SDI represents an attempt to shift away from the strategic primacy of offensive nuclear weapons. Secondly, once deployed, SDI would undercut (perhaps fatally) the doctrine of mutually assured destruction (MAD) which lies at the core of contemporary deterrence. Clearly, once cities and civilian populations can be protected against nuclear attack, then the balance of nuclear threat and counter threat would be broken (Weinrod, 1985, 95–114).

In the circumstances, with the US beginning to move on a variety of SDI fronts (including the testing of anti-satellite ([ASAT]) weapons), it should have come as no surprise that the Soviet Union offered in June 1984 to meet with the US in September at Vienna to discuss opening up negotiations to ban weapons in space. The Reagan administration was, however, anxious to employ the leverage it appeared to enjoy, and its response to accept the Soviet offer indicated the desire for a broader agenda including the question of the stalled Geneva arms control talks. In the event, while Reagan did meet with Soviet Foreign Minister Gromyko at the White House in September, it was not until January 1985 that US–USSR discussions about the resumption of arms talks took place. Meeting with Gromyko on 7 January (only days before Reagan's first term would end), Secretary of State George Shultz agreed the details for a new round of arms negotiations.

The resumption of arms control talks agreed by the US and the USSR was to be based on a merging of the INF and START areas of negotiation, with the addition of the new area of defensive systems (to include SDI, ASAT and ABM systems). Thus the fresh round of arms discussions scheduled to commence in March 1985 at Geneva was to be conducted with a single team of negotiators from each side, with subgroup panels to cover three sets of issues to be dealt with simultaneously: long-range strategic weapons: intermediate-range weapons; and defensive systems. The Reagan administration made determined efforts, however, to withhold the issue of SDI from the new Geneva arms agenda, or at least to maintain a strict separation of the negotiations on offensive and defensive systems. The fact that the US came to accept the inclusion of SDI within a simultaneous (and therefore essentially linked) framework of multiple issues indicated the extent to which the administration needed to get arms control negotiations restarted.

Assessment

Measured in terms of capacity to change America's national priorities to increase substantially the share of resources allocated to defence spending, Ronald Reagan's first four years were enormously successful. In spite of an economic recession in 1981 and 1982 (which added considerably to the pressure on federal spending), and a mushrooming federal budget deficit, the president's determined efforts to protect the defence budget from major cut-backs prevailed. Over its first term in office, the Reagan administration increased spending on defence in real terms at an average annual rate of 8.3%. While Congress made cuts that averaged $18.1 billion from the Reagan defence budget requests for each of the years, FY 1983–5, the fact was that these merely trimmed the requested budget increases: the upward pattern of spending continued.

The massive scale of the administration's defence spending prompted, however, serious questions about the content of its defence efforts. As noted earlier, in Reagan's first year Fallows contended that quantity appeared to be of greater importance than actual content, while Kaufmann argued that the administration's defence requests reflected more the priorities of the various military services than those of the Defence Secretary. To these charges the administration had essentially pleaded *nolo contendere*. In the circumstances of Reagan's first year, this was not altogether unreasonable given the institutional budgetary constraints which work against the capacity of incoming administrations immediately to effect significant changes in spending priorities (especially in defence). Nevertheless, the administration continued to be subjected to such charges throughout its first four years in office.

In 1983, the Reagan achievement of increased defence spending was heavily criticised by George Kuhn for its 'negligible results' in terms of obtaining improvements in force structure, readiness and overall fighting ability. In Kuhn's view, a major cause of this situation was structural:

Unrealistic DoD cost planning and force development decisions contribute directly to the escalation of costs beyond the cpacity of even generous budgets. Official cost projections are typically drastically below the levels needed to achieve stated goals. Whenever a period of increased spending occurs, planners pack the budget with new programs, since low estimates make it appear there is more room in the new budget than is in fact the case. The internal budget pressure generated by cost escalation in the various programs eats up all available funding so that even significantly growing budgets will not cover costs (Kuhn, 1983).

While Kuhn indicated serious structural deficiencies within the Pentagon's budgeting system, he also pointed out that the increasing dependence on sophisticated technology was contributing heavily to greater defence costs (both in procurement and operations). He concluded that the trend was for tactics to be 'driven by technology'. This criticism found some echo within the administration, with Assistant Defense Secretary Lawrence Korb noting in a 1983 address that the increased dependency on advanced electronic equipment seriously raised support costs for weapons systems from an average of 5–7 per cent (for previous, less-advanced systems) to at least 20 per cent of a new weapon's total acquisition cost. There was moreover a very real question, in his view, as to whether the Pentagon had budgeted sufficient support-funding to deal with this growing requirement (Gordon, 1984a).

For all its massive scale, therefore, the Reagan defence budget continued to be assailed for failing to come to terms with one of the president's priorities – military readiness. While more and more money continued to be spent on the procurement of new, more advanced weapons systems, this worked to the detriment of funding for training, spare parts and munitions. This problem was raised within the Defense Department by Assistant Secretary Korb in a memorandum in February, 1984 which warned Defense Secretary Weinberger: 'The stiff competi-tion for resources in the (Defense) Department does leave us with some underfunding of spares procurement in virtually every service, as well as some underfinanced maintenance backlogs that will remain' (Gordon,

1984a). Accordingly, while the administration could point to some improvements (notably in the quality of military personnel, combat training and Air Force and Navy fighter aircraft readiness), the fact was that its overall record on military readiness was 'mixed' to 'poor'.

As for the area of defence strategy, the administration was strongly attacked for its failure to produce any strategy statement in its first year. When it did move to do so in its second year, the result was largely to replicate the strategy of the Carter administration: an administration which it had so severely censured on defence. Indeed, as Huntington noted, 'Apart from the SALT II agreement, no broad military concept or policy of the Carter administration was rejected by the Reagan administration' (Huntington, 1983, 89). The major changes which were effected concerned US policy in dealing with the Soviet Union, with the Reagan strategies of economic warfare and horizontal escalation signalling a tougher, more confrontational stance than that of his predecessor.

At the heart of the expanding Reagan defence programme were the very large procurement programmes required to meet the administration's goal of modernising US military capabilities. These principally included: new strategic bombers (B-1B, and 'Stealth'); Trident submarines; Trident II (D-5) missiles; the MX missile; an increased ship-building programme (to achieve the goal of a 600-ship navy); and development of a survivable strategic C^3I system. Thus Reagan had moved to modernise substantially all three legs (i.e. ground, air and sea-based systems) of the US strategic nuclear triad. However, while there was a very real commitment within the administration to close the so-called 'window of vulnerability' opened up by the modernisation and expansion of Soviet military capabilities, no 'quick fixes' were effected. Worse still were the bungled efforts to obtain Congressional funding for the counterforce system designated to resolve much of the vulnerability problem – the MX missile. By its poor choice of MX basing modes, the administration undercut a great deal of the rationale for MX missile deployment and came close to a total denial of MX funding by the Congress. Significantly, by the end of his first four years, Reagan still had not managed to deploy any of the strategic systems he requested at the start of his term of office.

On arms control, the Reagan approach evidenced a major US policy shift with its demands for sharp reductions in weapons systems. By insisting on reductions rather than limitations (emphasised by the change in nomenclature, with SALT replaced by START), the administration certainly reshaped the arms control agenda. However, events external to the arms control negotiations combined to prevent real progress or agreements from being reached. The frailty of Soviet leaders intruded, with the deaths of Brezhnev and Andropov and the failing health of Chernenko making decision-making within the Kremlin uncertain and cautious. Moreover, the Soviet Union's withdrawal from all arms control negotiations in the Winter of 1983 effectively ended all prospects for arms control in Reagan's first term.

In consequence, Reagan's record of achievement in defense policy and arms control was decidedly mixed as his second term approached. His most impressive achievement was his endeavour to rebuild American military strength by means of an expanded military budget successfully won from Congress in the face of strong opposition. Less successful was his administration's ability to achieve the goals set for itself in such areas as military readiness, dealing with the 'vulnerability' problem, and deployment of new weapons systems.

Given that much still had to be done, the Reagan administration appeared to have created problems for itself as its second term approached. Not least of these was the fact that public support for increasing the defence budget (a factor in gaining Congressional approval of Reagan's defence requests) had vanished. Reagan's success in increasing the defence budget now began to count against him. According to a Harris poll taken in January 1985, whereas in February 1980 71 per cent supported defence increases, in January 1985 only 9 per cent were in favour. With Congress increasingly concerned with the growing federal deficit problem, the defence budget looked to be increasingly difficult to protect.

References and further reading

Brzezinsi, Zbigniew (1983). *Power and Principle: Memoirs of the National Security Adviser, 1977 – 81*, London: Weidenfeld & Nicolson.

Burt, Richard (1982). 'Evolution of the US START Approach', *NATO Review*, September, 1982.

Clark, William P. (1982). 'National Security Strategy', Address given to the Center for Strategic and International Studies, Georgetown University, 21 May 1982.

Cohen, Eliot A. (1985). 'Defense: Strategies Money Can't Buy', *American Spectator*, Feb., pp. 21–4.

Committee on the Present Danger (CPD) (1982). *Is the Reagan Defense Program Adequate?*, Washington, DC: Commitee on the Present Danger, Mar.

Congressional Budget Office (CBO) (1982). *Analysis of the President's Budgetary Proposals for Fiscal Year 1983*, Washington, DC: U.S. Government Printing Office.

Congressional Budget Office (CBO) (1984). *Analysis of Administration Strategic Arms Reduction and Modernisation Proposals*, Washington, DC: US Government Printing Office.

Congressional Budget Office (CBO) (1985). *Analysis of the President's Budgetary Proposals for Fiscal Year 1986*, Washington, DC: US Government Printing Office.

Fallows, James (1981). 'The Great Defense Deception', *New York Review of Books*, 28 May 1981.

Garfinkle, Adam M. (1984). *The Politics of the Nuclear Freeze*, Philadelphia: Foreign Policy Research Institute.

Gordon, Michael R. (1984a). 'Weinberger's War Readiness Claims Spark Controversy within the Pentagon', *National Journal*, pp. 1120–3.

Gordon, Michael R. (1984b). 'Next Time Could be the Last Chance for Foes in Congress to Halt the MX', *National Journal*, pp. 2240–4.

Green, William C. (1982). 'Department of Defense', in R. N. Holwill, ed., *The First Year*, Washington, DC: The Heritage Foundation.

Halloran, Richard (1982). 'Pentagon draws up first strategy for fighting a long nuclear war', *New York Times*, 30 May 1982.

Hoeber, Amoretta M. and Douglas, Joseph D., Jr (1980) 'Soviet Approach to Global Nuclear Conflict', in P. Duignan and A. Rabushka, eds, *The United States in the 1980s*, London: Croom Helm, pp. 445–68.

Huntington, Samuel P. (1983). 'The Defense Policy of the Reagan Administration, 1981–1982', in F. I. Greenstein, ed., *The Reagan Presidency: an Early Assessment*, Baltimore: Johns Hopkins University Press, pp. 82–116.

Iklé, Fred C. (1980). 'Arms Control and National Defense', in P. Duignan and A. Rabushka, eds, *The United States in the 1980s*, London: Croom Helm, pp. 419–44.

Kaufmann, William W. (1981). 'The Defense Budget' in J. A. Pechman, ed., *Setting the National Priorities: the 1982 Budget*, Washington, DC: The Brookings Institution.

Kaufmann, William W. (1982). 'The Defense Budget' in J. A. Pechman, ed., *Setting the National Priorities: the 1983 Budget*, Washington, DC: The Brookings Institution.

Kennedy, Edward M. and Hatfield, Mark D. (1982). *Freeze: How You Can Help Prevent Nuclear War*, New York: Bantam Books.

Korb, Lawrence J. (1981). 'The Foreign and Defense Policies of a Reagan Administration' in W. Valis, ed., *The Future Under President Reagan*, Westport, Conn.: Arlington House, pp. 121–36.

Kuhn, George W. S. (1983). 'Department of Defense: Ending Defense Stagnation' in R. N. Holwill, ed., *Agenda '83*, Washington, DC: The Heritage Foundation.

McCoy, Tidal W. and (ed) Kraemer, Sven. (1981). 'The Department of Defense' in C. L. Heatherley *Mandate for Leadership*, Washington, DC: The Heritage Foundation, pp. 89–162.

McMahan, Jeff (1984). *Reagan and the World: Imperial Policy in the New Cold War*, London: Pluto Press,

Smith, H., Clymer, A., Silk, L., Lindsay, R. and Burt, R. (1981). *Reagan the Man, the President*, Oxford: Pergamon Press.

Spanier, John and Uslaner, Eric M. (1985). *American Foreign Policy Making and the Democratic Dilemmas*, 10th edn, New York: Holt, Rhinehart & Winston.

Stares, Paul (1985). *Space Weapons and US Strategy: Origins and Development*, Washington, DC: The Brookings Institution.

Starr, Richard R. (ed.) (1984). *Arms Control: Myth versus Reality*, Stanford: Hoover Institution Press.

Thompson, E. P. (ed.) (1985). *Star Wars*, Harmondsworth: Penguin Books.

Towell, Pat (1984a). 'Reagan Critics Square off on Space Weaponry', *Congressional Quarterly*, pp. 837–40.

Towell, Pat (1984b). 'MX Survives in Senate as Bush Breaks Tie Vote', *Congressional Quarterly*, pp. 1417–20.

Van Cleave, William R. (1980). 'Quick Fixes to US Strategic Forces', in W. Scott Thompson, ed., *National Security in the 1980s: From Weakness to Strength*, San Francisco: Institute of Contemporary Studies.

Weinberger, Caspar W. (1981). 'The Defence Policy of the Reagan Administration', Address given to the Council on Foreign Relations, New York, 17 June 1981.

Weinberger, Casper W. (1983). *Annual Report of the Secretary of Defense to the Congress, F.Y. 1983*, Washington, DC.

Weinrod, W. Bruce (ed.) (1985). *Assessing Strategic Defense*, Washington, DC: The Heritage Foundation.

Williams, Phil (1984). 'Carter's Defence Policy', in G. M. Abernathy, D. M. Hill and P. Williams, eds, *The Carter Years: The President and Policy Making*, London: Frances Pinter, pp. 84–105.

The Reagan administration and intergovernmental relations: decentralisation and New Federalism

Transformation of the federal system was an important component of the domestic policy agenda of the Reagan administration in 1981. Together with the deregulation of inter-governmental programmes, it represented an ideological commitment to devolve power and responsibilities from the national government to state and local government, reduce government spending (especially by the national government) and lessen governmental interference and restrictions on private enterprise. The administration moved speedily and skilfully in the first half of 1981 to change domestic national priorities. The first major achievement was the passage of the Omnibus Budget Reconciliation Act in August 1981. This legislation reduced domestic spending, and shifted responsibilities from the federal or national level to the states. It led to the first absolute decline in federal spending on grants-in-aid to the states and to local government since the 1950s, and accelerated the slowing down of expenditures by the national government which had begun during the Carter presidency.

The other major reform was the New Federalism programme launched in the President's State of the Union Message in January 1982. Here the president promised 'a major effort to restore American federalism'. His proposal contained three central elements. A programme swap, whereby the states would assume full responsibility for two major welfare programmes (Food Stamps and Aid for Families with Dependent Children) while the national government took full responsibility for Medicaid (medical care for the poor). A 'turning back' of forty-four national grant progammes in education, social services, transportation and community development to the states with, at least initially, the revenues to fund them.

A federal trust fund would enable the states to finance these programmes for four years, allowing them time to decide whether to continue operating the programmes, or alter or even abolish them and direct the money to other progammes.

Together, these two initiatives envisaged 'a radical restructuring of intergovernmental relations' (McKay, 1985, 188), marking 'another round in the seemingly unending quest for an appropriate balance among national, state and local powers and responsibilities' (Sedgwick, 1984, 66). The consequences and implications of these developments in Reagan's first term will be examined here from several perspectives. It is apparent that there is no agreed consensus as to the extent of the changes that may have taken place, and how far the nature of the federal system has been changed by these initiatives, beyond the fact that the role and importance of state governments has been enhanced.

One observer has already concluded that the New Federalism reforms failed because of the Reagan administration's reliance on 'political expediency' and a 'crude decentralist ideology' (McKay, 1985, 202), and others also doubted if any fundamental realignment of domestic policy responsibilities had taken place by 1984, or that the president's commitment to the principles of federalism was as strong as his desire for budget cuts or regulatory relief (Conlan, 1984). Others, however, take a different view, suggesting for example that the first four years of the Reagan administration saw a marked deconcentration of power away from Washington, a devolution of power, programmes and funding, and the deregulation of federal rules and regulations (Leach, 1984). It has also been suggested that the New Federalism proposals of Reagan 'may turn out to be the major sleeper issue of his presidency', thus challenging the conventional wisdom that the Reagan administration succeeded in cutting domestic spending and shifting priorities to defence, but failed to obtain any real results in its federalism initiatives (Nathan and Doolittle, 1984a, 105).

Yet another interpretation suggests a more complex but equally plausible record of achievement in the first term. On the one hand, the radical devolution of programme authority implicit in the specific New Federalism proposals did not gain sufficient support. However, assertion of the general principle produced a devolution of programme implementation and management responsibilities which led to considerable activity by the states, and to major changes in the management of inter-governmental programmes. These changes were much greater than those achieved by previous administrations (Peterson, 1984, 218–19).

What was new about Reagan's New Federalism?

When Reagan came to the White House in 1981 he inherited an inter-governmental system that was complex and often chaotic. Every president since 1968 had attempted to reduce the role of the federal government, yet federal spending on grants-in-aid had continued to grow. Most of the proposals associated with the Reagan administration's New Federalism – grant consolidation, federal aid cuts, regulatory relief, programme trade-offs – were not new ideas. Federal aid as a proportion of state and local government expenditures had actually peaked in 1978. In this sense, the Reagan administration could be said to be running with the tide, not fighting against it.

However, behind the Reagan proposals lay a perception of the federal system rather different from the one which dominated thinking and political action since the 1930s. If anything, it argued for a return to what may be considered to be the original intentions of the federal system, or the first principles of federalism. This meant a return to a view of the states as at least equal partners to the national government with respect to programmes, and as being on balance more efficient, more accountable and more flexible in organising and financing programmes. The actions of the Reagan administration also constituted a more systematic attempt to reduce the financial and administrative obligations of the national government than had occurred for example following the revenue-sharing and other initiatives of the so-called 'new federalism' of the Nixon Republican administration a decade or more earlier.

The first attempts at change were undertaken through the federal budget process, by the increased use of block grants to the states as a means of reducing federal budget expenditures and increasing programme efficiency. This was evident in the proposals made in March 1981 to consolidate eighty five existing categoric federal grant programmes into seven new block grants. It was a deliberate attempt to offload the financial and administrative cost of certain programmes to the states. In the final reconciliation legislation this was amended by Congress to nine block grants incorporating over seventy seven existing categorical programmes. These included programmes in social services, community development, elementary and secondary education and health services. In all instances the states were assigned administrative responsibility, and many states decided to take over responsibility for most of the block grants in this legislation. While Reagan did not get all that he requested, he did achieve a major objective which over time could affect the existing patterns of inter-governmental relations.Even if the principal objective was to cut social spending, the 1981 legislation had several effects. By withdrawing from participation in certain domestic programmes, the national government forced the states to consider their position with respect to the structure and operation of existing welfare programmes, and their relations with local government in maintaining such programmes.

Central also to this development was the view that it was necessary to return to a situation where each level of government has separate and clearly assigned functions and, where possible, its own sources of finance to meet their responsibilities. The new role assigned to the states and localities had both a short-term and a long-term dimension. This involved cutting back on grants by the national government to either the state or local governments, the simplification of grant administration and regulation to allow states more flexibility, and the simplification of the complex work of cooperative activity and regulations that characterised many domestic programmes, especially social welfare policies. The longer-term effect would be to re-establish a separation of the different levels of government, the devolution of responsibilities to governments closer to the people, and in time less public spending throughout government (Benton, 1985).

While the term 'new federalism' was coined more in terms of the proposals made by Reagan in his 1982 State of the Union message, the objectives of the Reagan administration were more firmly established by cuts achieved in the 1981 reconciliation legislation. The effects of these, however, were felt especially hard by the poor, especially the working poor. In the words of one observer 'Reagan's 1981 reconciliation victory was a historic piece of social legislation – not just a spending measure, but a major substantive change in national policies toward the poor' (Nathan, 1983, 61). Deep cuts were also recommended for several domestic programmes in the Reagan budget for 1983, but it was the new New Federalism proposals that were intended as the next stage in the restructuring of inter-governmental relations. These proposals were to be put into effect over seven years and involved initiatives to swap some welfare programmes and to devolve others to the states, as well as creating new procedures for financing these programmes. It is not surprising that the proposals attracted much debate and a good deal of opposition, not just from Democrats in Congress (Sedgwick, 1984), or that the specific proposals were later modified. Debate over the New Federalism proposals, which led ultimately to a failure to achieve legislative change, demonstrated that there was no coherent support for the devolution of programme authority by the national government, but strong support for the devolution of responsibilities for implementing programmes. What the 'new federalism' initiative achieved, in the first Reagan term, was the beginning of a significant shift of management responsibilities to the state governments (McKay, 1982; Peterson, 1984).

The response of state and local government

The initial proposals of Reagan in 1982 were cautiously supported by the state governors, but city mayors were more wary. The welfare swap was seen as a mixed blessing by many governors, who supported the transfer of Medicaid costs to the national government, but would have liked it to keep AFDC and food stamps in exchange for the states assuming costs in other areas such as education. As to the new funding provisions, governors were concerned about the fate of the poorer states, when by 1991 the states would be on their own to raise funds for their programmes or be forced to cut back on services and benefits. These views reflected the problems of the very different financial and other situations of the fifty different states, but the Reagan administration was reluctant to consider some form of long-term revenue adjustment to help equalise financial disparities between states. The major issues raised by the New Federalism proposals were whether they could avoid hurting some states while helping others, while city mayors had mixed feelings about having to become more reliant on state governments for welfare programme funds. The Reagan administration responded to these concerns by dropping the proposal to transfer the food stamp programme to the states, and by seeking to ensure that local governments would be guaranteed the same share of aid from states as they had originally received from direct national grants. Reductions were also made in the 'turnback' proposals, but the legislation was never put before Congress in 1982, and was later essentially abandoned (Williamson, 1983).

In the first term therefore the major impact on inter-governmental relations came from changes which took place through cuts made by the Reagan administration to the federal budget. The changes that affected state and local government involved three types of grant-in-aid programmes – entitlement programmes like Medicaid where payment of benefits is administered by states and localities, operating programmes where the national government provided grants, and capital programmes where again the national government provided grants to states and localities for public projects such as highways. The biggest cuts were made in entitlement programmes, where both funds and eligibility were cut. However, as a result of the restoration of funds by Congress and the replacement of funds by state and local governments, the momentum of the cuts made in 1981 declined over the rest of the first term. The 1981 shift in the direction and administration of domestic policy was important, but it was neither as uniform nor as lasting in most areas, except for welfare, as some observers had predicted. Among other things, the states and localities were in a better position after 1982 to replace aid cuts with their own resources, and assume new responsibilities and pay for them (Ellwood, 1982; Nathan and Doolittle, 1984b; Nathan and Doolittle, 1985). After the 1982 elections, in the face of severe recession, Congress actually passed two new bills which provided funds for jobs in highway, mass transit and other community programmes.

States responded to the changes in entitlement programmes in different ways. These included reductions in the number of recipients in programmes like AFDC, cuts in the costs of treatment, or encouraging the use of less expensive services in Medicaid programmes. State governments were, of course, under the same pressures as the national government to cut taxes and costs, but also to respond to economic difficulties. Peterson has claimed that one of the ironies of these developments was that the most effective way of restraining spending proved to be providing penalties for high expenditures and rewards for spending restraints, a sharing of programme costs and saving that was 'perhaps the purest embodiment of cooperative federalism, an intergovernmental style which the (Reagan) administration in principle had repudiated' (Peterson, 1984, 241). In part this was the result of compromises made with opponents in Congress, and in response to pleas from state politicians.

The effect of increased block grant consolidation differed from state to state and programme to programme. States tended to test programmes in terms of public demand and service need before deciding on how to allocate the reduced grants, whether to restore funds, and which programmes to sustain. Important general factors were the relative ability to stave off immediate cuts, the general financial situation of individual states, and the strength of commitment to programmes by particular states. For example, in big states like California and New York where extensive state-funded health and social service programmes already existed, the cuts or changes in federal block grants proved generally less important than in states with a history of less activity and involvement with such programmes. By 1984 the predicted large decline in services had not become a permanent reality, but there was little evidence of either saving or greater efficiency as a result of the shift of responsibilities to the state and local governments.

Some specific programmes changed more markedly than others. For example, the public service job component of the Comprehensive Employment and Training Act (CETA) programme was eliminated in the 1981 reconciliation act, and in October 1982 CETA was replaced by the Job Training Partnership Act which began a year later. This new programme gave major administrative responsibility to the states, rather than to local governments as under CETA, and emphasised the role of the private sector. However, the rate and nature of the assumption of state control of administration differed considerably, and changes in the nature of the new programme were greater than the way in which states themselves came to administer it.

More states have found it possible to replace federal aid with respect to capital grant programmes. Most states and their localities increased their tax revenues in 1982 and 1983, except for states like California and Massachusetts, constrained respectively by the limitations of Proposition 13 and Proposition 2½ (Davies, 1985). Much of the state action was from necessity rather than desire, but it led to important structural changes in programmes, and the changes varied from state to state. States responded in different ways and for different reasons to the opportunities provided by the policy changes of Reagan's first term. States like New York or Massachusetts have sought to provide the resources to keep certain federal welfare programmes going because they support the objectives of these programmes. Other states like Arizona responded because they shared the decentralisation objectives of the administration, while other states suffering fiscal problems took the opportunity to cut programmes, but few states took the opportunity to 'kill off' programmes. To this extent, state governments proved to be more responsive than many observers predicted in accepting both devolved responsibilities and the need to control the costs of government. The major reservation appears to be to what extent these changes will exacerbate the considerable differences in the financial resources and administrative skills which exist between states, and to what extent local initiatives and cooperation will be stifled rather than encouraged as the changes work themselves out.

The implications of decentralisation

One of the strongest arguments in the 1960s for the greater involvement by the national government in the financing and administrative direction of many new programmes was the inability or unwillingness of many state governments to accept such responsibilities. The pressure nationally by the Reagan administration for a devolution or decentralisation of responsibilites, and the questioning as to whether government at any level should be involved in certain activities, came at a time when state and local governments in general were better organised to accept increased responsibilities, and make programme innovations in their own ways, even if many were also under financial constraints. Certainly many states seemed more capable of absorbing the new administrative obligations, and more flexible and ingenious in finding sufficient funding, than was initially envisaged. In turn, the actual changes occurring up to 1984 were not as great as the rhetoric of the Reagan administration suggested. Nevertheless, intergovernmental relations in 1985 were different from the situation when Reagan was elected. Some of the changes that occurred were already in the pipeline, some occurred with little pressure from the Reagan administration itself, while others followed as a specific response to the actions and the rhetoric.

Nor indeed have the changes all been in one direction. For example, in February 1985, in the case of *Garcia v. San Antonio Metropolitian Transit Co.*, the Supreme Court significantly enhanced the power of the national government to regulate state activities, overruling a 1976 decision that the US Constitution does not permit Congress to extend federal minimum wages and hours standards to state employees. Also, there have been serious arguments put forward that where the national government has 'withdrawn' from programmes by phasing out or reducing financial support, parts of the anticipated budget savings should go into a reserve fund which might be used to help localities where above-average unemployment or poverty is persistent, or to help equalise out the revenue capacity of the states.

Part of the argument of the Reagan administration for shifting control over certain domestic programmes from the national to the state level was the improved quality of state government, and there have been some positive developments here. By 1984, one observer found 'state and local leaders emerging as a new class of governmental entrepreneurs . . . taking the lead in spurring economic development, in continuing health care costs, in rebuilding public facilities and in improving education' (Howard, 1984, 4). The budget cuts made at the national level did not have by 1984 as disruptive an effect on state and local governments as was feared initially. This was in part because the complementary thrust for decentralisation through the New Federalism proposals never materialised. To this extent it cannot be said that the Reagan decentralisation initiatives produced a fundamental realignment of domestic policy responsibilities among the different levels of government by 1984, yet the policy process may now be more responsive to executive-led ideological appeals than was previously supposed.

There are also likely to be mixed consequences in the changes in state and local relationships as block grant devolution gives state governments more control over the allocation and distribution of funds for specific programmes, and the consequent adjustments in priorities and targeting policies that may occur (Ervin, 1985; Pelissero, 1985). The overall impact of decentralisation is more than one of 'moderate, incremental adjustments to the intergovernmental system' (Beam, 1984).

Conclusion

With respect to decentralisation and reshaping intergovernmental relations, while major changes occurred in the first term which will continue to have effects throughout the 1980s, developments were not such as to alter the nature of the federal system irrevocably. This is in part because public attitudes towards decentralisation are ambivalent, as many Americans pay lip service to these ideals but in practice are reluctant to sacrifice the benefits from certain federal programmes. The Reagan administration, in turn, seemed prepared to sacrifice the principles of New Federalism when they conflicted with other strongly held policy objectives. There were also inconsistencies in the rationale behind the Reagan initiatives, in particular over whether the principal reasons for decentralisation were those of economics (saving money), administrative efficiency, or political commitment. Any radical reform of the federal system will be opposed by powerful forces in Washington and in the states. However, the particular nature of the proposals and the reluctance of the Reagan administration to make it a top priority policy, meant that in the end the objective of decentralisation was left to be achieved through the vagaries of budget-cutting and block grants, plus the shifting of grant management to the states and localities.

Given these developments, it is surprising that so much change did take place in intergovernmental relations by 1984. They demonstrate that an ideological appeal by a president can strike a responsive chord, even if the political follow-through is not very systematic. These changes include a significant reversal of the trend towards financial dependence on the national government, and a revival of the ability of the state and local units of government to finance and administer public service programmes according to their own capacity and standards. It is also unlikely that in the immediate future the national government will assume new obligations with respect to social welfare programmes. As Peterson suggests 'the restrictiveness of the federal budget constraint is likely to force state and local governments to retain at least their present allocation of service and financing responsibilities', providing 'a recurring impetus towards further devolution' (Peterson, 1984, 258). The intergovernmental grant structure has become smaller but more flexible, and it is no longer axiomatic that the national government should have or will have the task of producing some measure of equity in the provision of public services or setting uniform standards. It is now more possible for particular states to choose to spend more say on child abuse prevention programmes than on family planning or day care, but the availability of funds to help states with school desegregation for example has diminished.

In many instances the reduction of federal funding has meant a reduction in the services provided by both public and voluntary or non-profit sector programmes. Whether programmes are more efficiently administered as the states have more flexibility is difficult to assess, since much of the reinvigoration of state and local administration has been self-generated, and began before the Reagan initiatives. The major developments in the first term may be simply summarised as an acceleration of the jettisoning of financial and other responsibilities by the national government, and the recognition that state and local governments can and should play a more innovative and activist role in the federal system. Separated rather than shared functions did not become the dominant pattern. It therefore seems likely that, despite change, intergovernmental relations post-Reagan will be as complex and as prone to tension as in the 1970s, even if the states, as partners with each other as well as with national and local units of government, seem set to play a more central role than has been the case for several decades.

References

Beam, D. R. (1984). 'New Federalism, Old Realities: the Reagan Administration and Intergovernmental Reform' in L. M. Salamon and M. S. Lund, eds, *The Reagan Administration and the Governing of America*, Washington DC: The Urban Institute Press.

Benton, J. E. (1985). 'American Federalism's First Principles and Reagan's New Federalism Policies' in D. R. Morgan and J. E. Benton, *Intergovernmental Relations and Public Policy: a Symposium, Policy Studies Journal*, pp. 563–663, 568–75.

Conlan, T. J. (1984). 'Federalism and Competing Values in the Reagan Administration' delivered at 1984 Annual Meeting of APSA, Washington, DC.

Davies, P. J. (1985). 'State and Local Government in a Tax-Cutting Era: the Case of Massachusetts', *Politics*, pp. 28–35.

Ellwood, J. W. (ed.) (1982). *Reductions in U.S. Domestic Spending: How They Affect State and Local Governments*, New Brunswick, NJ: Transaction Books.

Ervin, O. L. (1985). 'The State-Local Partnership and National Objectives: an Examination of the CDBG Small Cities Program', *Policy Studies Journal*, pp. 634–42.

Howard, S. K. (1984). 'De Facto New Federalism', *Intergovernmental Perspective*, p. 4.

Leach, R. H. (1984). 'Federalism and the Constitution: Whither the American States?', *Newsletter*, University of Virginia, Institute of Government, pp. 21–5.

McKay, D. (1982). 'Fiscal Federalism, Professionalism and the Transformation of American State Government', *Public Administration*, pp. 10–22.

McKay, D. (1985). 'Theory and Practice in Public Policy: the Case of the New Federalism', *Political Studies*, pp. 181–202.

Nathan, R. P. (1983). 'The Reagan Presidency in Domestic Affairs' in Fred I. Greenstein, ed., *The Reagan Presidency: an Early Assessment*, Baltimore and London: The Johns Hopkins University Press, pp. 48–81.

Nathan, R. P. and Doolittle, F. C. (1984a). 'The Untold Story of Reagan's New Federalism', *The Public Interest*, pp. 96–105.

Nathan, R. P. and Doolittle, F. C. (1984b). 'Overview: Effects of the Reagan Domestic Program on States and Localities', Woodrow Wilson School, Princeton University: Princeton Urban and Regional Research Center.

Nathan, R. P. and Doolittle, F. C. (1985). 'Federal Grants: Giving and Taking away', *Political Science Quarterly*, pp. 53–74.

Pelissero, J. P. (1985). 'State Revenue Sharing with Large Cities: A Policy Analysis Over Time', *Policy Studies Journal*, pp. 643–52.

Peterson, G. E. (1984). 'Federalism and the States: An Experiment in Decentralization' in J. L. Palmer and I. V. Sawhill, eds, *The Reagan Record*, Cambridge, Mass.: Ballinger, pp. 217–59.

Sedgwick, J. L. (1984). 'The Prospects of "Restoring the Federal Balance"', *Polity*, pp. 66–87.

Williamson, R. S. (1983). 'The 1982 New Federalism Negotiations', *Publius*, pp. 11–32.

Reagan and the social agenda

It is important to remember that the Republican victory of 1980 which put Ronald Reagan in the White House, and Republican senators in charge of the Senate and its standing committees, was seen initially by many observers inside and outside of Washington not merely as marking the beginning of a new electoral realignment in American politics but as the end of the dominance of liberals and liberal values in national policies. The radical right conservative policy agenda and its supporters, which had surfaced (and sunk) in 1964 when led by Goldwater and which was exploited and betrayed by Richard Nixon, now appeared to have a genuine spokesman in the White House.

Alongside the new domestic policy agenda of budget cuts, tax cuts and reform, deregulation, and decentralisation of the federal system, was a social agenda which was an important part of the Republican party platform in 1980. It included issues and attitudes which were strongly held by a coherent group of Republican activists and their spokesmen in Congress, especially in the Senate. As with many other things, this movement was aided by the Carter campaign in 1976 and his presidency. The brief Carter period in office heralded the electoral collapse of liberalism as the dominant public philosophy, and precipitated the emergence of a new national conservatism. In 1976 Carter was the first modern president to be an avowed born-again Christian, and the first to reassert small-town Christian morality as the heart of national political culture. He was also the first Democrat since Roosevelt to cast doubt on the continued virtue of big government in Washington. The Reagan movement had already demonstrated in 1976 that it possessed sufficient support within the Republican party to come close to capturing the nomination from an incumbent president. Its campaign was fuelled by morality, anti-statist attitudes and small-town Christian virtues. Reagan himself gave this religious influence a more politically positive role and force in the campaign, and in his first term as president. He also reached out beyond this religious base, his anti-statism promising freedom from national regulation, and more local control of morals and social behaviour unencumbered by Supreme Court and bureaucratic 'social engineering'. Reagan welded together religious right organisations such as the Moral Majority with more cosmopolitan economic libertarians, plus disenchanted former liberals upset at the excesses of domestic initiatives such as the use of 'affirmative action' programmes and busing to help achieve civil rights and end racial discrimination.

The different elements of this coalition had different priorities in terms of domestic politics, and once Reagan was in the White House they competed for his attention. The more cosmopolitan economic conservatives were keen to see policies effected which removed government regulations on industry and business and lessened government spending and taxing, while the more religious conservatives opposed big government in general but in fact favoured the expansion of governmental power and constitutional authority with respect to moral issues.

The kinds of social issues which concerned the different elements of the Reagan political coalition were set out in the Republican party platform of 1980. It included the enactment of constitutional amendments to forbid abortion and to allow states to permit prayers to be said in state schools, and legislation to provide tax credits for parents who pay to send their children to private schools. The platform also demanded that a specific effort be made to change the composition of the national judiciary, including the Supreme Court, by appointing judges more sympathetic to Republican views. As the platform stated succinctly: 'we will work for the appointment of judges at all levels of the judiciary who respect traditional family values and the sanctity of innocent human life'. Another, more complex, area of social policy which concerned in different ways the several elements of the Reagan coalition was that of civil and equal rights. Here again at issue were decisions of the Supreme Court, but also the actions of the Justice Department in implementing civil rights legislation. How did the Reagan administration in the first term handle these social policy issues? What were the consequences of their actions?

Abortion and the right to life

There were essentially two ways in which the Reagan administration sought, as Reagan put it in his January 1984 State of the Union address, 'positive solutions to the tragedy of abortion'. The first was through a constitutional amendment to outlaw abortion, and thus reverse the decision of the Supreme Court in 1973 in *Roe* v. *Wade*. By that decision the court established the rights of a woman to have an abortion, basing this on an implied right of privacy in the US Constitution. The decision legalising abortion on demand was a controversial one, with important political repercussions in the 1970s (Rubin, 1982). The second strategy was to cut funding for, or eliminate, federal government programmes intended to deter unwanted pregnancies or provide pregnant women with alternatives to abortion.

Throughout the first term, Reagan supported efforts to initiate in Congress a constitutional amendment and legislation on abortion, but by the end of 1984 little had been achieved. The administration was consistent in its rhetoric on the issue, but other policies had priority in terms of trying to persuade Congress to take action. As with other parts of the social agenda, the administration seemed prepared to involve itself with these issues only at the beginning or at the end of the 97th and 98th Congresses.

In 1983, in a 6 to 3 decision in *Akron* v. *Akron Centre for Reproductive Health*, the Court rejected arguments of the Reagan administration to give states and cities more leeway to regulate abortion. Reagan's appointee to the Court, and its first woman, Sandra Day O'Connor, dissented from the decision which effectively reaffirmed the previous position of the Court on the issue. In 1985, however, the Supreme Court agreed to consider another case (*Thornburgh* v. *American College of Obstetricians and Gynecologists*) which provided an opportunity for a new definitive decision by the Court on the abortion issue, perhaps permitting states some opportunity to regulate abortion. The Justice Department filed a brief in this case in support of allowing state and local government some authority.

In 1981 the Reagan administration took direct action by cutting the budget requests for three government programmes. Administration officials claimed that they were unhappy about any government involvement with family planning, reflecting the concern of many of Reagan's supporters about government providing information or services relating to contraception or sex education. Congress rejected two of these cuts, but almost a quarter of the funding for family planning under Title X of the 1970 Public Health Service Act was cut. While funding continued after 1981, despite attempts by the Reagan administration to incorporate this in a health block grant to the states, in 1984 it was below the level of funding in 1979 (*Congressional Quarterly Almanac*, 1984, 465–9).

During Reagan's first term, there were other initiatives to provide alternatives to abortion, but they were not proposed by the administration. They included a proposal by conservative Republican Senator Jeremiah Denton (Alabama) known as the Adolescent Family Life Programme. By 1984 the programme included some fifty-nine demonstration projects to discourage teenagers from risking pregnancy, and those who did become pregnant from having an abortion. Another initiative in 1984 was a modification of Medicaid (the health programme for the poor) to require state government help for first-time pregnant women. The Reagan administration was criticised for opposing abortion and also at the same time some family planning programmes. Officials claimed that the administration was concerned about alternatives to abortion, but believed that such programmes would be administered best by the states through block grants.

A major issue was whether the national government should provide funds to permit abortions for poor women, and by 1984 such funds were available only for abortions to save the life of the pregnant mother. The Supreme Court has upheld funding bans, and by 1984 only 15 states and the District of Columbia provided abortion funding for poor women. By 1984 some seven federal programmes existed to help prevent unwanted pregnancies or provide services to pregnant women, including the two new programmes. The most controversial was the family planning programme under Title X of the 1970 Act mentioned earlier. For fiscal 1982, the Reagan administration proposed a 23 per cent cut in funding which was accepted by Congress, and Reagan made clear his opposition to this programme, which anti-abortion groups such as the American Life Lobby also opposed. In the first term he was unable to end Title X, but it was reorganised in such a way as to reduce its effectiveness. The programme was no longer run by career public health officials, but was put under the control of Marjory Mecklenberg, a deputy assistant secretary at the Department of Health and Human Resources. A political appointee, she was a former president of American Citizens Concerned for Life. In

January 1983, the administration published a regulation requiring that parents be notified if adolescents received prescription contraception through the Title X programme. Later this rule was struck down by two federal district courts.

Efforts in Congress by anti-abortion legislators were affected by a split in the movement between those seeking a constitutional amendment and others seeking legislation. While the administration supported these activities, it gave no real leadership.

School prayer

Despite a variety of efforts by conservatives in Congress, backed sporadically by the Reagan administration, only modest progress was made towards a constitutional amendment to permit organised recited prayers in schools. The culmination came in March 1984 when the Senate rejected a proposed constitutional amendment on school prayer, supporters falling eleven votes short of the required two-thirds majority. However, in July Congress accepted a bill allowing student religious groups to meet before or after school in the same way as other groups. An attempt was made to add a provision requiring schools receiving federal aid to permit students to take part in silent prayer, but it was not accepted. At the beginning of Reagan's second term, the so-called 'silent prayer' issue was due to come before the Supreme Court, who agreed to consider the constitutionality of an Alabama law authorising a moment of silent prayer or meditation at the beginning of school.

The question of voluntary versus organised school prayer became a controversial political issue following two decisions of the Supreme Court in 1962 and 1963. Requiring students to recite a particular prayer daily, and requiring daily Bible readings in state schools, were deemed to violate the separation of church and state provision of the 1st Amendment of the US Constitution. Inside and outside Congress, opponents of the decisions sought throughout the 1960s and 1970s to get a constitutional amendment overturning the decisions, or preventing the federal courts from considering cases concerned with this issue.

In 1981 and 1982 efforts led by conservatives such as Senator Jesse Helms (N. Carolina) to add amendments to appropriations legislation were also defeated, but in 1983 and 1984 Reagan gave the campaign specific support. In his 1983 State of the Union address he made clear his opposition to the Supreme Court rulings, and his support for a constitutional amendment. In February 1985 he spoke on radio about the issue, and in March made a strong speech favouring some form of amendment. Reagan also lobbied several senators prior to the 20 March vote, but failed to persuade some of them to support the prayer amendment.

In April 1984, the Supreme Court reiterated its opposition to organised school prayer by sustaining a lower court decision declaring unconstitutional an Alabama law permitting teachers to lead students willing to pray in prayers at the beginning of class. However, the Reagan administration urged the Court to at least permit silent prayer, and filed a brief supporting the Alabama law on this issue up for consideration in 1985.

A related social issue concerning schools in the first term was that of tax credits for tuition fees for parents sending their children to private or religious schools. This was pressed by the administration, but in 1984, as earlier, while being recommended in the president's budget requests and budget message, it was not accepted by Congress.

The judiciary

In the first term the Reagan administration, principally through appointments to the lower federal courts, began the promised ideological transformation of the federal judiciary.

In 1981 Reagan was able to make history by appointing the first woman, Sandra Day O'Connor, to the Supreme Court, but it is in his second term that he has an unusual opportunity to affect the composition and attitudes of the Supreme Court, since five of the current justices were in their late seventies by 1985. On average they are older than the Court which Roosevelt challenged at the beginning of his second term in 1937. The extent to which Reagan can give the Court a more conservative cast depends on many factors, but it could have an important influence long after he ceases to be president. The policy agenda of a president is affected by the past and current decisions of the courts, especially if that agenda includes controversial social issues. One way therefore in which a president can help himself and his supporters is through his powers of appoinment (Birkby, 1985).

The extent of this influence can be seen by the evidence that by 1987, through filling vacancies and new judicial appointments, Reagan will have appointed a majority of the 750 or so lower federal court judges, effecting a change from a predominantly Democratic to a conservative Republican bench. These lower court judges deal with civil and criminal cases on a continuous basis. In his first term Reagan made over 160 such appointments. During his first two years in office there were certain general characteristics of these appointments. Firstly, they were more partisan than any president since Woodrow Wilson (almost 100 per cent Republicans), and were more likely to have been politically active and to be white than appointees of any of his predecessors since Kennedy. They tended to be high socio-economic status (over 20 per cent were millionaires) and two-thirds of those appointed to the courts of appeal were sitting federal or state judges with prior judicial records (Goldman, 1983).

By the end of the first term, Reagan had appointed seventeen women, including Sandra Day O'Connor, but he made only two black appointments. While eight Hispanics were appointed, three of these were to the traditionally Hispanic court in Puerto Rico. More than half of the female appointments were made in the last year and a half of the first term, after the so-called 'gender gap' had become an issue in the mid-term elections. The number of black appointees was the worst since the 1950s. As to the qualifications of the nominees, the ratings of the Reagan nominees by the American Bar Association show no significant difference in the 'exceptionally well qualified' and 'well qualified' categories in comparison with ratings of appointments made by Carter. One of the private groups active in 'screening' judicial applicants is the Center for Judicial Studies, which is supported by the Moral Majority Foundation and other conservative groups concerned about the social agenda.

There is little doubt, given statements made by Justice Department officials, that the Reagan administration made a systematic effort to appoint conservative judges, who would share Reagan's opposition to Supreme Court decisions on abortion and school prayer, and to busing and affirmative action programmes. By appointing conservative Republicans, Reagan has behaved little differently from previous presidents who held very different political beliefs, and it proved to be one way of assuaging the demands of his more conservative supporters. However, the full impact was not felt immediately, but will be reinforced by Reagan being able to make court appointments until the end of 1988 (Reston, 1985).

That this remains a sensitive issue is reflected in two events which occurred at the beginning of 1985. The first was the resignation of

Rex E. Lee after four years as Solicitor General, the Justice Department official who presents the administration case in the courts. At the beginning of his tenure he was criticised for being too conservative and too political. By the end of four years he was under attack from conservative hard-liners who felt that, despite some successes, he had not pushed hard enough for the administration position on abortion, school prayer, busing and civil rights. The second event was the refusal by the Senate Judiciary Committee in June 1985, to nominate favourably the appointment of William Bradford Reynolds as Associate Attorney General. This followed the long delays in approving the appointment of Edwin Meese, the former White House adviser, as Attorney General. Reynolds had been the head of the civil rights division of the Justice Department, where he had directed the campaign against quotas, affirmative action and busing. The Senate Judiciary Committee decision occurred, despite appeals by Reagan in a national radio speech, when moderate Republicans joined with Democrats to veto approval.

These developments show that, while conservatives were generally disappointed at the extent to which Reagan had been successful in the first term with respect to social agenda issues, this perception was not shared by others. This is in part because there is an important difference between what an administration may achieve through legislative and other formal change, and the changes that can be achieved by holding certain executive positions, through the appointing process, and by virtue of being able to decide how and whether existing policies will be implemented. This latter point is especially important with respect to that part of the social agenda which relates to civil and equal rights.

Civil and equal rights policy

Among the charges made by civil rights groups opposing the Meese nomination in 1984 were that he had helped to shape administration policy with respect to civil and equal rights. It was claimed that he had worked to make the independent and influential Civil Rights Commission more amenable to the views of the president, that he had initiated administration efforts to abolish the Legal Services Corporation, which provided legal services for the poor with respect to civil rights issues, and had been behind an unsuccessful attempt to change government policy denying tax breaks to private schools that discriminated. It was also argued that he had influenced the Justice Department to seek a narrow interpretation of the law which barred sex discrimination in education programmes financed by the national government. This had led to the Supreme Court ruling in 1984 in *Grove City College* v. *Bell* that this ban on sex discrimination applied only to programmes receiving federal aid, not *all* programmes at a school or college.

These were some of the initiatives taken by the Reagan administration in the first term which led many observers to conclude that a deliberate effort was being made to reverse policies encouraging forceful government action through legislation, court decisions and active implementation and enforcement initiatives by the civil rights division of the Department of Justice. Reagan himself was an opponent of the Equal Rights Amendment and of devices such as busing and affirmative action programmes to help minorities in employment and education (Sindler, 1984). His appointee as Attorney General, William French Smith, shared these views, and other officials such as Reynolds, who headed the civil-rights division, were opposed to an activist role by the federal courts or a vigorous enforcement programme by the Justice Department of civil rights legislation.

The Reagan administration in the first term consistently opposed racial discrimination, but argued that government policies should be colour-blind, and that affirmative action and other devices were not. So, attempts were made to reverse or slow down judicial and other efforts to achieve economic or social equality through such programmes. The results were mixed, especially with respect to court decisions.

One early example illustrates this. In the Republican platform and in campaign speeches in 1980 Reagan pledged to reverse an Internal Revenue Service policy denying tax exemptions to private schools who discriminated on the basis of race. In response to demands from Republican members of Congress, in January 1982 the Justice Department asked the US Supreme Court to dismiss suits involving schools facing the loss of their tax-exempt status, while the IRS was ordered to restore tax-exempt status to such educational institutions. These developments led to charges of racism, and the administration then sought to get Congress to make the IRS ruling law, making the policy decision one made by the elected representatives of the people not government bureaucrats. However, in 1983, by an 8 to 1 vote, the Supreme Court rejected the administration's claim that only Congress, and not the IRS, had the power to deny tax exemptions to private schools.

In 1984, however, the Supreme Court, in *Firefighters Local Union No. 1784* v. *Stotts*, did modify its earlier position on the inviolability of affirmative action programmes, asserting that federal judges should not override a valid existing seniority system in order to preserve the jobs of black workers who were hired under an affirmative action plan. The black workers had been hired under the terms of a court order requiring the integration of the fire department in Memphis, Tennessee. Solicitor General Rex Lee, as a friend of the court, supported the city and the seniority system, and immediately after the decision the Justice Department began to review and challenge all anti-discrimination agreements to which the government was a party, and later filed motions in the federal courts to modify affirmative action agreements made by other city police or fire departments. In 1985 the Supreme Court had the opportunity to make a more precise demarcation between permissible and impermissible affirmative action plans, in this instance with respect to school board recruitment of teachers, while the administration threatened to repeal rules setting specific targets for black or other minority employment contracts.

The Reagan administration also gave different signals to liberals and conservatives with respect to the issue of the extension of the Voting Rights Act of 1965. This legislation had been crucial in increasing the registration and voting of blacks in the South in the 1970s. While the administration could not be seen to oppose the extension of this legislation, it did not take the initiative with Congress, and gave unenthusiastic support to a new provision prohibiting state and local officials from employing voting procedures which resulted in discrimination. The administration also discouraged acceptance of a provision requiring federal clearance indefinitely of any changes in voting procedures in districts that discriminated in the past, and got this modified to twenty-five years. In 1982, Congress voted overwhelmingly for the extension and strengthening of the 1965 legislation. Reagan reluctantly signed the bill rather than have his veto overridden. At the same time he visited a Maryland black family who had just received damages after having been the victim of Ku-Klux-Klan harassment. Since the passage of the 1982 extensions the Justice Department has sought to monitor and review lower court interpretations of the new provision regarding voting procedures. In 1980 the Supreme Court ruled that anyone trying to challenge state voting rules had to prove discriminatory intent on the part of state legislators. The 1982 legislation modified this, but the Justice Department tried hard to get from the Supreme Court what it lost in Congress, and in 1985 the Court, on the urging of the Reagan administration and the Solicitor General, agreed to consider a case in North Carolina. Civil rights advocates believe that the court may come to make it more difficult to demonstrate that voting discrimination exists and is intended.

Modest changes in the attitude of the Supreme Court in 1984 suggested that, after re-election, the Reagan administration might get more favourable decisions from the Supreme Court on issues related to the social agenda. After rebuffing administration arguments in the first three years, on matters ranging from abortion to busing and affirmative action, in 1984 the Court found the arguments of Solicitor General Lee and his office more persuasive.

There is little doubt as to the views of the Reagan administration about the value of civil rights legislation and implementation, or of judicial involvement in these areas. In September 1982 the president affirmed that blacks 'would be appreciably better off today' if these and other Great Society reforms had not been initiated. This statement came after the chairman of thirty-two state agencies affiliated to the Civil Rights Commission declared that the president was responsible for a 'dangerous deterioration in the Federal enforcement of civil rights', and after criticism from lawyers that the Justice Department was doing little to encourage desegregation or guarantee minority rights. In the first six months of the Reagan administration, the Civil Rights division of the Justice Department filed only five lawsuits on racial discrimination issues, compared to 24 suits under Nixon in the same period in 1969 (Marable, 1984, 198–202). In June 1983, civil rights activists accused the Reagan administration of fostering racism by its opposition to court-ordered affirmative action programmes and to busing.

The total effect of the actions of the Reagan administration in the first term is not easily measured. Many changes do not have immediate effect, and part of the strategy has been to take no action or to oppose initiatives. Certainly the attitudes and composition of the Civil Rights Commission are very different from a decade ago, and its black chairman Clarence Pendelton is a strong opponent of racial quotas. The concern expressed in 1985 by moderate Republicans following the continued decline in black support for the Republicans, suggests that, if conservatives felt that the Reagan administration had not given such issues sufficient priority in the first term, others in the party believed that it had done more than enough.

Conclusion

Consideration of efforts by the Reaan administration to effect the essentials of the social agenda promised in the Republican platform and in the 1980 campaign, and dear to the hearts of the far-right conservative wing of the Reagan coalition, reveals several distinctive features. The actual actions of the administration to bring about changes were considerable. Individuals were appointed to key positions who shared many of the attitudes of the supporters of the social agenda in Congress. Many changes were achieved indirectly, through administrative action or inaction, through appointments or through efforts as part of a wider attempt to reduce government spending and involvement in certain policy areas. Though the president himself often employed the rhetoric of the Moral Majority, he rarely took the lead in pressing for constitutional amendments or legislation, and when he did it tended to be when other more pressing priorities had been dealt with, or when it was difficult to avoid having to do so. Moreover, Reagan was always careful not to alienate other elements in his coalition or his more moderate supporters in the country, in trying to satisfy the more extreme demands of the religious moralists, and the antipathy of the neoconservatives to the social engineering aspects of the federal government's implementation of civil rights legislation as represented by quota or affirmative action policies (Glazer, 1985). Because the problem of translating intentions into programmes is a difficult one in American politics, the ideological thrust of the Reagan administration and of many of its supporters was always likely to be limited and constrained by other forces, even though many of the issues raised were matters that had also been confronted in the Carter presidency.

However, while the existing social agenda was not one achieved solely by court action, the Reagan administration made a good start in the first term to begin to influence and modify judicial attitudes, and much more may be possible in the second term. Whether Reagan can continue to persuade or satisfy his conservative supporters that administrative and judicial influences may in the end outweigh or at least be as valuable as new legislation or constitutional amendments in forwarding the conservative revolution and making the new social agenda a reality, will become more evident as the events of the second term unfold.

In 1984 the Republican party platform made a pro-life position a condition for appointing federal judges, and in early 1985 Reagan was placed in a dilemma as to his reaction to a rash of 'terrorist' activities by a group known as the 'Army of God' against abortion clinics. Such events suggest that it will become more difficult in the second term for Reagan to keep his conservative support without more concrete efforts to fight for the central objectives of the social agenda. Consideration of issues related to the social agenda illustrates the development within the Republican party of the increasing significance of cultural values and social policy as the new organising issue which may be displacing the old organising issues of social class and economic policy in American politics nationally (Shafer, 1985). How the Reagan administration interprets the re-election mandate in 1984 may in the end determine whether they will try to deliver conservative public policy to the fundamentalist supporters of the religious right or leave this to the less direct, less immediate, but often equally effective consequences of judicial or administrative decisions.

References

Birkby, R. H. (1985). 'The Courts: 40 More Years?' in Michael Nelson, ed., *The Elections of 1984*, Washington DC: Congressional Quarterly Press, pp. 239–56.

Congressional Quarterly Almanac (1984). 98th Congress, 2nd Session, Washington DC: Congressional Quarterly Inc.

Glazer, N. (1985). 'The Social Policy of the Reagan administration: a Review', *The Public Interest*, pp. 76–98.

Goldman, S. (1983). 'Reagan's Appointments at Midterm: Shaping the Bench in His Own Image', *Judicature*, pp. 334–47.

Marable, M. (1984). *Race, Reform and Rebellion: the Second Reconstruction in Black America, 1945 – 1982*, London: Macmillan.

Reston, J. (1985). 'Reaganism Will Endure in the Courts of America', *International Herald Tribune*, 20 Sept., p. 6.

Rubin, E. R. (1982). *Abortion, Politics and the Courts: Roe* v. *Wade and Its Aftermath*, Westport, Conn.: Greenwood Press.

Shafer, B. E. (1985). 'The New *Cultural* Politics', *PS*, pp. 221–31.

Sindler, A. P. (1984). *Equal Opportunity: On the Policy and Politics of Compensatory Racial Preference*, Washington DC: American Enterprise Institute.

10 *John D. Lees*

Environmental deregulation and intelligence-gathering under Reagan – contrasting experiences of policy change

In attempting to evaluate the extent to which the Reagan administration in the first term succeeded in changing the nature and the direction of the national policy agenda, it is useful to consider specific areas in domestic and foreign policy where the Reagan administration was committed to defining and effecting new policy goals and priorities. Examination of the Environmental Protection Agency (EPA) and the Central Intelligence Agency (CIA) reflects the degree to which regulatory reform (especially deregulation) and a more assertive foreign policy were central features of the Republican party platform and the 1980 campaign which led to Reagan's election. Together they illustrate how the 'Reagan revolution', predicated on a radical reassertion of executive authority, combined negative and positive strategies – the domestic policy agenda being principally one of cutting taxes and government spending, and ending unnecessary and costly government regulations, and the foreign policy agenda one of increasing spending on defence and national security, and reasserting the importance of intelligence-gathering in protecting the United States from the threat of international communism. They are examples of executive 'intervention' into already controversial policy areas in the 1970s. On the one hand, the intention was to control and curb EPA activities, define new environmental policy priorities and appoint senior administrators to implement these policies under the watchful eye of the Office of Management and Budget (OMB) rather than Congress, and on the other to protect and defend CIA activities, and give the Director more latitude and legitimacy to implement national security policy, under the watchful eye of the National Security Council rather than the committees on Intelligence in Congress. In their different ways they are yardsticks of the capacity of the Reagan administration to achieve non-incremental or radical policy change.

The EPA and regulatory reform

Following its creation in 1970, EPA developed into one of the largest federal regulatory agencies. It was also one of the most controversial, since the environment was one of the new and major domestic issues of the 1970s, and EPA was given responsibility for a large number of complex and costly laws passed by Congress. Increasingly also EPA became enmeshed in the employment versus environment controversy as the economic decline at the end of the 1970s led business representatives to argue that the costs of complying with a variety of economic regulations retarded industrial expansion and recovery, and increased unemployment. Some of the administrative problems encountered by EPA were the result of Congress giving the agency more statutory responsibilities than it could perform effectively. A combination of too many programmes and often broad discretionary authority made it difficult for EPA to satisfy environmentalists without encountering stiff resistance to their attempts at implementation.

Pressures for regulatory reform were evident well before Reagan's election victory. Some deregulation occurred under Carter, and while he placed committed environmentalists in key EPA positions there was also some attempt to review their activities. The Reagan emphasis on greater executive control and intervention over regulatory decisions was therefore not new; what was new was the scale of the proposed control and intervention (Kraft and Vig, 1984, 416–21).

The policy goals of the Reagan administration regarding environmental issues were part of the broader thrust for regulatory reform as expressed in the creation of a presidential task force on regulatory relief, chaired by Vice-President Bush, to oversee a review of regulatory agencies with the intention of dismantling many federal regulations. This gave substance to pledges in the 1980 Republican party platform, which recognised a government role to maintain a healthy environment but deemed it 'imperative that environmental laws and regulations be reviewed' in terms of whether the benefits justified the costs, and that regulatory procedures be reformed. A transition task force on the environment was appointed to produce reform ideas. It included two former EPA heads, and recommended the re-examination of environmental legislation. The moderate proposals of the task force were later ignored, as the environmental policy agenda became influenced by the attitudes of James G. Watt, soon to become Secretary of the Interior, and other more conservative ideologues. This was reflected clearly in the appointment of Anne Gorsuch (later Burford), a protégé of Watt, as EPA head. The election victory in 1980 fuelled the belief that the Reagan administration had received a mandate for its political agenda, and should move immediately to implement it where possible in areas such as environmental policy.

Hence, despite the fact that public support for environmental protection remained high, the Reagan administration defined new policy priorities for the EPA, and a new strategy for maintaining firm executive control of the agency and its activities. The overall objectives, as set out in the annual reports of the Council on Environmental Quality, were moderate in tone, reflecting a general view that it was necessary to use more efficient and economic techniques in protecting the environment (*Environmental Quality 1982*, 1982). However, to do this required efforts to get the support and approval of Congress to revise or repeal existing legislation, and the major legislative priority in 1981 and 1982 was economic recovery through tax cuts and reductions in federal spending. The strategy adopted instead was one of achieving reform through administrative control. This involved centralising White House control through OMB, appointing leading EPA officials who were loyal and ideologically committed, and cutting the budget requests for the EPA and its programmes and personnel.

The persons appointed to the top positions in EPA in 1981 had similar backgrounds and attitudes. They were recruited primarily from business, often from industries regulated by the EPA. They had little or no experience in Washington DC, but shared a scepticism about many of the EPA programmes they were supposed to administer. Anne Gorsuch had been member of the Colorado House of Representatives (she later married the former House Speaker Robert Burford after he joined Watt in the Interior Department), and a lawyer for the Bell telephone company in Colorado. She was a compromise choice for the top position as Administrator at EPA, put forward by Joseph Coors, who was a member of Reagan's kitchen cabinet and a financer of conservative causes. As a state legislator she took an anti-regulatory line, and gave little support to the state government with respect to undertaking environmental regulation. She had no administrative experience in government at any level, or knowledge of national environmental policy. She had acquired a reputation for shrewdness and abrasiveness, and sought to improve administrative efficiency at EPA and implement effectively the deregulation agenda of the administration (Brownstein and Easton, 1982, 205–8; Lash, 1984, 3–14). She had little influence over the selection of other senior EPA administrators. Among them was Rita Lavelle, a former public relations officer for Cordova Chemical, a subsidiary of a California company Aerojet General, which had a bad pollution record in the state. A friend of White House aide Edwin Meese, she had criticised the implementation of hazardous waste policies. Against Gorsuch's wishes, she was appointed in 1982 as Assistant Administrator for Solid Waste and Emergency Response (Lash, 1984, 42). She had no previous experience in government, like other appointees to EPA who had either been lobbyists or lawyers for companies regulated by EPA.

It did not take long for EPA to begin to feel the effects of the actions of the new administration. Even before Gorsuch and other agency administrators were appointed, President Reagan issued Executive Order 12291 which required cost-benefit analysis to be applied to all major regulations, and gave OMB unprecedented oversight authority to control the regulatory process (*Presidental Control of Agency Rulemaking*, 1981). Also, OMB immediately used large budget and staff cuts to demonstrate its new authority. EPA suffered serious cuts which necessitated major reductions in personnel and in the efforts to implement existing regulations. The Regulatory Relief Task Force also identified many EPA regulations which industry in particular felt were onerous to them, and they were scheduled for review. Very quickly members of Congress became concerned that the budget cuts were being applied just as the agency was beginning to implement many of the laws enacted by Congress, such as the 1976 Resource Conservation and Recovery Act concerned with the disposal of hazardous wastes. This was the beginning of what developed into a major battle between Congress and the environment community, and the Reagan administration, in the guise of its political appointees to EPA, over the hazardous waste policy. In particular, attention centred on the so-called Superfund programme, signed into law by President Carter in December 1980 as a $1.6 billion emergency programme to clean up chemical dumps. Superfund became a catalyst, and an excellent example of the conflict which developed in the first three years of the Reagan administration over attempts to reform the regulatory activities of EPA.

SuperRon meets Superfund

The strengths and weaknesses of the strategy of the Reagan administration towards deregulation are all evident in the issue of Superfund. Ultimately it produced a major confrontation between the president and Congress in 1982 and 1983 which was reminiscent of the Nixon administration, and almost obliterated the very real legislative and other successes achieved by Reagan in 1981. Under Carter, EPA administrators had developed and worked for the Superfund legislation, and saw it as a programme that would get private organisations, where possible, to clean up their own hazardous waste sites, with the government stepping in if necessary and taking immediate emergency action. The Superfund was financed principally through a tax on industry, and there were clauses in the legislation designed to make the clean-up programme cost-effective. The intent was to use the federal government as a last resort, but the nature of the programme assumed a degree of conflict between industry and government, Congress and EPA believing that, on balance, industry would prefer not to spend money on cleaning up hazardous waste sites. The programme thus involved a mixture of cooperation and confrontation with industry.

In 1981 Superfund was under the overall direction of EPA Administrator Anne Gorsuch, and very quickly substantial modifications were made to the agency strategy. It soon became clear that enforcement activities would be minimal, and that the overall policy would be one of cooperation with industry. At the same time as the overall budget of the EPA was being cut by the administration, it was also under pressure not to spend very much federal money on clean-up programmes. Serious problems also surfaced within EPA, as the career administrators tried to work with their new politically appointed leaders. This was made more acute in the case of Superfund and the appointment in 1982 of Rita Lavelle, as she proved to be inept and incapable of understanding the complexities of the programme. Moreover, the combination of a reluctance to use litigation and a preference for private negotiated agreements with industry slowed the pace of actual clean-up, and angered environmentalists. (Vig and Kraft, 1984, 273–91).

The Gorsuch – Lavelle approach was supported by the political appointees at EPA and was consistent with the Reagan administration's anti-regulatory attitudes and policy. The manner in which it was applied at EPA, especially with respect to programmes such as Superfund, soon began to cause hostility and conflict within EPA itself. While most career members of the EPA had a grudging respect for Gorsuch this was not true of Lavelle, but the major failing of both proved to be an incapacity to recognise that the responsibility of an agency head or senior administrator is not solely to implement the priorities of the current administration. Unrest within the professional staff of the agency was exacerbated by evidence of hit-lists of personnel who were marked out for demotion or transfer (Lash, 1984, 29–62). As morale declined, so EPA professional staff began to look for help outside. A senior hazardous waste official complained to the press that the agency was being run by a 'radical group' dedicated to 'stopping the EPA from doing its job as mandated by Congress' (Brownstein and Easton, 1982, 214).

It did not take long before members of Congress, especially Democrats in the House, began to press for a closer look at the EPA's management of the Superfund programme. As early as November 1981, the Subcommittee on Oversight and Investigations of the House Energy and Commerce Committee, which has jurisdiction over most of the EPA's programmes, held hearings on EPA enforcement and administration of Superfund. The committee was chaired by John Dingell from Michigan. Despite being a defender of the automobile industry, and an opponent in the past of stringent pollution control requirements and no obvious friend of environmentalists, Dingell, like other Democrats on the committee, was concerned at the failure of EPA to enforce the law with respect to hazardous wastes and the use of Superfund. His staff collected extensive data on the weakened enforcement programme, aided by leaks from within the EPA itself. The hearings revealed evidence of litigation brought by the Environment Defence Fund to stop the EPA delaying the drawing-up and enforcing of regulations regarding existing hazardous wasteland disposal facilities. Concern was also expressed at the role of OMB in forcing substantial funding cuts of EPA which would weaken the capability of the agency to implement Superfund. Extensive and more critical hearings were held in April

1982, where Democratic members of the sub-committee and former EPA officials cited specific evidence and examples of the decline in the enforcement of the hazardous waste programme (*EPA Enforcement and Administration of Superfund*, 1982). A summary report based on the hearings was very critical of hazardous waste enforcement policy since 1981 (*Hazardous Waste Enforcement*, 1982).

On 17 September 1982, Dingell wrote to Anne Gorsuch requesting that EPA provide his Subcommittee with certain documents relating to the administration of the Superfund legislation, including material on three hazardous waste sites designated for priority action. These requests followed allegations that two senior EPA officials had engaged in misconduct and unethical behaviour in activities relating to one site in particular in California. In essence it was felt that the Superfund programme was being manipulated for political purposes related to the November congressional elections, and that both Gorsuch and Lavelle were involved. In early October, EPA and Department of Justice officials expressed concern about releasing some of the documents requested, and, after the failure of an initial attempt to come to a compromise agreement, the Department of Justice advised EPA to refuse to release some thirty-five documents described as 'enforcement sensitive'. As a result of the refusal to give up documents voluntarily, Gorsuch was served with a subpoena directing her to deliver to the Subcommittee documents concerning several hazardous waste sites. On 30 November 1982, after the elections, President Reagan claimed executive privilege with respect to EPA Superfund files, and directed Gorsuch to withhold documents relating to these sites, and also other Superfund documents subpoenaed by a second House subcommittee, that on Investigations and Oversight of the Committee on Public Works and Transportation. On 14 December 1982, Gorsuch appeared before Dingell's oversight Subcommittee, and refused to provide the documents requested in the subpoena. She stated that her refusal was based on the directive of the president to assert executive privilege. Later the same day, the Subcommittee voted to cite Gorsuch, as EPA Administrator, for contempt of Congress for refusing to provide the subpoenaed documents. A similar pattern of events occurred within the Oversight Subcommittee of the Public Works and Transportation Committee (*EPA Withholding of Superfund Files*, 1982; *Contempt of Congress*, 1982).

While Gorsuch herself was unhappy about withholding the documents, she acceded to the president's instructions. On 16 December, the House voted 259 to 105 to hold her in criminal contempt of Congress, the first such citation of an executive officer by Congress. Some fifty-five House Republicans voted in support of the resolution. The Justice Department immediately filed a court suit against the House, asking that the court block the contempt proceedings. The new Congress which assembled in January 1983 was more sensitive to environmental issues, as Dingell and his subcommittee sought to obtain the documents withheld by the administration. They were angered when Gorsuch refused to allow EPA staff to be interviewed alone by Subcommittee staff, and documents continued to be withheld while negotiations were conducted with administration officials.

At the beginning of February the Justice Department suit against the House was rejected. On 4 February, Gorsuch asked Lavelle to resign or she would be fired. She refused to resign, but on 7 February she was dismissed by the president. It transpired that during this period, in the words of a report of the House Committee on Energy and Commerce, 'members of Rita M. Lavelle's staff engaged in a concerted and comprehensive effort to remove government documents, including Superfund case files, from Ms. Lavelle's desk and office', with her full knowledge and approval (*Investigation of the Environmental Protection Agency*, 1984, 93).

These events led to intense media attention and scrutiny of EPA activities. While the House Public Works and Transportation Subcommittee on Oversight came to an understanding with the EPA involving limited access to documents, Dingell's Subcommittee served a further subpoena on Gorsuch requiring the production of certain specified documents by 10 March. On 9 March Gorsuch resigned, and the White House agreed to drop the claim of executive privilege and to permit the Dingell Subcommittee to see, and under certain circumstances make public, the Superfund documents previously withheld. Many of these documents were delivered a day later. On 21 march, the Dingell Subcommittee held hearings and subpoenaed Rita Lavelle to attend. She did not appear, and documentary evidence was recorded which indicated that she had been in contact with her former employers while she was in charge of the Superfund programme, and had involved herself in a decision regarding a hazardous waste site in California, thus violating assurances given during her Senate confirmation hearings. She had failed to appear at hearings held earlier in February after having been served with a subpoena, but did testify under oath before the Senate Committee on Environment and Public Works and the House Public Works and Transportation Subcommittee on Oversight (*Superfund Oversight*, 1983). On both occasions she testified that she had no access to records concerning her EPA work with respect to Superfund, and that these records were held by EPA. In April the Committee on Energy and Commerce adopted a contempt of Congress resolution against Rita Lavelle, and in May the House voted to prosecute her (*Proceedings Against Rita Lavelle, 1983*). In July a Federal District Court jury acquitted her of this charge, while the contempt of Congress citations against Anne Gorsuch were also dropped after her resignation and the abandonment of the claim of executive privilege by the Reagan administration.

Rita Lavelle's ordeal was not, however, over. In August 1983 she was indicted by a federal grand jury for perjury, obstructing a congressional proceeding and making a false statement on a government matter. These indictments involved her testimony and statements regarding the delaying or hastening of the clean-up of certain sites with political considerations in mind. She was later convicted and in January 1984 was fined, sentenced to six months' imprisonment and five years' probation during which community service was to be performed. Her appeal was rejected, and in September 1985 she was released from prison in California, having served all but three weeks of the six-month sentence.

If Lavelle was abandoned totally by the administration that appointed her, Gorsuch fared little better. It is clear that by early March 1983, the White House wanted her removed, yet two days after her resignation President Reagan claimed that he would never have asked for her resignation, that his administration had a proud record in environmental protection, and he blamed others for having forced her out of government.

So, for most of 1983 and 1984 the Reagan administration was obliged to try to restore morale in EPA, and through the appointment of William Ruckelshaus, who had been EPA's first administrator, to improve the management of programmes such as Superfund, and moderate the overall approach to environmental regulation. However, there is little doubt that the efforts of the federal government to clean up hazardous waste were significantly impaired by the attempts by Gorsuch and Lavelle to fit Superfund into the overall strategy of their administration to reduce regulations. Perhaps more than any other EPA programme Superfund was a specific response to the consequences for environmental quality of an absence of regulations, as many career EPA officials recognised. It was therefore perhaps not entirely accidental that the administration of hazardous waste policy exposed the extent and the limits of the capacity of a new administration to effect major changes in government operations.

The implications of the EPA scandals

Gorsuch and Lavelle were not the only sacrificial lambs. Before the 1984 election season began, James Watt had resigned as Secretary of the Interior, yet at no time did President Reagan accept that the policies that had forced him to make new appointments might need modification. The Reagan administration had been embarrassed but not converted. By the time Ruckelshaus ended his salvage operations, EPA was about the same size as it had been a decade or more before when he had first been in charge, but it had many more responsibilities. Budgetary restrictions imposed by OMB continued to constrain EPA activities, even if internal morale improved. The error of the Reagan administration lay in the appointment of key officials whose overt ideological and political commitment outstripped their administrative competence and skill. As a result, environmental policy was characterised as much by controversy as by lasting change. Reliance on administrative action, rather than changes in legislation, as an instrument for modifying policy, required a more careful choice of experienced administrators, and the judicious handling of career bureaucrats. In this instance, the scandals in 1983 which forced the resignation of Gorsuch and other top EPA officials, and the dismissal of Lavelle, meant that for the remainder of the first term Ruckelshaus was left with the task of restoring the credibility of EPA and improving public trust (Portney, 1984, 172), before handing over in 1985 to a new Administrator.

Attempts to cut the EPA budget lacked sophistication, and encouraged opposition from more than just committed environmentalists. The Reagan administration had the opportunity to make a thorough appraisal of previous environmental policies, and then begin a new approach, but the priorities of cutting spending and providing relief from regulations produced a strategy which served instead to invite controversy and incur opposition from Congress, especially the House.

The Reagan administration's 'intervention' into regulatory policymaking in the first term went far beyond that of previous administrations, and was not confined to environmental policy. Despite the public controversy, it proved to be more successful than it deserved to be. Congress was certainly able to embarrass the administration, though it did not prevent many of the organisational and enforcement changes and the cuts in funding from taking place. The final recommendations of the House Energy and Commerce committee investigations of EPA were also very modest (*Investigation of the Environmental Protection Agency*, 1984, 17–18), and the influence of environmentalists on EPA policies if anything diminished. While the publicity served to remind the Reagan administration that public opinion remained in support of strict environmental protection, especially with respect to cleaning hazardous waste, Reagan himself succeeded in avoiding blame for the EPA scandals.

The administration, despite its errors, was able in the first term to reduce the size and effectiveness of EPA, and to effect changes in priorities and procedures. However, much of this change was achieved by methods which took little account of the need to build public and congressional support, and damaged both the capacity and the inclination of career administrators to regulate efficiently or effectively. Certainly the foundations for a lasting change in environmental policy-making and implementation were not in place by 1985 as Ruckelshaus did little more than restore staff morale and moderate the aggressive politicisation of implementation priorities which, as the Superfund example demonstrated, showed that less regulation does not mean better administration. President Reagan also learned that executive prerogative is best preserved by jettisoning embarrassing subordinates rather than employing doctrines of doubtful constitutionality in defence of the indefensible.

The rejuvenation of the CIA – a new era of trust?

The election of Reagan and a new Republican administration in 1980 was greeted with relief at least at the Central Intelligence Agency. For this agency, unlike many others, the 1970s had been a period in which many of their activities had been subjected to unprecedented press and public scrutiny, and investigation by Congress. The legitimacy of the organisation and its policy role was seriously questioned. In 1974, the first statute to place controls on its intelligence-gathering activities (the Hughes–Ryan amendment, which required the president to approve and report to Congress all important covert actions) was passed. In January 1975, President Ford established the Commission on CIA Activities within the U.S., chaired by Vice-President Nelson Rockefeller, followed almost immediately by the creation of special committees of the House and Senate to investigate American intelligence operations. These were the inevitable fall-out of the Watergate revelations, where the CIA was accused of having been involved in extensive spying and illegal intelligence operations within the United States, and the frustrations of the involvement in the Vietnam war. The amount and nature of the information about CIA activities, obtained by the congressional committees in particular, led to the establishment of permanent select committees on Intelligence in the Senate and House in 1976 and 1977 respectively. This was followed by efforts to draw up a charter to supplement the original 1947 legislation which had created the CIA. While the 1980 Intelligence Oversight Act was something of a compromise measure, it represented a significant move towards greater legislative–executive cooperation in the making of intelligence policy. To the CIA itself the measure was a grim reminder of the determination of many in Congress to establish closer supervision over the intelligence agencies, and to establish a statutory right to be fully and currently informed of intelligence activities (Johnson, 1985; Maass, 1983, 240–6; Clarke and Neveleff, 1984).

Not every development, however, was problematic for the CIA during the Carter presidency. In 1979 two spy scandals and the overthrow of the Shah of Iran, followed by the capture of US embassy officials who were held as hostages, and the Russian invasion of Afghanistan, strengthened CIA arguments that they were being excessively restricted in their efforts to resist Soviet and other subversion. In his January 1980 State of the Union message, President Carter took a noticeably stronger line about the need to resist aggression abroad, adding that it was now necessary to tighten controls over sensitive government information and remove unwarranted restraints on intelligence-gathering. The Reagan nomination by the Republicans in July, and the choice of George Bush, a former Director of the CIA under President Ford, as his running-mate, was also encouraging. Both spoke of the need to strengthen the CIA, and the national intelligence section of the Republican party platform asserted that the Democrats had impaired the efficiency of the

intelligence community and underestimated the strength of the
Soviet Union, and pledged the strengthening of the intelligence
services and counter-intelligence facilities, together with the
improvement of intelligence capabilities for technical and clandestine collection, cogent analysis and covert action.

Expectations of a change in attitude towards intelligence-
gathering were reinforced by the nomination by Reagan of William
J. Casey as CIA Director. Casey was a member of the advisory board
of the National Intelligence Study Center at Georgetown University
in Washington, and had been a member of the Foreign Intelligence
Advisory Board in the Ford administration. He had experience of
international economic affairs, and served as an Undersecretary of
State in Nixon's second term. More pertinently, he had served with
OSS, the predecessor of the CIA, during the Second World War;
hence CIA officers saw him as someone prepared to defend the
agency and restore its morale, and its former status within the
executive branch. Casey was able moreover to establish that he had
direct access to President Reagan. Another apparent bonus was the
capture by the Republicans of the Senate, as it meant that Barry
Goldwater, defeated presidential candidate in 1964 and doyen of the
conservative Republicans, would chair the Senate Intelligence
Committee. Goldwater, though recognising the need to establish
'trust and confidence between the intelligence community and
Congress' also sought to revive the CIA's intelligence-gathering
capacity (Goldwater, 1983, 21). Goldwater preferred a military man
as Director rather than Casey, but went along when Admiral Inman
was made deputy director. He also appointed as staff director of his
committee a former high-ranking CIA officer.

Early in 1981 the White House gave serious consideration to a
draft executive order restoring some of the authority of the CIA to
operate domestically. Following the attempted assassination of
President Reagan, and as the foreign policy rhetoric of the administration became the reality of increased defence expenditures and a
tougher posture towards the Soviet Union and so-called Marxist–
Leninist regimes closer to home such as Cuba and Nicaragua in
Central America, so in December 1981 Reagan issued an executive
order. It replaced and revoked the 1978 order of President Carter,
and expanded the authority of the CIA to engage in foreign
intelligence-gathering, but also allowed the CIA to collect 'significant' foreign intelligence at home and to engage in counter-

intelligence and covert activities within the United States. The order reaffirmed restrictions on activities such as the tacit support of assassinations but, significantly, sought to reassert the role of the National Security Council in determining the scope and scale of CIA activities and ensure that accountability would be as much to the executive as to the new permanent oversight committees of Congress. This was followed in April 1982 by a further executive order tightening up on the procedures for classifying, declassifying and safeguarding national security information (*Compilation of Intelligence Laws and Related Laws and Executive Orders . . .* , 1983).

Two other pieces of legislation reflected both the determination of the Reagan administration to protect the CIA, and the diminution of pressures to keep the activities of the CIA under public scrutiny. The disclosure of the identities of several CIA agents working overseas in various books and publications seeking to inform the American public of the nature of the work of the CIA, led to the murder of a CIA station chief in Athens. Backed by the Reagan administration, who feared that such events damaged the overall effectiveness of covert operations, legislation was passed in 1982 known as the Intelligence Identities Protection Act. This prohibited any intentional disclosures of the identities of covert agents by anyone, and provided penalties in the form of fines or imprisonment. The legislation had implications with respect to the delicate balance between the necessities of national security and constitutional civil liberties, representing an important shift in the balance which took place between 1981 and 1985 (Clarke and Neveleff, 1984, 499–503).

The second piece of legislation represented a victory for the CIA in their efforts to return to a situation where their activities would be protected from disclosure. Hence the agency had long been unhappy at having to comply with the terms of the Freedom of Information Act (FOIA) of 1966, and the 1974 amendments. The Reagan administration, in turn, from the outset encouraged agencies to use internal procedures which might discourage public requests for information, and approved of efforts to amend the legislation to exempt foreign intelligence agencies from its coverage. The legislation applied to the CIA as it did to any other federal agency, but the CIA had particular problems in deciding what portions of records might be disclosed and what was exempt from disclosure. After several attempts to obtain legislation, in October 1984 Reagan signed a bill authorising the CIA director to close certain files from review under the Freedom of Information Act. The legislation was supported by the American Civil Liberties Union, principally because of a belief that the agency would be more prompt as a consequence in releasing files that were not exempt. A more extensive piece of legislation to overhaul the FOIA was not accepted by the House in 1984.

Thus by 1984 the CIA appeared to have shaken free from a range of restrictions and requirements imposed in the 1970s. In contrast to many other agencies, the CIA budget increased, and old veterans and new recruits bolstered the personnel available for intelligence-gathering. However, the real test for the administration in restoring the CIA to its former independence and secrecy of activity was provided by the continued existence of the House and Senate Intelligence committees, and in particular the attitudes of Congress towards the conducting of covert operations by the CIA.

Covert operations, CIA accountability and Central America
One of the major changes in the direction of foreign policy at the outset of the Reagan administration was an emphasis on the need to prevent the export of terrorism and subversion from Cuba through Central America. By the time Reagan took office in 1981, the CIA was convinced that the Sandinista government in Nicaragua had betrayed its nationalist roots and set the country on the path to Marxism–Leninism. In November 1981, Reagan approved a plan for US policy in Central America which included increased military aid to El Salvador and Honduras, and support for paramilitary operations against the Nicaraguan regime.

The issue of covert or paramilitary operations, and so-called 'special activities', was of continuing concern to those seeking to establish more permanent accountability for CIA activities ever since the fiasco of the Bay of Pigs invasion in 1961. It was an important area of consideration for the congressional investigations of the mid-1970s, as was evident in the Hughes–Ryan amendment of 1974 which required the president to approve and report to Congress all important covert actions on the part of the US intelligence agencies, and the Tunney amendment in 1976 which prohibited further funding for covert operations in Angola. The 1980 Intelligence Oversight Act made the Intelligence committees the major recipients of information on covert operations, and set out procedures determining how and under what conditions Congress was to be notified in advance of covert operations. The actions of the Reagan administration and the CIA made the issue of covert operations a central one, and led to demands for further legislation controlling such activities as a result of administration policies towards Central America in general, and Nicaragua in particular (*Congressional Oversight of Covert Activities*, 1984).

One consequence of the 1980 legislation was to legitimise and make part of the public record the conduct of covert operations. The CIA often had problems in the past with respect to covert activities and accountability, one of the disadvantages of counter-insurgency being the difficulty of justifying even to Congress activities that relied on secrecy and public denial of their existence as crucial prerequisites for success. Now, with the support of the administration, a more confident CIA could admit to and justify covert activities, while the need to inform the Intelligence committees in advance that highly sensitive covert actions were to be undertaken made the committees 'captives' of secret information. However, very soon in 1981 there were complaints that briefings on covert action and counterintelligence activities from the CIA under Casey were less satisfactory than in the recent past. Casey himself seemed to have little respect for the Intelligence committees.

The Reagan administration, in turn, developed a policy of clandestine operations against Nicaragua in an attempt to force the Sandinistas to change their policies, or to have them replaced by a government more congenial to the United States. While such covert operations constitute only a small part of the activities and funding of the CIA, they have become a major concern of the Intelligence committees in Congress. As the CIA appeared to be initiating operations to support the contra movement (opponents of the Sandinista government engaged in guerrilla attacks on their own country from bases in Honduras and Costa Rica), so the Intellience committees began to doubt that Casey was complying with the 1980 law and keeping them 'fully and currently' informed about ongoing developments relating to Nicaragua. The executive order of Reagan's in December 1981 gave an executive definition of 'special activities', and strengthened the confidence of the CIA in pursuing covert operations, since it was difficult for the Intelligence committees or Congress to veto such actions except by denying funds.

The House Intelligence committee, chaired by Massachusetts Democrat Edward Boland, became increasingly uneasy in 1982 about developments in Central America, and initiated what, in December 1982, became the Boland Amendment. This amendment to the fiscal 1983 Defence Appropriations bill sought to prohibit the use of CIA or Defence Department funds to provide military equipment, military training or advice, or other support for military activities, to any organisation not part of the armed forces of a country, for the purpose of overthrowing the Nicaraguan government or provoking a military exchange between Nicaragua and Honduras. It was passed by Congress despite assurances by the Reagan administration that they had no intention of overthrowing the Sandinista government or provoking a war with Honduras. Evidence of continued support for anti-Sandinista forces led to further concern in the House, and in April of 1983 Reagan agreed to address both houses of Congress. A secret meeting of the Senate considered the possibility of legislation to restrict covert aid to the contras, and a bill was introduced in the House to prohibit any funds being spent by the CIA or any other government agency in support of military or paramilitary operations in or against Nicaragua by any nation, group or movement.

The president, in his speech to Congress, defended the administration's policy of protecting El Salvador and other friendly Central American nations from the growing Marxist threat emanating from Nicaragua. Members of the House Intelligence Committee visited Central America to investigate intelligence activites, and on their return Democratic and Republican members disagreed over whether the Boland Amendment had been or was being violated. The House finally accepted a revised bill, but it became 'bogged down' in the Senate Intelligence committee. Meanwhile, a Democratic member of the House Intelligence committee, Wyche Fowler from Georgia, introduced a resolution which sought to give Congress a more direct say with respect to covert actions, permitting the Intelligence committees to disapprove major covert actions, and strengthening the conditions which must exist before covert action can be initiated. Extensive hearings were held on the issue in September (*Congressional Oversight of Covert Activities*, 1984), and by this time the administration and the CIA faced severe opposition, especially from the Democratically controlled House of Representatives, to any attempts to organise or finance covert operations in or around Nicaragua. Twice in 1983 the House voted on party lines to suspend aid to the contras. The Senate remained less hostile, and limited funding was made available, but this situation changed in 1984, principally as a result of two revelations.

The first came early in 1984 when Senator Goldwater and other Senate committee members discovered that the CIA had helped anti-Nicaraguan commandos to mine several Nicaraguan harbours. Goldwater, in particular, felt angry and betrayed by the administration, whose policy he had continued to support in the belief, erroneously, that he and his committee were being fully informed. He was especially aggrieved when it transpired that House committee aides had found out about the mining by persistent questioning at CIA briefings. Goldwater, now abandoning his previous opposition to congressional oversight of covert operations, made public a letter he wrote to Casey which in the strongest language charged the administration with violating international law and complained at the failure to inform him about such actions. In early April both the House and Senate voted to condemn the minings and demanded that no US funds be used for such activities. A few days later, Democratic Senator Daniel Moynihan resigned his position as Vice-Chairman of the Intelligence Committee in protest at the 'breach of trust' by the CIA in failing to keep the committee informed. He withdrew this only after receiving firm assurances that the committee would be informed in the future. This followed an apology by Casey, and negotiations between him and committee leaders, which led to a new agreement governing the CIA's reporting about covert operations. The agreement required the CIA to provide information as to specific activities planned as part of 'ongoing covert action operations, as well as regular information on implementation of each ongoing operation' (*Report of Senate Select Committee on Intelligence*, 1985, 15). Casey also agreed a similar procedure with the House committee.

In October 1984, the second revelation which damaged the CIA came when the press reported that in 1983 the CIA had secretly published a manual on psychological operations in guerrilla warfare which had been disseminated to the contras, and which among other things encouraged the killing and kidnapping of government officials. The manual seemed to constitute clear violation of the Boland amendment regarding the overthrow of the Nicaraguan government, and Reagan's executive order prohibiting US intelligence agents from encouraging others to take part in assassinations. It became an election issue briefly, both Mondale and Ferraro demanding some explanation from Reagan. In the final televised debate of the campaign on 21 October, Reagan was asked about the manual. He tried to explain that the CIA had excised certain passages in the manual but some unexpurgated copies had been issued. While the matter did not have any lasting effect in itself, it cast doubts on the capacity of the CIA to learn from its past mistakes, and emphasised the need for stronger controls on their activities by both the executive and Congress (*Psychological Operations in Guerrilla Warfare*, 1985).

The House and Senate Intelligence Committee investigated the affair of the manual, and condemned the CIA's handling of support for the contras but, in the wake of Reagan's re-election victory, did not charge the CIA with deliberately violating the Boland amendment or the executive order. They rightly believed, however, that it would effect congressional attitudes towards presidential requests for financial support for 'the Nicaraguan program'. At the end of 1984 Congress postponed any decision on providing any funds for aid to the contras which might be used by the CIA until February 1985 (*Congressional Quarterly Almanac* 1984, 1985, 86–93). In 1985, despite continued justification by the administration of covert operations in Cambodia, Afghanistan, and Ethiopia, it proved difficult to get anything other than money from Congress for humanitarian aid for the contras which was not to be administered by the CIA.

By the end of the first term, the Central Intelligence Agency, especially with respect to covert activities in Central America, had moved from being an instrument of foreign policy which in 1981 had bipartisan support through a period of partisan challenge by the Democrats to incurring the displeasure of both Republicans and Democrats on the Intelligence committees. It was perhaps fortunate that in 1985 both committees had new chairs and several new members, thus providing a temporary respite. However, the Congress continued to refuse to provide the funds or permit the CIA to provide official aid or support to opponents of the Sandinistas, while supporting financially covert action in support of anti-Soviet rebels in Afghanistan. If the Reagan administration succeeded in restoring the morale and status of the CIA, and reaffirming its position as the major intelligence-gathering agency in the executive, the Congress continued to demonstrate a desire to determine the degree of discretion available to it and to exercise accountability over its actions in areas such as covert operations.

Conclusions

These examples from the first term suggest in their different ways that when executive policymaking is dominated by ideological partisans who have little real respect for congressional attitudes and who rely on public support for the president rather than evidence of support for their policy initiatives, change can be achieved but it is likely to be transient rather than permanent. Neither of these policy areas were dominant issues in the 1984 election, but they remain important bellwethers of the 'success' of the 'new beginning' during Reagan's second term. One evaluation of the policies of the Reagan administration in the whole area of natural resource policy concluded that it is doubtful that they will have a lasting effect, suggesting that the opportunity to reassess past environmental policies and 'lay the groundwork for a new approach to environmental policy' was lost in the first term because of a reliance on the wrong kind of management team, and a preference for administrative action rather than changes in legislation as the method of redirecting policy (Crandall and Portney, 1984, 76–7).

With respect to the EPA in particular, the resignation of Ruckelshaus in late November 1984, suggested that while the agency remained vulnerable to cuts in programme funding, within the EPA itself administration was returning to established procedures. Reagan appointed Lee Thomas, an experienced administrator who had been in charge of the hazardous waste programme after the dismissal of Lavelle, as the new EPA chief, and the major concern for the immediate future was how far the OMB and the White House would support the reauthorisation of, and provide adequate funding for, several environmental laws including Superfund.

The contrasting experiences of the EPA and the CIA illustrate the particular strategy employed by the Reagan administration of appointing at the head of such agencies officials who were primed to transform the internal behaviour of their organisations, together with the use of executive orders to provide the guidelines for new behaviour. The new activities of these agencies, on the one hand the constriction of the enforcement actions of the EPA and on the other the revival and restoration of old practices such as covert actions, incurred the disapproval of Congress, especially the Democratic majority in the House. The final result was a major adjustment, if not a total reversal, of the policy objectives of the administration in the latter part of the first term with respect to these two agencies. One of the first actions of the Senate Committee on Intelligence in 1985 was to consider recommending legislation which would substantially downgrade the role of the CIA director.

The evidence suggests that the Reagan administration tried to educate public opinion to accept a new political consensus about what government in Washington should or should not do. However where public sentiment was lukewarm about changes, as was the case with respect to covert action in Central America or a reduction in efforts to protect or improve the environment, the results were mixed. This is due to a combination of political opposition, and defective strategy on the part of the White House, perhaps the most notable example being the resurrection of executive privilege to thwart House investigations of EPA decision-making. Such setbacks did not lessen the popularity of President Reagan, or affect the success of his re-election efforts in 1984. Nevertheless, they did blunt the thrust of the 'new beginning', and diminished the extent and permanence of the changes sought by the Reagan administration.

References

Brownstein, R. and Easton, N. (1982). *Reagan's Ruling Class: Portraits of the President's Top 100 Officers*, Washington, DC: The Presidential Accountability Group.

Clarke, D. L. and Neveleff, E. L. (1984). 'Secrecy, Foreign Intelligence, and Civil Liberties: Has the Pendulum Swung Too Far?', *Political Science Quarterly*, pp. 493–513.

Congressional Oversight of Covert Activities (1984). Hearings before Permanent Select Committee on Intelligence, House of Representatives, 98th Congress, 1st Session, Washington, DC: US Government Printing Office.

Congressional Quarterly Almanac 1984 (1985). Washington, DC: Congressional Quarterly Inc.

Compilation of Intelligence Laws and Related Laws and Executive Orders of Interest to the National Intelligence Community (1983). House Permanent Select Committee on Intelligence, 98th Congress, 1st Session, Washington, DC: US Government Printing Office.

Contempt of Congress (1982). Report of Committee on Public Works and Transportation, 97th Congress, 2nd Session, Washington, DC: US Government Printing office.

Crandall, R. W. and Portney, P. R. (1984). 'Environmental Policy'. in P. R. Portney, ed., *Natural Resources and the Environment: The Reagan Approach*, Washington, DC: The Urban Institute Press.

Environmental Quality 1982 . 13th Annual Report of the Council on Environmental Quality, Washington, DC: US Government Printing Office.

EPA Enforcement and Administrtion of Superfund (1982). Hearings before Subcommittee on Oversight and Investigations of the House Committee on Energy and Commerce, 97th Congress, 2nd Session, Washington, DC: US Government Printing Office.

EPA Withholding of Superfund Files (1982). Hearings before Subcommittee on Investigations and Oversight of the House Committee on Energy and Commerce, 97th Congress, 2nd Session, Washington, DC: US Government Printing Office.

Goldwater, B. (1983). 'Congress and Intelligence Oversight', *Washington Quarterly*, pp. 16–21.

Hazardous Waste Enforcement (1982). Report of Subcommittee on Investigations and Oversight of the House Committee on Energy and Commerce, 97th Congress, 2nd Session, Washington, DC: US Government Printing Office.

Investigation of the Environmental Protection Agency (1984). Report by the Subcommittee on Oversight and Investigations of House Committee on Energy and Commerce, 98th Congress, 2nd Session, Washington, DC: US Government Printing Office.

Johnson, L. K. (1985). 'Legislative Reform of Intelligence Policy', *Polity*, pp. 549–73.

Kraft, M. E. and Vig, N. J. (1984). 'Environmental Policy in the Reagan Presidency', *Political Science Quarterly*, pp. 415–39.

Lash, J. (1984). *A Season of Spoils: the Reagan Administration's Attack on the Environment*, New York: Pantheon Books.

Maass, A. (1983). *Congress and the Common Good*, New York: Basic Books.

Portney, P. R. (1984). 'Natural Resources and the Environment: More Controversy than Change' in J. L. Palmer and I. V. Sawhill, eds, *The Reagan Record*, Cambridge, Mass.: Ballinger, pp. 141–75.

Presidential Control of Agency Rulemaking (1981). Report for Use of Committee on Energy and Commerce, U.S. House of Representatives, 97th Congress, 1st Session, Washington, DC: US Government Printing Ofice.

Proceedings Against Rita M. Lavelle (1983). Report of the Committee on Energy and Commerce, House of Representatives, Washington, DC: US Government Printing Office.

Psychological Operations in Guerrilla Warfare (1985). New York: Vintage Books.

Report of Senate Select Committee on Intelligence (1985). 98th Congress, 2nd Session, Washington, DC: US Government Printing Office.

Superfund Oversight (1983). Hearing before Senate Committee on Environment and Public Works, 98th Congress, 1st Session, Washington, DC: US Government Printing Office.

Vig, N. J. and Kraft, M. E. (1984). *Environmental Policy in the 1980s: Reagan's New Agenda*, Washington, DC: Congressional Quarterly Inc.

Part 4

The Reagan Revolution: problems and prospects

The first four years in retrospect

The first term of the Reagan presidency was distinctive on several counts. By the end of it, when he was re-elected in a massive personal election victory, Reagan had demonstrated how premature were many of the predictions made in the aftermath of Watergate about the demise of presidential government. Indeed, by the end of 1981 he had shown that an elderly, 'laid-back' chief executive could, through a combination of circumstances and activities – an apparent electoral mandate, the swift initiation of a new legislative programme, partisan and ideological majorities in Congress and the adept massage of public opinion – effect a radical change in public policy (Greenstein, 1983). This was achieved by the development of a political strategy which was congruent with prevailing politial and economic realities and involved swift, perceptible action, a narrowing and simplification of the policy agenda, the centralisation of executive policy management in the Executive Office of the President (and in the Office of Management and Budget in particular), and the special communicating skills of Reagan himself. In order to use the active presidency as the instrument to attain conservative objectives and reorder the priorities of the national government, it was necessary for Reagan to 'adopt the approach of Wilson and Roosevelt' in pursuit of very different objectives (Palmer and Sawhill, 1984, 41).

The successes of 1981 were inevitably too good to last. The year of the president was followed by periods of stalemate and even reversal, as preceding chapters have demonstrated. Yet the consolidation, indeed the affirmation, of the switch from the policies of 'public action', which had its origins in the latter part of the Carter presidency, was achieved in the first year. In fact, as earlier analysis shows, many of the policy initiatives associated with the Reagan administration, such as deregulation, were already evident in embryo during the ill-fated Carter years.

The strategy of the Reagan administration combined short-term and long-term considerations, and was designed to affect all segments of the political activities of the president – the federal bureaucracy, Congress, the judiciary, interest groups and state and local government. It was intended to have an immediate impact – a 'new beginning' which would lay the foundations for a permanent change in the priorities and the obligations of the national government. By 1985 the record was one of qualified success, the gains on balance outweighing the losses, a mixed result which was reflected in the 1984 election results, where Reagan won a second term by a comfortable margin but the Republicans made insufficient gains in the congressional elections to provide the bedrock for a new momentum in 1985 of the kind that occurred in 1981.

The initiatives of 1981 were designed to help to achieve four central objectives – cuts in the federal budget, a stronger defence posture, deregulation and the decentralisation of many domestic programmes, and the reassertion of certain moral values through a series of social reform measures. By the end of the first term fiscal restraint had become a domestic priority, and a defence build-up was well under way, but the pace of deregulation and decentralisation had been erratic, and the implementation of the social agenda of the conservatives became a long-term goal rather than a substantive reality. Moreover, the combination of tax cuts and increased defence spending produced a large and growing federal deficit which cast a shadow over the policy agenda for the second term, requiring more than 'Grace and Growth' (a *blitzkrieg* on the federal bureaucracy, privatisation and economic growth) to reduce.

Nevertheless, Reagan came to the White House with a strong commitment to retrenchment in the public sector, and made substantial changes in the first term. While many of the efforts to change the domestic social policies and priorities of the national government failed to achieve the stated objectives, the cumulative effect of these efforts advanced retrenchment goals significantly. Promises to abolish the Departments of Education and Energy, established by Carter, and efforts to eliminate organisations such as the Appalachian Regional Commission were unfulfilled, but an important and possibly permanent shift in intergovernmental relations and

responsibilities was set in train. For example, many state governments began to play a stronger leadership role in education, welfare
and even environmental policy areas, though in some other areas the
independent authority of the states was limited where they might act
to inhibit the free market. Here and elsewhere, while the capacity of
the national government was reduced its autonomy was asserted in
new or alternative areas. The agenda of the national government was
simplified, and the initial domestic agenda was obtained with speed
and firmness.

The strategy of the administration in 1981 was to take the
initiative in a manner reminiscent of Roosevelt in 1933, though in a
more programmatic manner, with the goal of reducing not rescuing
or enlarging liberalism. If the accomplishments of the first term were
limited, in the first year they included two major pieces of legislation, the Omnibus Budget and Reconciliation Act and the
Economic Recovery Tax Act, which changed the direction of
national economy policy and altered the terms of the debate about
national policy objectives.

The Reagan administration believed that inflation and low
economic growth were the central problems of the American
economy in 1980. This was a common view, although not everyone
was so certain that the economic policies of the 1970s had failed
(Schwarz, 1983). However, the economic strategy employed by
Reagan to deal with the problem comprised a rather messy *mélange*
of the disparate economic approaches of fiscal conservatism (with a
commitment to spending cuts and balanced budgets), monetarism
(stressing control of the money supply), deregulation, and supply-
side theory (holding out the promise of accelerated economic growth
by tax-cutting incentives). Politically, there was a broad consensus
supporting Reagan's goals of faster economic growth, reduced
inflation and unemployment, tax cuts and a balanced budget.
Economically, the administration was riven internally by the various
competing economic schools – each of which was embodied as a
component part of 'Reaganomics' (Stockman, 1986).

The short-term economic resuts of the 1981 Reaganomics package
proved to be disastrous. A sharp recession followed excessively tight
growth in the money supply and this compounded the federal
budget deficit problems flowing from reduced revenues (caused by
the Reagan tax-cutting package and lowered inflation) and increased
defence spending. While the administration adopted mid-course

corrections in 1982 (which included tax increases delicately termed 'revenue enhancements' in deference to Reagan's hostility to raising taxes) and the economy staged a recovery in 1983 and 1984, the longer-term prospects worsened. The federal deficit had turned into a seemingly unstoppable juggernaut, racing to 'a permanent structural deficit in excess of $225 billion per year, or five percent of GNP' (Stockman, 1986, 425).

The economic legacy of the Reagan revolution was thus a burdensome one. While the administration's first term ended with promising economic indicators of low inflation, lowered unemployment and increased growth, these took on a transient appearance in the light of a federal deficit burden whose funding consumed some two-thirds of the nation's net private savings. Considerably dented, the radical right's 'new beginning' with supply-side economics came under censure, but some viewed this as scapegoating for the hotchpotch nature of Reaganomics (Roberts, 1984).

The Reagan administration utilised several organisations in the attempt to impose a lasting influence on the governmental process in Washington. Of greater significance than the much-publicised system of Cabinet Councils were the Office of Management and Budget, with its director David Stockman and its top-down budget strategy, and the Legislative Strategy Group led by senior White House aide Baker and the head of the White House congressional liaison office. The Cabinet contained only five appointees who had been close to Reagan before 1980, and only three (Weinberger, William French Smith and CIA Director Casey) had been linked with Reagan in California. However, the significant innovation was the systematic attempt to appoint to sub-Cabinet positions in departments like-minded officials 'committed to the administration's objectives' and 'willing to challenge career officials in order to incorporate these ideas into the administrative processes' (Nathan, 1984, 375). This was a tactic which was also pursued in terms of ideological commitment when making nominations to the federal judiciary.

The increased politicisation of the OMB and the attempt to centralise the executive budget process worked well in 1981, but was less effective in later years. Also within OMB, the Office of Information and Regulatory Affairs was used to achieve some control over regulatory agencies. This central control aroused hostility and opposition in Congress, as was reflected in the oversight investigations of the EPA. Together with the coherent attempt to appoint political executives who would direct the implementation of policies, it represented a more systematic and legitimate attempt to be at the centre of policy implementation and control the actions of the bureaucracy than that attempted by the Nixon administration. To the extent that this strategy has relied on changing administrative actions or inaction rather than changing statutory authority, it may make it easier for a new administration in the future to reverse policy actions taken. Moreover, the management team chosen to direct the EPA, and to a lesser extent that of the Interior Department, proved to be considerable embarrassments to the Reagan administration in the latter part of the first term. It was therefore not enough to want to effect change, it was also necessary to know how to get it. This showed that career bureaucrats are capable of defending themselves, as the EPA 'whistleblowers' demonstrated, with the help of friends in the divided Congress.

What Reagan achieved with respect to the governmental process in the first term was obtained while his initial popularity remained high. He shifted defence spending patterns, cut taxes and reduced the level of domestic spending. As this popularity and party loyalty and support in Congress declined, so some of the original objectives had to be modified. The Reagan strategy of using the budget in 1981 to achieve specific policy goals was a limited success. It shifted priorities in spending to the military from the civilian sector of the budget, and also shifted many costs from the national government to the state and local or to the private sector. State and local governments received far less federal funding, and there were considerable reductions in the tax burden of corporations and high-income taxpayers. While the revenue available for domestic programmes was reduced, the tax cuts failed to free new money for investment, as much of the savings went into helping the treasury finance the rapidly growing federal deficit.

The Reagan budget initiative had the same goals as that of the Nixon administration. Nixon also had sought to cut welfare and other social programmes, substitute reduced block grants to the states and cities for categorical grants and increase military spending. However, Nixon's use of impoundment and other arbitrary actions failed while Reagan succeeded by acting legally, by winning votes in Congress, and gaining public support. His use of the technical device of reconciliation, ironically part of the legislation passed by Congress in 1974 as a reaction against the Nixon onslaught, was daring but not unconstitutional, and he obtained the necessary spending and tax cuts, and increased military funding, by the skilful manoeuvring of Congress, turning close calls into narrow victories. As Schick suggests, 'the president had a hit list of federal programs, and the budget was his instrument for eliminating them' (Schick, in Ornstein, 1982, 42). The price of this was the budget deficit, and after 1981 it became more and more difficult for Reagan to control the agenda and to obtain the necessary support in Congress (Sinclair, 1985).

The strategies employed and the legislation obtained in the early part of the first term also served to change the balance of interest group influence in Washington, and to modify some of the existing issue networks. Interest groups concerned about federal expenditure or human resources tended to lose influence, while groups supporting moral issues and elements of the social agenda became more vocal and gained more sympathetic attention, especially in the Senate (Peele, 1984). Overall, however, the first term saw if anything an increase in the activities of interest groups, and a shift of some group activity to the states. However, these groups were forced to operate within a policy framework determined by the president's ability to control the political debate. If future administrations also operate in a situation of scarcity then group competition for resources is likely to increase rather than decrease.

Reagan's foreign affairs and defence policy goals were no less dependent on the administration's vigorous budetary strategy. The enormous expansion of the military budget was considered to be crucial for the endeavour to restore the United States to active leadership of the western world and to strengthen the American position in superpower relations with the Soviet Union. While the five-year growth in defence spending won from Congress in 1981 underpinned the hard-line approach in the administration's conduct of US foreign policy (exemplified by Reagan's Central American policy and the Grenada invasion), the effect of this military build-up on the USSR was much less clear. For once, Ronald Reagan suffered a streak of bad luck as his first term dealings with the Soviet Union were punctuated by constant leadership changes in the wake of the deaths of Brezhnev, Andropov and (in 1985) Chernenko. Arms negotiations were thus checked, leaving to his second term the question of how successful the Reagan policy of 'negotiation from a position of strength' would turn out.

More than any other US president, therefore, Reagan has used the federal budget to articulate and pursue his policies. His main success has come domestically in changing the national social policy agenda from problem solving to budget cutting. The focus of Washington, DC, consequently shifted away from developing new federal welfare programmes, creating new government regulatory agencies and from promoting the common good by activist federal intervention. Policy debate now features discussion of privatization, enterprise zones and individual choice in welfare by means of vouchers (in housing and even health care). Ironically, Reagan's unintended economic legacy of a massive federal budget deficit virtually eliminated room for any agenda change for the foreseeable future.

Contributing in large measure to the successes of his administration were the style and persona of Reagan himself. His manner as president in his first term revealed a blend of the political pragmatist and the rigid ideologue which was combined with considered passivity and passionate assertiveness. Thus, in 1981 he could be likened to Franklin Roosevelt or Lyndon Johnson in terms of his ability to galvanize both the country and the Congress behind his agenda. Thereafter, the comparison is with Dwight Eisenhower – with the 1984 campaign conducted somewhat in the manner of Ike's 1956 campaign.

As an individual, Reagan embodies similar characteristics to those attributed to Franklin Roosevelt by Oliver Wendell Holmes: according to Holmes, Roosevelt combined a first-rate political instinct with a second-rate mind. In the case of Reagan, his political instincts for both popular sentiment and attitudes in government are clearly first-rate while his capacity for dealing with detailed and complex argument is considerably less impressive (Dallek, 1984). These characteristics fit well, however, with his operating style in political office. He operates his presidency as a chairman of the board – dealing with the broad contours of the policy agenda, while leaving the programmatic details to his appointees, and acting as chief publicist and salesman for the Reagan agenda. Accordingly, he stands in direct contrast to Jimmy Carter who, as president, was so immersed in programmatic detail that he had little or nothing left over for policy direction. Unlike Carter, Reagan is possessed of considerable ability to communicate effectively with the public: Carter's televised speeches over the heads of members of Congress to lobby the people directly for support of presidential proposals languishing on Capitol Hill carried little of the conviction or persuasive power of Reagan. Yet, despite his deserved reputation as 'the Great Communicator', Reagan's popularity as measured by opinion poll ratings was by no means consistent throughout his first term. In the early/middle part of 1981 he enjoyed approval ratings of 60–70 per cent, but this declined to below 40 per cent by the beginning of 1983 as the recession bit deeply and unemployment peaked. Thereafter, his popularity rose (helped in October 1983 by the support generated for his intervention in Grenada) to around 62 per cent approval by the end of the first four years.

The task confronting Reagan and his administration in January 1981 was that of transforming a brittle mandate into the foundation of real policy change. Initially, there was success in achieving substantive change as well as the generation of personal and symbolic support for the president – if not for all of the policy agenda of the conservative movement he headed. The capacity of the administration to maintain the momentum for substantive changes dissipated considerably between 1982 and 1984 as the traditional checks and balances of the political system struck back. Reagan's re-election win in 1984 poses the question of whether this was simply a mandate for more of the same from him in a symbolic sense if not in substantive terms. If so, Reagan seems set to survive on popularity until January 1989. However, the situation would appear to be much more difficult for whoever succeeds him. In particular, the Democrats have really very little to feel happy about, since they give every appearance of providing neither a real symbolic alternative nor a coherent policy alternative.

What the Reagan presidency shows is that the system can be given a short, sharp shock. Moreover, it raises the intriguing point of whether the system is not as pluralist and opposed to change (for good or ill) as has previously been believed. At the same time, Reagan has not – and perhaps could not – changed the system of politics, but was able merely to shift the focus and emphasis of the policy agenda. However, this latter achievement does in itself represent a significant accomplishment in restoring the leadership role to the White House after the turbulence of the 1970s. In this sense, the second Reagan term may well prove to be more of a transition than a consolidation of the first term – moving towards a new political consensus about what the national government in Washington, DC, should do (setting out a new balance between

government, the business community and the individual) as well as
the limits of what people believe is legitimate for governments.

References

Dallek, R. (1984). *Ronald Reagan: the Politics of Symbolism*, Cambridge,
Mass. and London: Harvard University Press.
Greenstein, F. I., ed. (1983). *The Reagan Presidency: an early Assessment*,
Baltimore: The Johns Hopkins University Press.
Nathan, R. P. (1984). 'Political Administration is Legitimate' in L. M.
Salamon and M. S. Lund, eds, *The Reagan Presidency and the Governing of
America*, Washington, DC: Urban Institute Press.
Ornstein, N. J., ed. (1982). *President and Congress: Assessing Reagan's First
Year*, Washington, DC: American Enterprise Institute for Public Policy
Research.
Palmer, J. L. and Sawhill I. W., eds (1984). *The Reagan Record: an
Assessment of America's Changing Domestic Priorities*, Cambridge, Mass.:
Ballinger.
Peele, G. (1984). *Revival and Reaction: the Right in Contemporary America*,
Oxford: Clarendon Press.
Roberts, P. C. (1984). *The Supply-Side Revolution*, Cambridge, Mass.:
Harvard University Press.
Sinclair, B. (1985). 'Agenda Control and Policy Success: Ronald Reagan and
the 97th House', *Legislative Studies Quarterly*, pp. 291–314.
Schwarz, J. E. (1983). *America's Hidden Success: a Reassessment of Twenty
Years of Public Policy*, New York: W. W. Norton Co.
Stockman, D. A. (1986). *The Triumph of Politics*, New York: Harper &
Row.

The future looking back: Reagan's second term

Even before it began in January 1985, Ronald Reagan's second term marked a significant milestone in contemporary American politics. After Eisenhower's re-election victory over Adlai Stevenson in 1956, only one other president (Richard Nixon in 1972) had succeeded in winning a second term of office. In the wake of the 'imperial presidency' of the Johnson and Nixon years and the 'imperilled presidency' of the later Nixon, Ford and Carter years, Reagan's victory over Mondale in 1984 signalled for many a return to the 'normalcy' of the two-term presidency (Bonafede and Kirschten, 1985). Indeed, throughout the first year and well into the second year of his second term, Reagan appeared to be consolidating this renewed sense of 'normalcy' by registering consistently high levels of job approval ratings in public opinion polls. His second term average of 61 per cent approval even prompted *Time* magazine in the summer of 1986 to feature what it termed the president's 'Yankee Doodle Magic' as its 7 July cover story.

However, Reagan's 'magic' abruptly disappeared in November 1986, with disclosures about deals made by administration officials involving the trading of arms for Iranian-held American hostages and the recycling of the arms sales profits for the funding of contra operations in Nicaragua. Immediately the presiden't job approval ratings plummeted. Decribing the result as the most astonishing reversal in the history of presidential approval polling, the *New York Times* reported a CBS/*New York Times* poll on 1 December which showed a dramatic fall in Reagan's approval rating from 67 per cent to 46 per cent in a single month. Almost overnight, the spectre of the 'imperilled presidency' reappeared to haunt White House politics.

The prospects for swift policy innovation as Reagan's second term got underway were poor for a variety of reasons. First, in common with other second term presidents, he lacked the cushion of a customary 'honeymoon' grace period accorded by Congress to newly-elected presidents: there would be no repeat of Reagan's legislative 'lightning' strikes of 1981. Second, in the 1984 congressional elections Reagan had failed to provide the necessary presidential coat-tails to effect favour-able changes in the composition of Congress (indicating his 1984 mandate to be a personal rather than a policy one). Third, the 1984 elections in any event had featured an absence of genuine tumult and presented little in the way of new policy debate. Finally, the president's 'new beginning' agenda in the first term was a *conservative* agenda explicitly designed to lower public expectations and to re-educate the public away from the belief that problems required the creation of new and bigger federal programmes. The continuation of the 'Reagan Revolution' clearly precluded the resort to innovative programme initiatives.

Accordingly, it came as no surprise that Reagan's second term agenda should essentially comprise a continuance of his first term agenda. In his second Inaugural Address and in his 1985 State of the Union Message, the president enunciated themes which held a familiar ring. On economic and budgetary policy, he proposed a major reform of taxation measures to simplify the tax code and restated proposals for creating urban enterprise zones and for the deregulation of natural gas and banking. He also indicated his support for a constitutional amendment requiring a balanced budget and for a line-item veto to give him presidential power to veto individual items in appropriations bills. On defence policy, he gave priority to maintaining funding for the MX missile and for continued research and development funding for the Strategic Development Initiative (SDI). In the area of foreign policy, his focus was largely on maintaining the provision of US assistance for 'freedom fighters' (especially in Central America and Afghanistan) and on the need for an aid and trade assistance programme for the Third World. Finally, concerning the conservatives' 'social issues' agenda, Reagan called unambiguously for a ban on abortion and for legislation to allow voluntary prayers in public school classrooms. He also urged Congress to ease the 'exclusionary rule' in criminal law cases (which prohibits the use of evidence obtained illegally by the police) and to enact measures allowing the death penalty 'where necessary'.

As his second term began, therefore, Ronald Reagan underlined the essential incompleteness of his 'new beginning' by straddling anew most of the same issues with which he began his presidency. More significantly, major hold-over problems from the first term remained, including: the escalating federal budget deficit; obtaining an arms reduction agreement from a new and dynamic Soviet leadership under Mikhail Gorbachev; the maintenance of economic recovery (to hold down both inflation and unemployment); and, on Capitol Hill, the difficulties involved in putting together bipartisan coalitions (particularly in the House) to gain passage of administration-backed proposals. For Reagan as a second-term president, the difficulties of the task would be compounded over each succeeding month by the need to stave off a growing sense of 'lame duck' status attaching itself to a gradually expiring administration.

The 1984 and 1986 elections and the Reagan agenda

On the face of it, Reagan's presidential election victory in 1984 was even more stunning than his 1980 defeat of Jimmy Carter. Carter was after all an unusual Democratic candidate who stood as much against elements of his party's New Deal/Great Society continuum as for them. His defeat was attributed by many as stemming more from the perceived incompetence of his administration than from the appeal of Reagan's conservative agenda. In contrast, Reagan's 1984 opponent, Walter Mondale, was an orthodox, establishment Democrat – a protégé of the late Hubert Humphrey, he was closely identified with the party's liberal tradition and presented himself as the standard bearer of the New Deal coalition. Reagan's defeat of this standard bearer by the record Electoral College margin of 523 to 13 votes thus appeared to provide emphatic proof of public rejection of liberalism's 'big government' values and of electoral support for the conservative agenda.

Certainly, in terms of total popular votes cast, the margin of Reagan's win was emphatic: Reagan gained 55,451,450 votes compared to a total of 37,574,305 votes for Mondale. However, once more the American voter had engaged in ticket-splitting on a grand scale. While Reagan ran ahead of Mondale in 370 of the 435 Districts of the US House of Representatives, the Democrats retained control of the House with only a slightly reduced margin of 253 to 182 seats over the Republicans. Moreover, the net Republican gain of fourteen seats did little to alter the ideological stripe of the House, since at least four of the defeated Democrats had been consistent supporters of the president's conservative coalition. In the Senate races, the Democrats managed to hold on to thirteen of the fourteen seats they were defending while gaining three Republican-held seats. The Republicans thus retained control of the Senate, but their majority had been reduced by four seats to a margin of 53 to 47 seats (Cohen, 1985). The voters were indicating therefore their desire for continuity in broadly maintaining the status quo at each end of Pennsylvania Avenue. In short, the outcome represented a personal mandate for a popular president from an electorate which held reservations about his policy agenda and which sought to retain congressional checks on his administration (see Nelson, 1985; Ranney, 1985).

The 1984 election results masked, however, the continuance of significant shifts within various segments of the electorate. According to exit polls conducted on election day by the *Los Angeles Times* and by ABC News/*Washington Post*, Reagan's biggest gains came from men (who supported him by a margin of 63 per cent to 37 per cent), easterners (59 percent to 41 per cent), Catholics (59 per cent to 41 per cent), independents (63 per cent to 37 per cent), Republicans (97 per cent to 3 per cent), moderates (59 per cent to 41 per cent), conservatives (82 per cent to 18 per cent), white voters (67 per cent to 33 per cent) – especially southern whites (73 per cent to 27 per cent) and 'born again' white Protestants (80 per cent to 20 per cent). The Democrats did evidence some improvement over their 1980 performance, with Mondale gaining increased levels of support from union voters, blacks, Jews, northern whites, westerners, college educated voters, Democrats and liberals. Much of this increased support came from the return of Democratic voters who had supported the independent candidacy of John Anderson in 1980, with Mondale gaining two out of three former Anderson voters. Reagan's gains confirmed, however, the further demise of the old New Deal coalition; the South was now broadly conforming to national voting patterns, while Catholics were voting in a similar manner to Protestants. More devastating for the future prospects of the Democrats was their very low level of support amongst young voters. Here, a septuagenarian president had opened up a generation gap by gaining the endorsement of under-thirty voters (historically, the most consistent Democratic voting group) by a margin of 60 per cent to 40 per cent (Schneider, 1984).

While Reagan's 1984 mandate was largely personal (as indicated by the widespread ticket-splitting), exit poll data obtained by the *Los Angeles Times* indicated that the president's position on key budgetary and spending issues was broadly supported. Thus some 49 per cent were in favour of cutting federal spending as the best means of dealing with the budget deficit problems. Moreover, those who favoured reductions in government spending supported Reagan over Mondale by the margin of 70 per cent to 21 per cent. On the debit side for Reagan policy was the exit poll finding that some 38 per cent of the electorate wanted reductions in defence spending (Schneider, 1984). However, as Wolfinger has noted, hard evidence about policy preferences from the 1984 elections is too scant to draw any clear picture. He summed up the results with some shrewd advice: 'In short, people who want to know who will run the government should look at election results. Those who want to learn about public opinion should consult a good pollster' (Wolfinger, 1985, 296).

On the question of whether the 1984 elections provided evidence of dealignment (denoting the weakening of party identification as the basis of the voter's decision) or realignment (denoting the switching of one or more groups from partisan identification with one party to the other), the analysts were uncertain or divided (Ginsberg and Shefter, 1985; Lowi, 1985; Wilson, 1985; Wolfinger, 1985). There was a broad measure of agreement that some dealignment is evident, but no sense of certitude about the degree to which Reagan's 1980 and 1984 results signal a Republican realignment. In 1980, Republican conservatives had claimed there had been a realignment comparable (in a mirror-image sense) to that of 1932, but such an analysis was effectively torpedoed by the poor Republican performance in the 1982 congressional races. In 1984, the mixed presidential and congressional election signals prompted no great aspirations about what the 1986 off-year elections might portend.

In 1986, the congressional election results bore the appearance of bad news for the Reagan administration. In the Senate, the Republicans suffered a net loss of 8 seats and surrendered majority control to the Democrats by a margin of 45 to 55 seats. In the House of Representatives there was only minimal change, with the Democrats gaining 5 seats to increase their majority to 258 to 177 seats. Not only had the Republican party suffered losses (with the major casualty being control of the Senate), but these had come in the wake of a major electioneering effort on the part of the president. Reagan had compaigned hard for Republican contenders in twenty-two states, hoping that his massive level of personal popularity would help his party's candidates. However, his lack of success led commentators to suggest a 'reverse teflon' effect: while adversity does not stick to Reagan, neither does his popularity rub off!

When the 1986 election results are put into context, however, they suggest that there was no Reagan factor at work. First, in the Senate the Republicans were always going to be the more vulnerable of the two parties since they held twenty-two of the thirty-four seats open for election. They could win most of these and still lose control of the Senate. In the event, while they lost eight seats, it has been estimated that a switch of only 55,000 votes spread over a handful of states would have seen them retain the Senate. Second, the division of the vote in the congressional and gubernatorial elections was remarkably close, with a narrow overall Democratic margin of 51 per cent to 49 per cent. Third, the 1986 turnout was desperately low, even by off-year election standards; at 37 per cent, it was the second lowest since 1942. Fourth, in the House races the incumbency factor proved decisive: out of 391 incumbents running for re-election, only 6 lost their seats (5 Republicans and a single Democrat). Fifth, once again ticket-splitting was prevalent, with voters splitting the ticket between the parties in almost half of all states featuring both senatorial and gubernatorial contests. Finally, on the basis of the tentative findings from the CBS News/*New York Times* exit poll data, the 1986 votes were not influenced by any particular issues (*Congressional Quarterly*, 1986; *National Journal*, 1986).

The crumb of comfort to be drawn from the 1986 elections for Ronald Reagan was that the results did not indicate any rejection of the Reagan agenda nor any swing back to the Democrats away from the Republicans. However, in terms of advancement of the conservative cause, the outcome of the elections was a considerable disappointment. In some ways, the 1986 results could be viewed as being broadly in line with those of 1984; with the voters in 1986 registering popular support for the president (as measured by his job approval ratings in the opinion polls) while providing a congressional check on him with their House and Senate selections. Unlike 1984, the status quo at each end of Pennsylvania Avenue was not now maintained. For the last two years of his presidency, Ronald Reagan would face a Democratic majority in *both* houses of Congress.

Budget deficits and tax reform

Dominating the first two years of Reagan's second term were the issues of the federal budget deficit and tax reform. Each carried with it considerable implications for the success or failure of Reagan's 'new beginning'. First, while the accelerating level of the federal deficit was in itself problematic (in FY 1985 the budget deficit reached $212 billion – 5.4 % of GNP), the effects of the deficit were both harmful and beneficial. In Reagan's first term, deficit spending had worked to stimulate the economy (assisted by the Federal Reserve's money supply policy holding inflation down and by the influx of foreign investment which held down US interest rates). In the *short term* at least, a significant reduction in the level of the deficit could harm the pace of economic recovery. However, the deficit problem also presented a growing *long term* threat to the nation's economic health; it was an increasing drag on the economy which would produce an eventual reduction in living standards as consequential high interest rates and the burden of government borrowing began to bite. Second, the issue of tax reform similarly carried with it some costs and benefits. Presidential backing for tax reform which redressed the balance in favour of the small taxpayer would enable Reagan to demonstrate that his administration was concerned about fairness and equity. However, the issue also held dangers. By lowering the tax burden on the poor and lower-paid, and by increasing the taxes paid by corporate concerns while at the same time only minimally changing the tax position of middle-income Americans (i.e. those with an annual income in the range of $30,000 – $50,000), the bedrock constituency of support for the Reagan Revolution could well become agitated.

Reagan's preferred line of approach to the deficit problem was to place an institutional barrier against deficit budgeting in Congress by means of a constitutional amendment requiring a balanced federal budget. Essentially, this approach reflected public choice theory which argues that budget deficits are produced in large measure because of the relative freedom possessed by legislators to accommodate their self-interest (or what they hold is in the interest of their individual constituencies) in the budgetary process by log-rolling and bargaining. Since there are no institutional barriers to limit such accommodations and few adverse political consequences for individual legislators (in practice, their re-election prospects may well be enhanced by such behaviour), there are little or no costs immediately incurred in the legislative budgetary process. Public choice theory argues that a proscription against deficit budgeting would change the behaviour of legislators by requiring them to factor into their budgetary considerations the benefits *and* costs of their actions. In effect, a zero-sum framework would be created within which proposals to increase areas of spending would need to be offset by spending cuts elsewhere (Buchanan and Wagner, 1977).

Despite the fact that by the spring of 1985 some 32 states had passed resolutions calling for a constitutional convention to consider a balanced budget amendment, the prospects of gaining the necessary 34 states (two-thirds) under Article V of the Constitution to force Congress to call such a convention were not promising. Moreover, Congress itself was unwilling to take up the president's call to pass a balanced budget amendment or to grant him a line-item veto. However, in the autumn of 1985 a new remedy for the deficits problem emerged: the Gramm–Hollings–Rudman balanced budget bill.

Introduced in September 1985 by two freshman Republican Senators, Phil Gramm (R-Texas) and Warren B. Rudman (R-N.H.), and their more senior Democratic colleague, Sen. Ernest F. Hollings (D-S.C.), the essence of the Gramm–Hollings–Rudman proposal was that it set declining ceilings on the federal deficit for each fiscal year until 1990 or 1991. At the start of each new fiscal year, budget projections would be made by the Office of Management and Budget (OMB) and the Congressional Budget Office (CBO) to determine whether the budget approved by Congress for that year would meet the target deficit ceiling. If it failed to do so, the president would be required to impose spending cuts on new federal spending on a uniform basis over most federal programmes and activities (only social security spending and interest on the national debt would be exempt) by a flat percentage necessary for meeting the deficit ceiling (Wehr, 1985).

For the Reagan administration, there were both advantages and disadvantages to be had from the Gramm–Hollings–Rudman approach. The major advantage was that it embodied the public choice theory benefits which the president sought from a balanced budget constitutional amendment. By imposing a zero-sum condition on the budgeting decisions in Congress, Gramm–Hollings–Rudman would either require spending increases to be offset by spending reductions or additional revenue-raising measures would need to be enacted. In either case, hard choices would be imposed. At the same time, there was a significant disadvantage concerning the defence budget: it would put paid to the president's use of the budget deficit to finance the continuing military build-up. If Reagan failed to agree with the Congress a federal budget which would meet the schedule of deficit reduction, the defence budget would be cut equally with all other programmes to produce the total of spending cuts to meet the targeted deficit ceiling. As Rep. Thomas S. Foley (D-Wash.) strikingly put it on 8 November 1985: 'Gramm–Rudman is about the kidnapping of the only child of the president's official family that he loves (meaning the defence budget), and holding it in a dark basement and sending the president its ear. . . .There will not be an exemption for defense. . . . The president will stand alone on that' (Foley, 1985).

Reflecting congressional concerns about the deficit problem, the Gramm–Hollings–Rudman proposal was quickly passed by the House and the Senate and was signed into law by President Reagan on 12 December, as the Balanced Budget Act of 1985. Under the terms of the new legislation, the federal deficit was timetabled for reduction to zero on the following schedule:

FY 1986 – $171.9 billion
FY 1987 – $144 billion
FY 1988 – $108 billion
FY 1989 – $72 billion
FY 1990 – $36 billion
FY 1991 – zero

A key feature of the 1985 Act was that it established a mechanism for imposing automatic spending cuts ('sequestrations') to keep the budget within the deficit ceiling. This required the OMB and CBO to estimate on the basis of spending projections the amount by which the deficit would exceed the targeted ceiling. Their estimates would be submitted to the General Account Office (GAO) which was charged with the task of making a final determination on the size of any budget ceiling overrun. Based on the GAO's report, the president was required to order sequestrations to reduce the overall budget to meet the stipulated ceiling. These sequestrations (automatic cuts) were to be divided equally, with half of the total to come from the defence budget and the remaining half from non-defence programmes not exempted by the 1985 Act (Rauch, 1986).

However, the mechanism for making automatic cuts was declared unconstitutional by the Supreme Court on 7 July 1986, on the grounds that it violated the separation of powers requirement of the US Constitution. The focus of the decision was on the role of the Comptroller General who, as head of the GAO, had responsibility under the 1985 Act for reviewing (and altering if necessary) the estimates of the OMB and CBO on the level of deficit overrun. It was these estimates which determined the imposition of sequestrations. The court held that since the Comptroller General was subservient to the Congress, it went against the separation of powers principle that he should be delegated what was in essence an executive responsibility. As Chief Justice Warren summed it up in his majority opinion: 'To permit an officer controlled by Congress to execute the law would be . . . to permit a congressional veto' (Rogers and Wermeil, 1986).

The framers of the 1985 Act had anticipated possible difficulties with the automatic cuts procedures, and the legislation therefore provided an alternative mechanism which required both houses of Congress and the president to approve across-the-board spending cuts to stay within deficit ceilings. Accordingly, as a result of the Supreme Court's 1986 decision, a president who was determined to resist defence budget cuts and a Congress equally determined to oppose cuts in social programmes were both now thrown back on the need to make critical budget reductions to comply with the Act's targeted deficit ceilings. Public choice theory thus re-appeared onstage, with a vengeance.

As the mid-point of Reagan's second term beckoned, it became clear that the Gramm–Hollings–Rudman measure was fast becoming more a symbol than a real force for tackling the federal deficit problem. The Act's budgeting deadlines slipped badly in Congress in the latter part of 1986, with various budget stages falling seriously behind the schedule for dealing with the FY 1987 budget. Moreover, there was every indication that the president and Congress were engaging in expenditure postponements and various budget accounting practices which would effectively put off critical programme-cutting decisions. Hard choices, as ever, were difficult to make.

The issue of radical tax reform was also the focal point of difficult political choices. The vast multiplicity of tax exemptions, deductions, loopholes and preferences in the US Tax Code provided in itself sufficient explanation to account for the fact that the last major overhaul of the tax system came during Eisenhower's first term as president. The fact was that tax reform stirred up a hornet's nest of special interests, each committed to defence of its individual tax breaks. In spite of this, Reagan declared his commitment to reform in his Economic Report to Congress on 5 February 1985: 'Our tax system needs basic reform. It is extraordinarily complicated; it leads to substantial economic inefficiency; and it is widely perceived to be unfair . . . . (We need) a program that will increase fairness, and stimulate future savings, investment, and growth.'

The administration had done some prior development work on tax reform with a Treasury Department report to the president in November 1984 entitled 'Tax Reform for Fairness, Simplicity and Economic Growth'. Working within a presidentially imposed condition that reform of the tax system should be 'revenue neutral' (i.e. should not increase or reduce the total revenues under the existing tax code), the Treasury report proposed that personal income should be taxed on a 'flat tax' basis, with three rates at 15, 25 and 35 %, and that overall taxation on individual income be reduced by an average of 8.5 %. To compensate for this, total *revenues* from corporate taxation would be raised. In the corporate sector, it was proposed to abolish investment tax credit and to decrease the benefits from asset depreciation; as a quid pro quo for these changes corporate tax *rates* should be lowered from 46 to 33% (Clark, 1984).

The Treasury Department's flat tax plan was in large measure similar to earlier proposals developed by Democratic Senators Bill Bradley (D-N.J.) and Richard A. Gephardt (D-Mo.) and by two Republicans, Sen. Robert W. Kasten (R-Wi.) and Rep. Jack F. Kemp (R-N.Y.). Given the broad array of vested interests opposed to any major reform of the tax system, the existence of the Bradley–Gephardt and Kasten–Kemp proposals respectively on the left and right of the Reagan administration presaged necessary coalition support for any Reagan reform endeavour.

The Reagan reform proposals were announced on 28 May 1985, and were broadly in line with the tax plan measures previously set out in the Treasury Department report, with a flat tax for individuals set at three rates of 15, 25 and 35 per cent. The major benefit in personal taxation reform would be given to individuals in the lower income brackets – a point for which the administration was given credit by several welfare groups (Clark, 1985).

After intensive lobbying in both the House and the Senate by all kinds of lobbyists, and after strong opposition to the reform measure by House Republicans (who were concerned about the detrimental effects of reform on their support constituencies), agreement was reached on a final reform package in September 1986. The measure signed into law as the Tax Reform Act of 1986 by the president on 28 September abolished fourteen rates of personal taxation and replaced these with a flat tax set at two rates, 15 and 28 per cent. Significantly, Reagan's goal of achieving simplification of the tax system on a 'revenue neutral' basis had been accommodated: under the 1986 Act, the tax burden on individuals would be reduced by a total of $121.9 billion over the five-year period FY 1987–91 while over the same period corporate taxes would increase by $120.3 billion (Clark and Cohen, 1986; Shanahan, 1986).

The 1986 Tax Reform Act was a major legislative landmark in Reagan's second term. Not only did it redeem his personal pledges for reform and simplification of the tax system, it also made it more difficult to find easy ways of increasing taxes. By eliminating at a stroke a broad swathe of tax loopholes, concessions, deductions and exemptions, the 1986 measure effectively removed the hidden means by which revenues could be raised. As the historical record shows, Congress had become decidedly adept at avoiding direct tax rate increases – preferring instead to resort to the device of withdrawing one or more of a variety of exemptions and concessions to raise revenues. With the 1986 reform legislation, President Reagan's position of opposition to tax increases appeared, therefore, to have been considerably strengthened.

Foreign policy, defence and arms control

Increased defence spending was the foundation on which Reagan had endeavoured to build a 'new beginning' in US foreign policy during his first term. As Table 12.1 indicates, his success in obtaining defence budget increases on a large scale was remarkable. But, after several years of growth, the mood in Congress began to swing against further increases. Indeed, in the fiscal years FY 1983–5, Congress moved to impose cuts which averaged $18.1 billion from each of the administration's annual defence requests. Accordingly, Reagan's prospects for maintaining the pace of defence budget expansion in his second term were considered poor.

Table 12.1:   Defence Budget Authority, FY 1981–85

FY	Budget authority granted (current dollars, totals expressed in billions)	Annual real increase
1981	180	12·7
1982	217	12·6
1983	245	8·4
1986	265	4·8
1987	292	4·8

Source: House Armed Services Committee.

However, few were prepared for the extent of defence cuts imposed by Congress for FY 1986 and FY 1987. In 1985, Reagan's request for $313.7 billion in defence budget authority for FY 1986 was reduced by Congress to $297.4 billion. This was bad news for the administration, but worse was to come with the first application of the 1985 Balanced Budget Act. In January 1986, the Defense Department was required to find cuts totalling $13.8 billion from its FY 1986 budget authority to provide the defence budget's 50 per cent share of automatic spending cuts imposed to meet the target deficit ceiling for FY 1986. The result produced a net total of $283.6 billion in FY 1986 defence budget authority, which was $9 billion less than the $292.6 billion granted by Congress for FY 1985. Thus, for the first time since the early 1970s, the defence budget showed a decline in absolute terms (Towell, 1985, 1986a; Morrison, 1985).

In February 1986, the administration requested $320.3 billion in defence budget authority for FY 1987 – an increase of 8 per cent in real terms over the final total granted for FY 1986. Despite a nationally televised presidential address lobbying public support for increased defence spending, Congress paid little heed and in October granted the reduced total of $292 billion for FY 1987. While this represented a dollar increase over the previous year's total, in real terms it was a decrease. More to the point, at $292 billion the FY 1987 budget authority was below the $292.6 billion approved by Congress two years earlier for FY 1985.

Congress had therefore effectively halted the future expansion of defence budget. Yet, while the upward trend of defence budget authority had been checked, increased defence *spending* (budget outlays) had not immediately been stemmed. In the defence sector, the multi-year nature of procurement and construction programmes typically builds up a 'backlog' of monies which have been authorised (by budget authority) but not yet expended (as budget outlays). It has been calculated that even if Congress had approved zero dollars in FY 1987 defence budget authority, the Department of Defense would still have in hand a total of $194.8 billion in unspent budget authority from prior years, with $113.6 billion of this committed for outlays in FY 1987 (Epstein, 1986). In consequence, almost regardless of any action Congress might take on defence budgets in his second term, Reagan was assured of success in locking the United States into a substantial military build-up extending to the end of the 1980s.

Less successful were the president's second term endeavours in the area of arms control. In November 1985 he held his first face-to-face meeting with a Soviet leader when he held a three-day summit with Mikhail Gorbachev at Geneva. While the meetings failed to produce any concrete accord, the two leaders pledged to speed up the Geneva arms control talks. In particular, they identified two areas for possible early agreement: making a 50 per cent reduction in the nuclear weapons held by each side; and, effecting interim cuts in intermediate-range forces (INF) in Europe. Significantly, Gorbachev reiterated Soviet opposition to the continuance of Reagan's Strategic Defence Initiative (SDI). Finally, the Geneva summit was to be followed by exchange visits by the two leaders; Gorbachev would come to the United States in 1986, with Reagan visiting Moscow in 1987.

In the absence of subsequent progress in the forum of the Geneva arms talks process, the two leaders met again in October 1986 at Reykjavik, Iceland, following a surprise invitation for discussions from Gorbachev to Reagan. While the Gorbachev entourage went to Iceland with a prepared and detailed agenda of arms reduction proposals, the Reagan team came relatively unprepared in anticipation of a preparatory 'pre-summit' to set up the subsequent agenda for Gorbachev's US visit. In the event, the Gorbachev–Reagan talks dealt from the outset with major issues: proposals for substantial cuts in both strategic nuclear weapons and INF deployment; consideration of a comprehensive test ban agreement; and, extensions to the provisions of the 1972 anti-ballistic missile (ABM) treaty including restricting SDI research to laboratory work. Unable to accept Soviet insistence on restricting SDI development to laboratory research, Reagan offered a counter proposal on day two: the 1972 ABM Treaty would be complied with by both sides for 5 years; strategic nuclear weapons would be reduced on both sides by 50 per cent; after 5 years, all remaining offensive ballistic missiles from each side's nuclear arsenal would be dismantled over a further 5-year period; during the entire 10-year period, each side would be free to engage in research, development and testing of ABM systems (including SDI); only at the end of the 10-year period would deployment of ABM/SDI be permitted. Predictably, the talks ended without agreement, with Gorbachev refusing to accept any proposals which would permit the substantial development of SDI to deployment stage (Jackson *et al.*, 1986).

Although the Reykjavik talks ended in impasse over the development of SDI, progress was made in some important areas. First, both sides worked out a formula for effecting 50 per cent reductions in the strategic nuclear arsenals of each side over a 5-year period. Second, agreement was established on major reductions of INF weapons: the Soviet total of longer-range INF missiles would be cut back from 1400 to a tight limit of 100 missiles world-wide imposed on each side. From the perspective of the Reagan administration, the ending of talks at Reykjavik did not shut the door on future progress in achieving arms reductions. The items for proposed agreement would be put to the Geneva negotiations process. However, the SDI stumbling block remained: Reagan was committed to the concept of a defensive shield against nuclear weapons and refused to view it as a negotiating 'bargaining chip'. Gorbachev was equally adamant that no significant arms reductions were possible without considerable modification of the Reagan position on SDI. Realistically, at the mid-point of his second term, Reagan's prospects for concluding a substantive arms reduction agreement with the Soviet Union appeared to be dwindling fast.

On the broader foreign policy front, the administration came under considerable challenge in several key areas during the first two years of Reagan's second term. First, international terrorism tested the mettle of the president's firmly stated resolve to meet terrorism with 'swift and effective retribution'. Despite being made to look helpless over the TWA aircraft hijacked to Beirut by Islamic Jihad in June 1985, he acted with decisiveness in January and April 1986 to punish Libya for its assistance and comfort to the perpetrators of various acts of terrorism: in December, at Rome and Vienna international airports and, in April, at a West Berlin nightclub frequented by US servicemen (Morrison, 1986). Commenting in a nationally televised address, after combined operations by American air and naval forces struck at Libyan targets on 14 April, the president declared: 'I warned that there should be no place on Earth where terrorists can rest and train and practice their deadly skills. I meant it. I said that we would act . . . alone if necessary to ensure that terrorists have no sanctuary anywhere. Tonight, we have.'

Second, the credibility of the Reagan Doctrine appeared to be seriously at risk in February 1986, as the Marcos regime in the Philippines desperately sought to cling to power in the face of adverse ballot box results. In spite of clear indications of over-whelming election fraud by the Marcos campaign, President Reagan initially discounted reports of such fraud and implied that President Marcos' election opponent, Mrs Corazon Aquino, should accept the outcome even if it were corrupt. Given the stress on freedom, self-determination and democracy that lay at the core of the Reagan Doctrine, the president was clearly in danger of undermining his own principles by his apparent support of Marcos. However, he was persuaded by Sen. Richard G. Lugar (R-Ind.), chairman of the Senate Foreign Relations Committee (who headed the team of US observers at the Philippines election), that the Marcos-claimed 'victory' was indeed fraudulent. The result was a presidential U-turn which saw Reagan giving encouragement (tacitly) to a Marcos resignation and endorsing the accession of Mrs Aquino to the Philippines presidency (Felton, 1986a).

Third, the Reagan administration's policy of 'constructive engage-ment' with the South African government became the object of growing congressional criticism for its failure to produce adequate progress in ending apartheid. Essentially, the Reagan policy sought to pursue a 'dual track' approach: pressing on South Africa American concerns about ending apartheid, while at the same time wishing to maintain its pro-Western, anti-communist government. In September 1985, the president moved to pre-empt passage of an anti-apartheid, economic sanctions measure in Congress by issuing an executive order which imposed milder economic measures. This tactic allowed him to retain his executive prerogative as president in conducting foreign policy. However, in the wake of the declaration of a state of emergency by the South African government in the summer of 1986, both the Senate and the House passed much tougher sanctions measures. Arguing that such sanctions would be more harmful to South African blacks than to the white minority government, Reagan vetoed the sanctions bill on 26 September. In a stunning defeat for the president, both houses overrode his veto – the House voted for override by a margin of 313 to 83, while the Senate voted likewise by 78 to 21. It was the first time that a presidential veto on a substantive foreign policy issue had been overridden since Congress enacted the War Powers Act of 1973 over Richard Nixon's veto (Felton, 1986b; Madison, 1986a).

Fourth, the most controversial of the administration's foreign policy goals – assisting the contra 'freedom fighters' in their struggle against the Nicaraguan Sandinistas – continued to generate controversy and conflict between the president and Congress. The president's difficulties grew with the enlargement of his Central America policy objectives. Initially, he had worked to pressure Nicaragua to cease its support of left-wing guerrillas in El Salvador, and US support of the contras grew from that objective. By the spring of 1985, however, the administration's policy was clearly geared to pushing for pluralist democracy in Nicaragua; a goal for which Reagan sought on-going funding for the contras. This development created considerable unease both within Congress and across a nation still bearing the scars of US involvement in Vietnam.

Reflecting the growing unease about the direction of Reagan policy, in 1985 Congress approved only $27 million in 'non-military' aid for the contras over 1985–6. In February 1986 Reagan requested an additional $100 million in contra aid, which would comprise $70 million for military purposes and $30 million for 'humanitarian' purposes. However, despite a nationally televised presidential address lobbying for public support for contra funding, the House narrowly rejected the $100 million request while the Senate approved it on a 53–47 vote. Undaunted, Reagan pushed hard to reverse the House decision and succeeded in gaining a 221 to 209 House vote on 25 June in favour of providing the $100 million in contra funding. Once more, congressional players had gone out 'to win one for the gipper'. The Senate similarly approved the Reagan request by a 53–47 vote margin. Yet, despite his success in reversing the House vote, it was clear that there was considerable disquiet about the president's backing of the contras. Members of Congress evinced very real concerns about the use of contra funding and the conduct of the contras themselves (Felton, 1986c; Madison, 1986b).

The credibility of the Reagan administration's foreign policy was abruptly shattered in November 1986, with the revelations about its secret dealings with Iran to arrange arms sales in return for Iranian assistance in freeing several US citizens held hostage in the Lebanon, and the linked endeavour to recycle the net arms sales profits to fund contra operations in Nicaragua. Initially, at his nationally televised press conference in 19 November, the president disclosed only the Iranian aspect of operation: 'Our purposes were fourfold: to replace a relationship of total hostility with something better, to bring a negotiated end to the Iran-Iraq war, and to bring an end to terrorism and to effect the release of our hostages.' The subsequent disclosure six days later of the contra link with the arms shipments to Iran was widely regarded as a political bombshell. The fact that Reagan indicated that he had not been 'fully informed' about the linkage only appeared to make matters worse: it raised serious questions about his grasp of the issues.

At the mid-point of his second term, therefore, the credibility of major elements of the president's foreign policy was beginning to crumble. In the first place, his 'hang tough' policy in dealing with terrorism was largely undercut by his administration's exchange of arms in return for assistance in releasing American hostages. Worse, these dealings on the issue were with a state he still regarded (at least in part) as terrorist. Secondly, the administration's position on the Iran–Iraq war had previously been one of studied neutrality. Thus, in the troubled region of the Middle East, his secret dealings with Iran caused fresh doubts to be sown about American credibility. Thirdly, coming as they did so soon after the president's success in getting the House of Representatives to reverse its vote on contra funding, the revelations of covert 'short-circuiting' of Congressional budgeting procedures were particularly harmful. The Iran–contra link put considerably at risk future congressional support for the contras.

The second-term Cabinet and White House

A major feature of Reagan's second term was the extent of personnel changes effected in major Cabinet and White House posts. The most immediate, unexpected and far-reaching of these came in January 1985, with the announcement that White House Chief of Staff James Baker and Treasury Secretary Donald Regan would swap posts.

This Baker–Regan switch brought in its wake substantial staff-turnovers within the White House and Treasury Department teams. In Baker's case, in addition to taking his White House colleague, Richard Darman, with him as Deputy Treasury Secretary, he appointed no fewer than eight White House aides to various Treasury posts. Similarly, Regan assigned five of his Treasury colleagues to senior White House positions.

Three other prominent presidential advisers left their posts within the Executive Office of the President (EOP) to take up Cabinet appointments; presidential counselor Edwin Meese succeeded William French Smith as Attorney General; White House Personnel Director James Herrington took over from Donald Hodel as Energy Secretary, with Hodel moving to replace William Clark as Secretary of the Interior; and, US Trade Representative William Brock became Secretary of Labor, replacing Raymond Donovan who was forced to resign while on leave to deal with criminal indictments against him for business fraud. These Cabinet changes produced still further personnel turnovers at the White House, with seven presidential aides moving with Meese to the Justice Department and three others assigned to Energy Department posts by Herrington. The scale and pace of staff changes within the EOP was startling. In the first five months of his second term, only 60 of the top 322 members of the President's EOP staff remained in post. Of greater significance was the fact that virtually all of the key leadership posts were filled with new appointees by the end of Reagan's fifth year – as Figure 12.1 indicates.

The appointment of Donald Regan as White House Chief of staff carried with it, however, much more than mere personnel changes: it signalled a major restructuring of White House operations. Whereas in Reagan's first term the White House had operated on a collegial basis with a troika of key presidential advisers (Meese, Baker and Deaver) coordinating and directing policy, strategy and operations and personnel, in his second term all of these critical responsibilities were brought together under the sole aegis of Regan as Chief of Staff. Donald Regan was now in a position to determine the major EOP appointments (extending to influence on the selection of James Miller to succeed David Stockman as OMB Director in the summer of 1985) as well as controlling directly the policy and operational aspects of the White House. By reviving the Legislative Strategy Group (LSG) under his personal chairmanship, he also

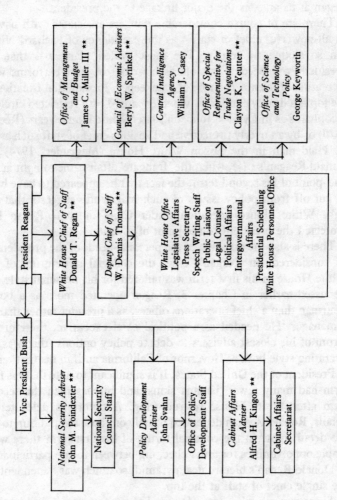

Figure 12.1: The Executive Office of the President (as at 31 December 1985)

Vice President Bush

President Reagan

National Security Adviser
John M. Poindexter **

National Security
Council Staff

White House Chief of Staff
Donald T. Regan **

Deputy Chief of Staff
W. Dennis Thomas **

White House Office
Legislative Affairs
Press Secretary
Speech Writing Staff
Public Liaison
Legal Counsel
Political Affairs
Intergovernmental
Affairs
Presidential Scheduling
White House Personnel Office

Policy Development
Adviser
John Svahn

Office of Policy
Development Staff

Cabinet Affairs
Adviser
Alfred H. Kingon **

Cabinet Affairs
Secretariat

Office of Management
and Budget
James C. Miller III **

Council of Economic Advisers
Beryl. W. Sprinkel **

Central Intelligence
Agency
William J. Casey

Office of Special
Representative for
Trade Negotiations
Clayton K. Yeutter **

Office of Science
and Technology
Policy
George Keyworth

** Second Term Appointees

sought to make himself the principal presidential strategist. In consequence, Ronald Reagan's second term White House became structured on the basis of a hierarchical pyramid featuring Donald Regan at its apex as the major linkage to the president.

There are of course considerable dangers associated with having an all-powerful chief of staff – as the presidency of Richard Nixon can so eloquently testify. The most evident danger is that the President will become cut off as his chief of staff performs with increasing efficiency the role of gatekeeper. Presidential isolation at the top is a deadly condition, whether caused by a restricted circle of sycophants as in Lyndon Johnson's later White House years (Reedy, 1970) or by an overly protective and zealous chief of staff such as H. R. Haldeman in the Nixon White House (Magruder, 1974). In Ronald Reagan's case, when the 'Irangate' affair came to light at the mid-point of his second term, the fact that he appeared to have been so cut off from policy issues of such magnitude suggests that the tight White House operation under Chief of Staff Regan had protected the president to the point of isolation.

There is also the question of the personal needs of the president to be considered. In Reagan's case, the collegial structuring of the White House in his first term was tailored for his personal style. As discussed earlier in Chapter 3, Reagan operated more as a board chairman than a chief operations officer, as a presider rather than as a manager. He needed as a political chief executive, therefore, a forum of his closest advisers to debate policy options: that was his operating style both as Governor of California and, in his first term, as President of the United States. It is significant to note that his first term had many fewer 'banana skins' and hitches than the second term after White House restructuring. A notorious delegater of details, Ronald Reagan depended heavily on those around him to get the detail right. In the collegial forum of his first term there were ample opportunities for cross-checking between forum participants: in Donald Regan's hierarchical pyramid, so much was dependent on the single chief of staff at the top.

There was a further area of second term restructuring which had some significance for the operation of the Reagan administration: in April 1985, the seven Cabinet councils were disbanded to be replaced by two councils, an Economic Policy Council and a Domestic Policy Council. The two new councils were much more streamlined than the seven they replaced and had sharper lines of authority: the Economic Policy Council (chaired by Treasury Secretary James Baker) would deal with all aspects of economic policy, while the Domestic Policy Council (chaired by Attorney General Edwin Meese) would deal with all other domestic policy issues. Given the evident reality that most of the seven disbanded Cabinet councils failed to develop as adequate policy forums, their passing was no great loss.

There were, however, some potential disadvantages from the new Cabinet council process. First, it created the possibility of 'Super Cabinet' status for Baker and Meese, but in practice the demands imposed by their respective departments blunted that prospect. Second, the streamlining of the council process to two bodies made it easier for Donald Regan as Chief of Staff to exert control over policy; his was the major voice in determining what issues would be dealt with by the Cabinet council. In the event, Regan failed to provide much in the way of policy impetus, however. As shrewd observers have noted of the second term:

With the White House less aggressive in setting the administration's policy tone . . . authority has passed to the few Cabinet Secretaries with aggressive programs of their own. . . . Reagan's second term is characterized by a few isolated areas of intense activity – Baker on international economics, Shultz on foreign policy, Meese on some social and legal issues – surrounded by vistas of uninspiring steady-state management (Brownstein and Kirschten, 1986).

Back to the future

In February 1986, in the course of delivering an up-beat State of the Union Address peppered with no less than sixteen references to 'the future', President Reagan reviewed the progress of what he termed 'this Great American Comeback': 'Tonight the American people deserve our thanks – for 37 straight months of economic growth; for sunrise firms and modernized industries creating nine million new jobs in three years; interest rates cut in half and inflation falling from over 12 per cent in 1980 to just under four today.'

Not only was America back, to everyone's relief the presidency itself appeared to be back: the years of the flawed presidencies of Johnson, Nixon and Carter were all now relegated to dark memories. The dreaded 'six-year itch' which turns presidents into 'lame ducks' for the remainder of their second terms seemed to have been repelled by the teflon coat of 'SuperRon'.

Yet, despite the continuance of the economic recovery well into his second term, it was clear that much of the original impetus of the Reagan Revolution had dissipated. Whereas the first term was characterised by energy, policy dynamism and innovation, the second term held an air of relative stasis. Much of this was due of course to the departure from the Executive Office of the President of virtually all of the key figures at the heart of Reagan's 'new beginning': Meese, Baker, Stockman, Deaver, and Darman. Nonetheless, in 1985 and 1986 the administration displayed little of its earlier drive: besides the achievement of the landmark 1986 Tax Reform Act, there were few legislative successes. First term initiatives such as New Federalism and urban enterprise zones remained unfulfilled, while the 'social issues agenda' were reduced to 'pipe dream' status. Significantly, not even the Reagan 'Yankee Doodle Magic' could save the expanding defence budget (the *sine qua non* of the president's 'walking tall' foreign policy) from vigorous congressional pruning.

At the mid-point of Reagan's second term it is much too early to write the president off, caught as his administration was in the grip of special investigators and congressional hearings examining the entrails of 'Iranscam'. However, the fact that yet another presidency has been drawn into the black hole of the 'six-year itch' may give rise to some revival of the single-term, six-year proposal. In the past, the debate on this reform focused on the desirability of removing party politics from the presidency and was properly rejected for its inherent folly. Nonetheless, the last president to complete two full terms was Eisenhower in the 1950s; this should at least give some pause before the idea of a single, six-year term is rejected.

References

Bonafede, D. and Kirschten, D. (1985). 'Presidency No Longer Seems to Be Imperiled', *National Journal*, pp. 66–73.

Brownstein, R. and Kirschten, D. (1986). 'Cabinet Power', *National Journal*, pp. 1582–9.

Buchanan, J. M. and Wagner, R. (1977). *Democracy in Deficit*. New York: Academic Press.

Clark, T. B. (1984). 'Business Hit Hardest Under Treasury Tax Plan', *National Journal*, p. 2312.

Clark, T. B. (1985). 'Crunching the Numbers', *National Journal*, p. 1386.

Clarke, T. B. and Cohen, R. E. (1986). 'Resolving the Differences', *National Journal*, p. 1658-65.

Cohen, R. E. (1985). 'Despite His Landslide 1984 Win, Reagan Trailed House

Winners in Most District', *National Journal*, p. 854–9.
Congressional Quarterly (1986). 'In New Hands' (special election issue), pp. 2670–720.
Epstein, J. M. (1986). *The 1987 Defense Budget*, Washington, DC: The Brookings Institution.
Felton, J. (1986a). 'New Slate, Fresh Problems for the Philippines', *Congressional Quarterly*, pp. 483–8.
Felton, J. (1986b). 'Hill Overrides Veto of South African Sanctions', *Congressional Quarterly*, pp. 2338–41.
Felton, J. (1986c). 'After House Defeat, Reagan to Push for "Contra" Aid', *Congressional Quarterly*, pp. 648–53.
Foley, T. S. (1985). 'Verbatim Comment', *National Journal*, pp. 2575.
Ginsberg, G. and Shefter, M. (1985). 'A Critical Realignment? The New Politics, the Reconstituted Right, and the Election of 1984', in M. Nelson, ed., *The Elections of 1984*. Washington, DC: Congressional Quarterly Inc.
Jackson, J. O. *et al.* (1986). 'Sunk by Star Wars,' *Time*, 20 October, pp. 11–15.
Lowi, T. J. (1985). 'An Aligning Election, A Plebiscite', in M. Nelson, ed., *The Elections of 1984*. Washington, DC: Congressional Quarterly Inc.
Madison, C. (1986a). 'Breaking the Engagement', *National Journal*, pp. 1820–4.
Madison, C. (1986b). 'Triumph and Challenge', *National Journal*, pp. 2492–5.
Magruder, J. S. (1974). *An American Life*. New York: Atheneum.
Morrison, D. C. (1985). 'Budget Balancing Legislation Would Put Defense Spending on the Chopping Block', *National Journal*, pp. 2655–8.
Morrison, D. C. (1986). 'The Shadow War', *National Journal*, pp. 1100–5.
National Journal (1986). 'The 1986 Elections: Governing in the Cross-currents' (special election issue), pp. 2803–73.
Nelson, M., ed., (1985). *The Elections of 1984*. Washington, DC: Congressional Quarterly Inc.
Ranney, A., ed., (1985). *The American Elections of 1984*. Washington, DC: American Enterprise Institute.
Rauch, J. (1986). 'Politics of Deficit Reduction Remains Deadlocked Despite Balanced Budget Act', *National Journal*, pp. 15–21.
Reedy, G. W. (1970). *The Twilight of the Presidency*. New York: World.
Rogers, D. and Weirmeil, S. 'U.S. Supreme Court Rejects Key to Deficit-Reducing Law', *Wall Street Journal*, 8 July 1986.
Schneider, W. (1984). 'An Uncertain Consensus', *National Journal*, pp. 2130–2.
Shanahan, E. (1986). 'Senate Clears Massive Tax Overhaul Measure', *Congressional Quarterly*, pp. 2344–58.
Stockman, D. A. (1986). *The Triumph of Politics*. New York, Harper and Row.
Towell, P. (1985). 'Pentagon Asks $313.7 Billion for Defence Buildup', *Congressional Quarterly*, pp. 229–35.
Towell, P. (1986). 'Reductions in Hundreds of Pentagon Programs', *Congressional Quarterly*, pp. 111–12.

Wehr, E. (1985). 'Confrerees Strive to Fathom Senate Budget-Balancing Plan', *Congressional Quarterly*, pp. 2091–4.

Wilson, J. Q. (1985). 'Realignment at the Top, Dealignment at the Bottom', in A. Ranney, ed., *The American Elections of 1984*. Washington, DC: American Enterprise Institute, pp. 247–310.

Wolfinger, R. E. (1985). 'Dealignment, Realignment and Mandates in the 1984 Election', in A. Ranney, ed., *The American Elections of 1984*. Washington, DC: American Enterprise Institute, pp. 177–296.

Index